The Open Society and its Friends

א ALEF
Series of works on universal logic and philosophy directed by
Michele Malatesta and Rocco Pezzimenti
A Allgemeine Logik Und Philosophie
L Universel Logik Og Filosofi
E Logica Universale E Filosofia
F Logica Universal Y Filosofia

Volume 2: Rocco Pezzimenti, *The Open Society and its Friends, with letters from Isaiah Berlin and Karl R. Popper*

In memory of my friend Davide Nardoni

The Open Society and its Friends

with letters from Isaiah Berlin and Karl R. Popper

Rocco Pezzimenti

GRACEWING

First published in 1997
This revised and expanded edition published in 2011
2020 - First reprint with a new preface

Gracewing
2 Southern Avenue
Leominster
Herefordshire HR6 0QF
United Kingdom
www.gracewing.co.uk

All rights reserved. No part of this publication may be reproduced, stored in a retrieval system, or transmitted in any form, or by any means, electronic, mechanical, photocopying, recording, or otherwise, without the written permission of the publisher.

©1997, 2011, 2020 Rocco Pezzimenti

ISBN 978 0 85244 739 0

Pericles: "We live under a form of a government which does not emulate the institutions of our neighbours; on the contrary, we are ourselves a model which some follow, rather than the imitators of other people".

Thucydides, *History of the Peloponnesian War*, II. 37,1.

Caesar: "Our ancestors, Fathers of the Senate, were never lacking either in wisdom or courage, and yet pride did not keep them from adopting foreign institutions (...) In fine, whatever they found suitable among allies or foes, they put in practice at home with the greatest enthusiasm, preferring to imitate rather than envy the successful".

Sallust, *The War with Catiline*, LI. 37-38.

Contents

Preface to the first edition	11
Preface to the new edition	12
1. Roman juridical experience. The reflections of Cicero.	13
2. The apogee of the principality and the long crisis.	47
A) *Cicero once again is witness to an era of transition.*	47
B) *The guarantee of legal rights and its role in social osmosis.*	53
C) *Law, institutions and the army: towards the Principate.*	59
D) *Early theorists of the Principate.*	65
E) *Seneca.*	67
F) *Tacitus.*	73
G) *More on the Army.*	81
H) *Ammianus Marcellinus and Zosimus.*	87
3. The beginning of the conflict and dilemma between religion and politics: Eusebius of Caesarea, Augustine of Hippo.	97
4. The rebirth of dissent: John of Salisbury.	119
5. Between secularism and theocracy. Aquinas *versus* the theorists of papal supremacy.	135
6. Dante. The problem of peace in the conflict between universal authority and local autonomy.	153

7. Marsilio of Padua. William of Ockham.
   The difficult search for consensus guaranteed by law. 163

8. Classical Historiography Miscellanea. 187

9. The Roman and Augustinian Heritage and others. 221

   A) *Liberty and will in Duns Scotus.* 221
   B) *The role of the aristocracy and the importance of not feeling oneself superior.* 225

10. The Greek Heritage in Medieval Islamic Political Thought. 231

Appendices

11. Concerning *Imperium*. 251

12. The case of Aristotle. 255

13. Letters from K.R. Popper and I. Berlin. 267

Works cited 285

Index of Names 301

Preface to the first edition

As I take leave of these pages, I am reading the latest book by Giovanni Sartori: *Democrazia: Cosa è,* and I paused at a basic statement with which I am fully in agreement: "We should note that loss of roots is also, often, freedom from chains. We must not idealise the *good times* of long ago excessively" (p. 26).

This work does not intend to halt the difficult path of the *open society,* nor is it inspired by a nostalgic dream of a return to the past. It simply seeks, to paraphrase Sartori again, to speak of politics in realistic terms, and not in those of abstract reasoning, in the conviction that the latter way, the way of the *tabula rasa is* both untenable and dangerous. The past, then, should neither be reduced to myth nor rejected; instead it should be sifted so as to avoid dangerous errors and to safeguard what has been attained with so much effort. It seems to me in fact that Sartori is saying the same thing, when he writes: "It matters little that that past was largely mythical: it matters that the Glorious Revolution was, in intention, a recovery. As for the so-called American Revolution; it was not a revolution at all; it was a secession" (pages 38-39). For Sartori, and I believe that he is right, in politics there is a perennial contrast between realism and rationalism, a conflict which for me was present, just because it is perennial, already in the ancient world; and the excerpts from the speeches of Pericles and Caesar, which are quoted in the opening chapter, are a reminder of this. As I read it, in chapters VIII and IX of the same book by Sartori, it is possible to find a great deal of what I too am saying.

In remains for me to make a final comment on certain medieval writers whose works will be found in the following pages, and who often show the typical contradictions of those who have sought to combine together positions which at times differ. They should be read and interpreted by extracting, for example, from the Aristotelian context (I am thinking in this case of Aquinas), what remains of the teaching deriving from the Latin sense of the concrete. It is precisely this teaching, as will be seen from the following pages, that lies at the basis of the modern notions which have been so well theorised by Locke, Vico, Montesquieu and the Federalists.

Preface to the new edition

On its appearance, when presented with this study of open societies, a significant number of people raised the criticism that the contribution Greek thought made to the development of Western democracy had been neglected. I do not intend to criticise my critics who, in part, are right. This, however, was a deliberate neglect. If I had also considered the Greek roots, whose contribution I do not in the least seek to underestimate, I would have gone over an itinerary that can be taken for granted and is obvious. In addition, perhaps, I would not have allowed the reader to consider another itinerary which is more connected with a practical and juridical philosophy enriched on one side by Christian thought. I see this latter itinerary as being equally important for the retrieval and reassessment of the leading values of modernity. It is certainly no accident that writers such as Vico, Montesquieu, Hume and others, the precursors of our political systems, refer more to the Latin than to the Greek tradition. It was, therefore, in order to rebalance the arduous itinerary of our idea of society, which I see walking on two legs and not just one, that I engaged in this study.

1. Roman juridical experience. The reflections of Cicero.

> *Legum ... servi sumus ut liberi esse possimus.*
> ... obey the law to the end that we may be free.
> (*Oratio pro Cluentio*, 53)

1.1 The intention of this essay is to identify the long and difficult path which has led to the achievement of the open society, showing that it is not a gift bestowed by nature upon humankind, nor the fruit of chance or fate. For this reason, the analysis of this path begins from the basis of Latin culture, for far too long regarded as lacking originality, or more often as indebted to the Greek world for everything of value that it possessed. It is not my intention here to indulge in superficial denials of the merits of one culture in order to exalt the merits of another. I merely wish to state that we are here dealing with two cultures which are profoundly different, even though they are closely connected, and while one of them (the Greek) may not, as Popper maintains, have the required qualities to allow us to see in it any prologue to the open society, the second has embryonic elements which lead us to think the contrary. First of all, there is a very original way of conceiving law, frequently considered by many philosophers and scholars, unfortunately, as an inferior form of culture, almost as if it did not carry the implications of its own philosophy in the background, even though these must obviously be of a practical rather than theoretical nature. With regard to law, we should point out at once one of its characteristics which can already be seen in the Roman era, and which will accompany it throughout in history: i.e. the fact that it has guaranteed stability on the one hand, and progress on the other. A formula of which I am particularly fond speaks of a dynamic equilibrium, because while on the one hand law in Rome remains fixed to such an extent that it is possible to speak of the "certainty of law", on the other hand it was constantly adapting itself to the needs of the time and developing in a rich and original fashion. We need only point out, for example, that certain scholars have reached the conclusion that the juridical rules of the Republican age, anticipating criteria which Europe was to adopt after the Glorious Revolution of 1688 in England (and a long time later in many European countries), held that the person of the citizen should be inviolable in his own house, and that his arrest could only take place outside the same; that preventive detention should be avoided, and that any citizen accused and not yet condemned must be granted the right to avoid the consequences of the condemnation (cf. Mommsen, I, 407).

1.2 It is evidently not just by chance that Mommsen arrives at the assertion that the Roman republic is the first liberal society in history (cf. Mommsen, I, 77). This is not only on the basis of the law, however, but because of the mentality and the culture which gave life to that law. In Greece, the person who did not speak Greek was a "barbarian"; in Rome, Ennius could say that he had three souls because he spoke three languages (cf. Ennius, 8, note). Local languages and cultures were not wiped out. On official occasions documents were drawn up in several languages: we could mention, for example, among many others, the inscription on the Cross of Christ, whose accusation was written in three languages because the punishment for the crime must be comprehensible to all, whether they were natives or foreigners. In Greece, slavery was justified by reference to natural criteria, but in Rome according to legal criteria (I shall return to this very delicate and important subject later). Rome never had philosophers who dreamed of a perfect world, nor even prophets who predicted future worlds (cf. Nardoni, SPP, 23); it did have jurists who indicated the way to constant improvements in legality. In this sense, it had philosophers of law and of practice. In Rome, the category of merits (the *cursus honorum*) existed, as did the category of freedom of conscience which found its highest expression in freedom of religious belief. The Latins had their traditional religion, but, in Rome there was also room for the oriental and other divinities; indeed the Pantheon signifies the equalization of all the Gods (cf. Nardoni, SPP, 24). Even the Jews, at the time of the greatest splendour of the capital, had as many as 13 synagogues (cf. Nardoni, SPP, 25). This freedom of religion signifies freedom of circulation of culture, languages, races, and so on. All this is due to the tradition, the experience of the city which owed its birth and growth to the meeting of diverse forces, and hence to differing cultural expressions.

1.3 From here were derived the ideas of a league and a federation, which were to undergo such an important development in the western world. There are those who would ascribe the criteria which inspired the American federalists to these notions, and it was from them that the distinction and limitation of powers arose – so dear to Montesquieu, whose inspiration was Roman before it was English. In this context it is enough to read *Considérations sur les causes de la grandeur et de la décadence des Romains,* and his other previous writings on Roman antiquity. It was also in Rome that the idea was born, and the realization took place, of the various local autonomies which were to develop so extensively after the millennium, as modern Europe began to take shape. Anyone who seeks proof of this need only remember that mercantile society, the communes, the formulation of contracts, the notaries and the juridical faculties all derived, as we shall see, from the rediscovery of Roman Law.

1.4 Right from its origins, the history of Rome presents us with a somewhat singular fact, absolute and hard-headed domination of one people over the others does not exist. "What has usually been defined as Roman domination over Italy seems to us to be the union of all the Italian tribes in a single state; among these tribes the Romans were the most powerful, but nevertheless only a branch of them" (Mommsen, I, 6). Already by the time of the Latin League, every "citizen" of this "Federation" could have legitimate offspring from any woman of other tribes, could possess funds and carry on business in every area of the League. This means that right from the beginning, this Federation has juridical content which in effect makes it not an occasional and extemporary, but a deliberate and a durable entity.

1.5 The Roman-Italic Federation is very similar to present-day federal systems. To Rome, seat of the central government, belonged direction over foreign and military policy. On all internal, administrative and juridical matters, every city or member-state of the Federation enjoyed full autonomy. Even in cases of military victory, the advantages were equally shared between Rome and the federate cities. The same took place in the foundation of the colonies, and also in the contributions which they had to make in peacetime, but more especially in wartime, to the Federation. This explains why very soon the conscience of nationality arose among the Italic tribes, which neither Carthage nor the barbarians, nor any other enemies ever succeeded in destroying, despite the threats and the bribes which were issued in difficult moments. This also proves the political wisdom of Rome, which always magnanimously refrained from imposing intolerable burdens on its subjects even when the enemy, apart from a few rare exceptions with historical rivals, was defeated. It should be remembered that the actual *debellatio* about which so much has been written, does not mean so much total destruction, as is so often claimed today, as merely removing the instruments of *bellum,* of conflict, from the enemy. Among many examples, we may cite Taranto during the war against Pyrrhus. In exchange for the *debellatio* the city was offered the possibility of retaining its own autonomy.

1.6 Why did the achievement of Federation, or the League, turn out to be quite natural for Rome? The answer lies in the fact that the city did not invent these institutions little by little; it began with these conditions. The diversity of the tribes which made it up (a very interesting point is the etymology of the word tribe from *tribuere* – to divide in three) made the achievement of a League necessary. The king who ruled the city in its origins had nothing in common with oriental or African kings. There is nothing theocratic in his figure. "Indeed, in terms of law, every citizen of sound mind and body who had reached the required age, could accede to the throne" (Mommsen, I, 62). Because of this, it is not claimed that the king is better than the citizens, and if these obey him, in reality their obedience goes to the laws and not to him in person, since the king "had only the faculty of putting the law into effect, and not changing it" (Mommsen, I, 62). This is why, in terms of law, anyone could become king. It is proved by the fact that Servius

Tullius became sovereign even though he was the son of a slave (cf. Cicero, DR, II, 21).

1.7 The institution of monarchy, even when it was exalted by the Romans as, for example, in the words of Scipio in the famous Ciceronian passage, should never mislead us under any circumstances. The king, in the Roman tradition, even in the actual period of the monarchy, has nothing in common with the various kingdoms of universal history. The sovereign is virtually a president of the republic, elected for life. On his death, authority returns into the hands of the vital forces of the city, since there is no criterion of succession. Moreover the king guarantees *aequabilitas*, (splendidly expounded, as we shall see, by Cicero), among the various social "classes", succeeding in tempering the conflicts between patricians and plebs by guaranteeing to the latter a natural support (cf. Homo, Part I, Ch. 1).

1.8 The king, although he administered the finances, was not allowed to confuse the public good with his own private goods. These two spheres were to remain so distinct throughout Roman history, that even in the periods of decadence of the later empire, we do not find a single emperor who was able to retain even a small portion of territory as his private property so as to leave it to his heirs or bestow it as a dowry (a typical aspect of other monarchies), or to divide the empire itself between his heirs. When this took place, at least in the crisis period, it was always to be because of public necessity. Family relationships themselves can have different contents when they are expressed in the public sphere rather than the private, even though they may be between blood relations. A person who "in his position as a son was subject to his father, could nevertheless in certain cases command him as his overlord" (Mommsen, I, 69).

This explains why in Rome the law is not an order issued by the sovereign to his subjects, but a pact, a binding link (hence *lex)* established between all the various components of the state, which places them all on the level of equality: different citizens among themselves, different communities in the League, different powers in the state. However, all this does not signify levelling down all the different members of the *civitas* into a ridiculous equality without merit. The law of property does in fact exist, where the concrete liberty of the individual finds its full expression, and without which it is impossible to understand what we mean today by the open society, the Lawful state. So much so that even today, all the juridical concepts of free societies are expressed in words of Latin origin.

1.9 It is law which confers on every individual the complete possession of his goods and the faculty of disposing of them without limit or restraint. This not only went for the original inhabitants of the capital, but also for the "Latin colonists living in Rome, not by favour of the King or of any other citizen, but by virtue of federal law" (Mommsen, I, 79). Here too, the equality typical of private law prevailed, which granted every free member of the league the right to settle in any corner of Latin territory (a right of movement which even today is not granted in very many states), and to hold possessions there. This explains why in Rome more than in any other civilization, the various tribes were notably intermingled.

1.10 This same rich variety of tribes enhanced the juridical experience which succeeded in establishing individual guarantees, many of which the modern states have recently attained. Mention could be made, for instance, of the guarantee of the property and the safeguarding of the persons of those incapable of defence of their own inheritance, such as minors, the handicapped, and so on, or of the interest due from debtors. It also seems that in the relations between private individuals, the state (or rather the public authority) was seen as a third party to whom recourse should only be had if agreement could not be reached. But a third party which, although it intervened only in a supplementary role, nevertheless had already eliminated the vendetta, specifically in order to guarantee security to private individuals. However, it could in no way absorb the family with its activities or the private affairs of individuals. Perhaps no-one put it better than Mommsen in summing up in a few words the greatness of this situation: "In Roman Law all is clear and concise; no symbols are adopted, and no institution is superfluous. This is not cruel: everything necessary is carried out without hesitation, even the death sentence (...) it is in this that the greatness of Rome is founded and contained: that the people had imposed on themselves, and had accepted, a law in which what dominated, and still does dominate today, were the eternal principles of freedom, property and legality, not falsified or mystified" (Mommsen, I, 150).

1.11 The very concrete nature of the forms of law can be seen in the limitations which the political authority met in carrying out its mandate. From the earliest times of the republican era, "the right to decide a question between private individuals according to their own will was immediately taken from the Consuls" (Mommsen, I, 231). Not only so: it was laid down that once the term of his office had expired, the Consul be subjected to the ordinary Courts like any other citizen for crimes committed during his mandate. The institution of limited immunity therefore existed, though for the period institutionally conceded.

Apart from immunity, the representatives of the people had special assurances and guarantees. The tribune, as far back as the 5th century B.C., could not be interrupted while he was speaking, and his person was declared inviolable.

1.12 At the very origins of the Republic a group of statesmen, who remain nameless to us, already gave the city a political system in which the powers are mutually balanced and limited. With the consuls, and in extraordinary cases with dictators, the sovereign power of law is maintained even if limited *de facto*. With the Senate, a multi-task body was introduced which would guarantee stability even in difficult moments, as would be the case with the House of Lords in England. With the rise of the plebs, not only would the voice of the people (a typical Latin concept) be guaranteed, but also that dualism which would guarantee vitality to the state, and the fullest solidarity and agreement in difficult moments. We might say that this was the same arrangement which would take place in England between the Whigs and Tories. All this dynamism always remained subject to the law, above which nobody, in this context, could ever place himself.

1.13 This explains why class conflicts, even during the period of the so-called Republica Patriciana would never lose sight of the fact that the safety of the state is placed above all party interest. In this way, just as in English history, the interests of the two conflicting forces were tempered. We need only mention that the centuriate system, in its period of maximum development, included all citizens without any distinction in the provisions for a census, – i. e. both patricians and plebs. While the citizens are then classified in the political organisation in terms of and in proportion to their wealth, which gradually replaced the criterion of birth, it should also be said that there is parity between patricians and plebs in the military and financial context, given that the state imposes certain obligations proportional to the wealth of each person (cf. Homo, Part I, Ch. 1). To sum up, it was a political system which would be described by Montesquieu as a *République aristocratique,* because the "upper class" and the people had equally important weight and roles, even though they were distinct.

1.14 Another basic aspect of the Roman republic, which collapsed only in the period of decline, is the very clear distinction between political and military matters. When a commander made use of a military situation to speak out on purely political affairs, his action remained "without effect, as if it had been effectively forbidden" (Mommsen, I, 238). The time when the Army would dictate the rules of the political game was a long way off, but by then, as Ammianus Marcellinus has convincingly shown, it would be out of place to speak of institutions of any type: the force of arms was to take the place of the force of law. During the republican period, it was exactly the opposite which took place: political reason always prevailed over military, and public opinion was fully behind this phenomenon. In our own times, it seemed astonishing that while the USA conducted the war in Vietnam a great open internal conflict should have been going on in its midst. In Rome, as long ago as 495 B.C., at a moment when the debtor citizens could not satisfy the heavy demands of their creditors, a whole band of conscripts deserted although a difficult war was imminent, so that the Consul Publius Servilius suspended the laws against the debtors. It was as if (as is right and proper) the civil world was forcing the hand of the political and military world, and the latter, it goes without saying, never took control over civil society until the crisis of the institutions. This means that there was present in the Roman republic the concept of limitation, often not expressed in formal legal language, but nevertheless recognized by all as constituting the basis of a genuinely legal state. And moreover that law, even when not expressed in juridical formulae, constituted a kind of *habitus* for the Roman citizen which gave a standard form to his own life.

1.15 The greatness of law in Rome lies not only in the fact that it constituted the theoretical and practical instrument of politics, but also in the fact that law itself enjoyed an autonomy of its own to such a degree that all that is juridical is isolated from what is moral, and from religion (in this context it is possible to trace the roots of tolerance). This derives from the fact that the aim and basis of law was quite different in Rome from what it had been in Greece. There the concept of justice was in fact the product of a philosophical deduction, while in Rome law arose from the demands of organization (cf. D'Addio, 148), for which reason there were no Utopian illusions to follow; nor were there ideals to be pre-established as models. Law was therefore the rationalization of the practical life of individuals.

1.16 In the Roman tradition, the *ius* is custom, probably inherited, at least in its fundamental structure, by the various peoples (Latins, Sabines, Etruscans) from among whom the first population of the city was made up. What is surprising, even from the first development of this population, is the distinctly individual concept of property. This is an expression of freedom (strange that the liberals like Hume were later on to take up this concept), since it is the lordship of man over things. Freedom is manifested up to the *ius abutendi,* which expresses the faculty of alienating, abandoning and even destroying the thing possessed. This is a matter of extreme solutions which, however, show that the freedom of everyone cannot tolerate interference of any type (cf. *Digesta*, 8, 5.8 §5). We have only to think that usucaption itself cannot harm the rights of others; thus the thinking would seem to be that the *bona fides* of usucaption implies having acquired civil property *ab initio*. In the absence of this *ab initio*, it would be possible in one way or another to damage the right of another person.

1.17 This is the reason why private law still holds such importance for us today, because in it "an uninterrupted tradition which binds our juridical thinking and the substance of our law to ancient Rome is recognizable" (Arangio-Ruiz, 8). In relation to this an important point should be noted: the traditional distinction between *ius publicum* and *ius privatum* means something more than the mere distinction between two juridical spheres, since "*ius publicum is* not so much the law which concerns the state, as the law which emanates from the state, in counter position to the rules which private individuals give to their own or other people's conduct" (Arangio-Ruiz, 9). Hence the *ius privatum* emanates from below, and is therefore not the fruit of legal imposition, but the result of a free relationship between individuals (an etymological analysis of the verb *instituere* fully confirms this conception). The spirit of Roman law therefore, reveals an intrinsic internal dynamism which is expressed case by case in the various "transactions" and becomes regulatory at the actual moment in which it becomes subjectivised. When these norms form the *ius civile,* the criterion of equity of the praetor is counterposed to their possible rigidity.

1.18 The limitations on property must either be dictated by public interest or that of neighbours, and whatever the case may be, they cannot be dictated by individual and arbitrary will. It is important that the concept of property, which as previously stated is not a theoretical concept, is strictly linked to work. For example, with the development of intensive agriculture and the consequent use of the large numbers of the plebs, the patrician minority had no further juridical reason to justify the ownership of large latifundiae: "(...) the triumph of this form of agriculture is translated into the claim of each peasant family, no longer precarious and subject to cancellation, but permanent and untouchable, over its own allotment of land" (Arangio-Ruiz, 184). This explains why the patricians, in order to avoid similar problems, preferred to extend and exceed the limits of the phenomenon of slavery, which itself was a cause of many contradictions, and of many problems to the free populace.

1.19 Slavery developed specifically during the intensification of civil disputes, along with the conquest of the Orient where the concept of property existing among the Latins had not developed. In the East the idea of property was strictly linked to that of sovereignty, both of which were exercised by the Hellenic dynasties. The subjects worked on behalf of their sovereign, and the prince was owner of everything. It seemed quite natural, therefore, that slaves from the orient should pass from the service of one lord into that of another. For the Latins, this was not the case. The private citizen justified his property with his work, and hence he had no juridical armoury to forbid it to these plebeians who, by working, sought to become proprietors. Property in Rome was not in fact by original title, as it was for oriental sovereigns, but by derivative title: how, then, could it be denied to the plebeians?

1.20 The nature of law itself still poses problems over slaves. To those among the latter who showed a spirit of dedication in moments of difficulty for the city, freedom and citizenship were recognized. This is what happened, during the second Punic War, in the case of those "soldier-slaves" who fought at Benevento under the orders of Tiberius Gracchus, the namesake of the future tribune. We should remember too that the possibility of learning to read and write was granted to rural slaves. This is proof that when Rome enlarged its citizenship territorially, it was in process of building a civilization which, as Mommsen states, could no longer be termed Hellenic, but humanitarian and cosmopolitan.

1.21 "*Utpote cum jure naturali omnes liberi nascentur*" (*Digesta*, 1.1.4). Here we are faced with a typically Roman conviction, which is opposed both to the Aristotelian presumption, (by which it is nature which lays down who is free and who is a slave), and to general Stoical cosmopolitanism. Before Stoicism had developed, and long before the formula of the Digest was codified, natural equality has a de facto existence: the slave has in fact full capacity to act. Slavery is a juridical condition for the Romans, not a natural one (cf. Nardoni, GR, 47 and ff.), and it is in reality quite rare in ancient Rome, where the *pater familias* most frequently had recourse to the services of *clientes:* i.e. of plebeians. However it may be, the slave can perform any kind of act on behalf of the master: be nominated heir, obtain the assignation of a small patrimony from him and he may (amazingly enough) pronounce the tract of land where his master is buried to be *locus religiosus,* and thus not on the market (cf. Arangio-Ruiz, 49-50). It is even more incredible that during festivals, such as religious feasts, the slaves also have the right to abstain from work and from their tasks (cf. Cicero, DR, II,12).

1.22 As we have stated, slavery does not depend on natural principles; it is *ope jure*. The Romans also furnish an indirect proof or confirmation of this line of thought. The re-acquisition of freedom takes place through a juridical transaction by which the slave is proclaimed free. The *manumissio* (this was the name by which the transaction is known) immediately created a de facto freedom. If slavery had depended on natural causes, how would it have been possible to provide for an immediate change of *status*? The practical character of the Romans, who made use of slaves even in the fields of education, letters and arts, knew very well that the nature of slaves is independent of juridical questions and political motives. It was conscious of all this because it had experienced the fact that even within the City a man might become a slave if, for instance, he did not fulfil certain of his civic obligations.

1.23 From the foregoing it can be understood that the Roman world was chiefly characterized by its historico-political interest in what could be called a practical philosophy, as against the more doctrinaire and theoretical kind peculiar to the Greek world. A proof of this may be found in the fact that when the Roman speaks of "virtue" he does not use the word in the way the Greek does, in strictly ethical terms contained within a philosophical dimension. For the Roman, virtue reposes in tradition, in the *mos maiorum,* and not in any philosophical analysis of the Schools. In fact philosophers prove to be effective and convincing only for a few people; legislators, on the other hand, possess in the law a real authority which they derive from tradition, and they are capable of leading all to moral and virtuous action. Cicero maintains (cf. Cicero, DO, II, 11) that the will of the laws succeeds in tempering passions and restraining injustices, avoiding the feverish disputes of theoretical philosophers who, closed within the confines of their own schools, never succeed in reaching definitive or even momentary conclusions. I have deliberately added the word "theoretical" to the term "philosophers", because it is the adjective which was displeasing to the Roman rather than the noun. For them, a philosophy which is not related to life, and does not become a norm for living was meaningless. *In other words, philosophy has a value for the Romans*, and Cicero in particular, *if it becomes politics, becomes law, affairs, and social relationships*, and inspires all these matters, and culls additional inspiration from their dynamism.

1.24 For the Romans, philosophy is a profession of life. It is useless, therefore, to isolate oneself in order to contemplate metaphysical truth; what is useful is to live for certain truths, the first of which is that of ensuring peaceful coexistence and social peace. The latter – in contrast to the claims of absolutists such as Hobbes (cf. point 1.33) – does not depend on the strength of tyrants, but on the certainty of the law. The study of any discipline thus has a social purpose, otherwise it is a pure waste of time. Man receives everything from his social dimension, and thus the duties which he has to society are superior to the personal *otium* of culture. Culture and action, in an inseparable partnership, truly contribute to the improvement of humanity; otherwise, if separated, they render mankind empty, presumptuous, and constantly searching for unreal models. Roman culture therefore has a natural pragmatic value, which seems to have passed into the inheritance of the Anglo-Saxon world, even as regards the juridical dimension.

1.25 For a confirmation of the above, we have only to think for a moment of the definition of a Republic given by Cicero (to which we shall return later): "*Est igitur res publica res populi, populus autem non omnis hominum coetus quoque modo congregatus, sed coetus multitudinis iuris consensu et utilitatis communione sociatus*" (Cicero, DR, I, 25). The definition finds no parallel in the whole of Hellenic civilization, and despite the efforts of many scholars to find it, none in Stoicism either. Apart from the concept of law, which is quite vague in the latter, the definition we have cited expresses certain typically Roman concepts. The *Communio utilitatis* expresses the whole of Latin pragmatism, which finds the real reason for the operation of individuals in their utility. Utility, however, outside the *consensus iuris* would produce anarchy, not a state; the *Consensus* implies an agreement which constitutes the real basis of society. It can also be said that it is from the *consensus iuris* that we pass on to that *consensus gentium* which is at the basis of Roman cosmopolitanism. It should be added that private utility, safeguarded by law, which was to be at the basis of modern liberal systems, makes it clear (on this Cicero is unequivocal) that law must protect the weakest, who, on equal terms with the rich, must also have the enjoyment of their utility. In short the *aequabilitas* which I shall discuss later (cf. points 1.31-35) is built into the concept of the Republic. Moreover the *communio utilitatis* of which Cicero speaks had already been expressed for many years in the Twelve Tables which safeguarded the property and the rights of individuals.

1.26 A most important point must be made on the subject of property: it is the proof that for the Romans, natural man whom the Greeks considered to be a "political animal", is different from social man. In the natural dimension, where all belongs to everyone, property does not exist; it is born with the juridical dimension (as Marx was to show clearly in a negative sense), at the point when the multitude becomes a society: i.e., when it gives itself laws: *ubi societas, ibi ius*. This highlights another important aspect: the forms of government decay for the Romans not, as the Greeks argued, when their fundamental institutions degenerate, but when the *consensus iuris* which safeguards the rights and liberties of individuals collapses. It is these which are no longer recognizable in the governing powers.

1.27 The foregoing paragraphs may serve as an introduction to a consideration of Cicero's thinking, to understand which it is necessary to set aside a number of doubts. Many scholars have stated that Cicero's political thought is the product of an eclectic mentality, which makes use of a refined education and influences from many writers. But in reality, Cicero's mind, like the minds of many Romans of his rank, derived from the cult of civic virtue, and hence of tradition. From this, as we have mentioned, there comes the entirely novel definition of the state which has no parallel in other cultures. In Cicero's opinion, men do not unite so much because of the need for mutual help as because of their social propensity to become "a people" and to remove themselves from the condition of the multitude where *there is* no law which is respected.

Marcus Tullius **Cicero** was born into a family of the knightly order in the early days of 106 B.C. At a very young age he took part in the Social Wars, but then dedicated himself to legal activities. After a long voyage of study in Greece, he began his political career as quaestor, aedile and then consul together with Anthony in 64. During this period he entered the public arena by repressing the famous Catiline Conspiracy, an episode which enabled him to extend his fame as a great jurist and orator. When his political fortunes declined, with the advent of the first Triumvirate, he went into exile. There followed years of intense opposition to the new regime which was in process of formation, but they were also years of intense reflection which produced his best-known writings: *De republica, De legibus* and, only after the death of Caesar, *De officiis*. He died in 43, killed by the partisans of Anthony after having been placed on the condemned list by the second Triumvirate. His letters are particularly valuable for an insight into his personality.

1.28 The state is therefore portrayed as the context of consensus based on laws. Where there is no juridico-political organization it is impossible to exercise civic virtue (cf. Cicero, DR, I, 26), which can only be manifested when a juridical tradition has been established and consolidated. It would also be interesting to study the degree of difference between Latin morality and Greek ethics. It is not a matter of claiming superiority for one over the other, but of pointing out the difference between them. We may notice, for instance, that dissent, one of the highest forms of moral life, is in Cicero's opinion only concretely possible and useful in a state of law. Dissent is discussion and controversy between friends, not a conflict between enemies. It is the law which allows that dissensions between friends may take place (cf. Cicero, DR, Frag., IV, 20). Dissent is thus distinguished from sedition, which seeks the ruin of the state and its foundations (cf. Cicero, DR, Frag., VI, 3).

1.29 For this reason, Cicero defends the mixed constitution; not only because it permits greater stability, but because in moderating the various powers and the various classes it allows for dissent in civil fashion, giving dissent the strength to be heard. In this context we may consider the constitutional rise of the plebs as developed in the historical excursus of *De republica*.

1.30 Law, the product of history, places politics beyond all forms of utopia. In fact laws are not to be thought of as perfect stereotypes which guarantee the eternity of the state. "Every constitution reflects the disposition and will of those who hold power" (Cicero, DR, I, 26). This is true above all when the highest power resides in the people, which in these circumstances must not only understand but also defend its own liberty. The latter, than which there is no more precious good, exists solely within the context of an equality of rights (cf. Cicero, DR, I, 31). Liberty is therefore not a convenient affirmation, but a liberty within the law, a *liberty of*, about which so much has been said in the western tradition. In short it is a practical liberty, theorized into law, which reveals the enormous practical genius of the Roman world – that same practicality which from the very first led it to found the city in a certain fashion (here too we can find the geopolitical conceptions formulated in the writings of Scipio, in the place where the city was founded).

1.31 Equality before the law was the fruit of the tradition and it constituted the soul of Roman society. It was attained after centuries of struggle and debate, but in the end it guaranteed the stability of the Republic. It is a matter of what Cicero called *aequabilitas:* a balance between the various classes of society. This *aequabilitas is* not to be understood as planning, because in such case not only would the liberty of individuals be an offence, but so would even their merits, which, on the contrary have great importance in the Latin tradition. Cicero explains this clearly: "*ipsa aequabilitas est iniqua, cum habet nullos gradus dignitatis*" (Cicero, DR, I, 27). The equality which does not distinguish individual merits is therefore not to be tolerated. Equality of rights signifies equality of possibilities and recognition of values. And it could not be otherwise, or else there is not even a possibility of a concrete state. "*Quid est enim civitas nisi iuris societas?*" (Cicero, DR, I, 32). Equality before the law, therefore, but without that levelling equality *(ipsa aequitas iniquissima est)*, which does not distinguish between individuals, thus denying their differences of capacity.

1.32 Thus the Republic should neither allow any place for arrogance on the part of the capable, nor offend the humble.

It must harmonize all its components, recognize merits, and guarantee the same possibilities to all. In brief, its task is to harmonize equality and liberty without utopian illusions, and without seeking to turn either of the two principles into an absolute. As we see from Ch. 42 of the second book of *De republica,* Cicero is very specific about this as well. He is of the opinion that the just order in a state is based on the balanced fusion of the most diverse elements. If this is not achieved then the result is civil disharmony.

1.33 What is the fundamental precondition for the achievement of a state of this kind ? Before everything else, peace. Like Hobbes in a later age, Cicero lived during a time of very serious social conflict, but the solution which he proposed would not be, like that of the English thinker, an authoritarian system. Peace cannot be attained by delegating all powers: it is born from below, like positive law. "Tranquil coexistence (...) is the first aim of living together in society, and this must be pursued by the state in laws and institutions" (Cicero, DR, IV, 3). Dictatorships and authoritarianism do not guarantee either peace or order; on the contrary they are the death certificate of democracies which have been emptied of their most basic contents.

1.34 On this issue too, Cicero leaves no room for doubt. Our Republic did not arise from the work of a single man, who gave it definitive laws (it is not a Leviathan: it will be recalled that Tullius Hostilius dared not assume the royal insignia before requesting popular authorization). Nor did it come about as the work of a single generation; it was produced by the contribution of many ages and the agreement of numerous men (cf. Cicero, DR, II, 1). We shall return to this issue later; it may be noted here that besides an inalienable law, there also exists a positive law, which is the fruit of historical experience. All Roman legislation is thus the expression of a dynamic process which expresses itself within a very small number of fixed sound principles, established because they are held to be natural. These are the grounds on which the great politician must be measured; he must be *peritissimus* both in natural and civil law (cf. Cicero, DR, V, 3). The degree to which Cicero differs from Plato and the Greeks is very clear here, and it is most unfortunate that his writings suffer, at this point, from substantial and irremediable gaps, though it is possible for us even so to deduce the essence from the few lines which have come down to us.

1.35 It is easy to understand how Cicero could say that the institutions of Rome did not derive from foreign models, but are the fruit of both "innate" qualities and of "the history of our people" (cf. Cicero, DR, II, 15). The latter, full of practical good sense even in its most primitive state, never considered nobility of blood as a priority factor; so much so that it preferred to call in foreign rulers, or elect kings who were even the sons of slaves or of client peoples (Servius Tullius is a case in point), in order to guarantee the stability of the state (cf. Cicero, DR, II, 13). From this, the criterion of *aequabilitas* can be seen again in all its clarity; among other things it was a guarantee of the marriage between aristocracy and people, who together ensured stability and continuity (inalienable right and positive law). Even this partnership itself derives from tradition: the *optimati* with their resources also had greater responsibilities; the populace (defined as *proletarius* but not in the pejorative sense in which it is used in contemporary reactionary rhetoric) with its offspring guaranteed the hope of continuity to the city (cf. Cicero, DR, II, 22).

1.36 That Rome's political experience lies at the basis of its political theory is demonstrated by Polybius himself. The originality of his political thought, in my opinion, finds its logical culmination in Cicero. We may take a brief glance at it at this point before turning back to Cicero himself. It is neither a cultural nor a chronological imposition. What would have become of Polybius' speculation if he had not come to Rome? If we are honest, we must describe his thinking as Hellenic-Roman. Those who reject this view should ask themselves how scholars like Schumpeter, Marcuse and many others could have carried out their research in the present century without settling in the USA. Polybius was also well aware of this, and recognizes the "enormous contribution" (Polybius, VI, 1, 2) which came from the Roman experience in the context of the various types of government. It is not important that this first work of history in the Roman world was written in Greek if we bear in mind that an open society such as that of Rome not only accepted but encouraged bilingualism, and at local level fostered various languages and cultures. In any case, who would dream of asserting that authors like Bacon or Descartes, who centuries later were to write in Latin, were embodiments of Latin philosophy rather than English pragmatism or French rationalism? We can understand why Cicero, when speaking of the historian, should refer to him as *"Polybius nostrum"* (Cicero, DR, II, 14).

Polybius of Megalopolis was born circa 203 B.C., and was an interpreter of the period which saw one of the major transformations of the ancient world: the passage from a Greek to a Roman vision of the world. His stay in Rome (167-150) offered him the possibility of attending the Circle of the Scipios, and thus of following the politics of Rome at first hand, thanks to various journeys in Italy, Spain and Africa. He was also present at the sieges of Numantia and Carthage. His *Histories,* which have come down to us only in substantially incomplete versions, give us a precise picture not only of the events of those years, but also of the Roman institutions, by which he was profoundly impressed. He probably died in 123 or 121, though some place his death in 118.

1.37 Polybius himself leaves no room for doubt on this point. When speaking of the Roman world, he writes: "I hold that an analysis of this kind not only constitutes an integral part of my history, but may prove to be very useful to scholars and politicians with a view to the reform or preparation of other constitutions" (Polybius, VI, 1, 5). He is equally clear when he has to describe the practical philosophy of Rome, showing that it emerges from what we would today term an open society. "More than any other people, the Romans (...) are capable of changing their customs and striving for the better" (Polybius, VI, 25, 11). It is no mere chance that Caesar could one day boast before the Senate: "Senators – our greatest men have never lacked either prudence or ardour, nor were they prevented by pride from imitating the institutions of others, if they appeared, point by point, to be good" (Sallust, LI, 37).

1.38 According to Polybius, the complexity of the Roman constitution derives from the richness and variety of its tradition (cf. Polybius, VI, 3, 3). History and politics are so intertwined in republican Rome that it makes no sense to make distinctions between them. From this inseparable coupling, there emerges a typical characteristic of a number of constitutions, one which in the city (as we have seen and will see again in Cicero) assumes a highly original guise: consensus. It is true that every form of legitimate government is based on a sort of tacit agreement between the various parties involved, but the stability of the Republic of Rome depended de facto on the circumstance that it had succeeded in providing for consent even in extraordinary circumstances. In short, it was even capable of "constitutionalising dictatorship" (D'Addio, 152).

1.39 To claim that the Romans had formed such a political system slowly and almost unconsciously, simply because no-one had proved capable until the first century B.C. of systemizing it in literary form, is an absurd error, in Polybius' own view. The citizens of Rome were fully aware of the greatness of their political system – so much so that any kind of transcription of it would have seemed meaningless. Polybius, who is himself very much aware of this, knows that he is not writing about it for their benefit, but for others outside: "I know very well that to these who are born and live in this state, my explanation will seem somewhat incomplete (...) they have had direct experience of all the dispositions provided for by this system because of the familiarity they have had with it and with its institutions since their childhood" (Polybius, VI, 11, 3-4). It should not be forgotten that one of the bases of primary education was the learning by memory of the Twelve Tables and other fundamental institutions. Something which seemed quite out of the ordinary to a foreign scholar, and therefore worth handing down to posterity, was a normal fact of everyday life for a Roman.

1.40 It is certainly not just by chance that political thought and philosophy began in Rome when the republican system was heading irrevocably towards crisis. The same thing occurred in Greece. The philosophy of Plato and Aristotle is the expression of a crisis in the *polis*. Thus before we state baldly that there was no philosophy in Rome, we should remember that the Roman crisis occurred in various times, and that to find their philosophy, we have to analyse authors from Cicero and Tacitus through Ammianus Marcellinus to Saint Augustine. The latter is the expression of the Roman world in disintegration, as Plato and Aristotle are of the Greek world.

1.41 Another matter of note that Polybius found in Rome is the question of weights and counterbalances – little considered because it is far from the view of the idealists who have interpreted Polybius up to the present, but very evident in some of today's systems, notably that of the USA. In the eyes of the Greek historian it is extraordinary not only that in the Roman constitution all the components are harmonized with each other, but that "each of these components can, if so wished, either be in opposition to the others or collaborate with them" (Polybius, VI, 15, 2). Yet more extraordinary is the fact that those who fill elective offices, "on leaving those offices (here he is referring to the Consuls) must give account to the people of what they have done" (Polybius, VI, 15, 11).

1.42 How the various forms of government are integrated in the Roman constitution, and how it achieved a division of the powers into three, on which Montesquieu would later reflect, is too well-known to dwell on here. What astonishes Polybius even more is what we would today call the interior or moral resources of the so-called mixed constitution: the separation, and at the same time the collaboration, existing between the various powers. This makes it possible "to confront each situation adequately, so that it becomes impossible to find a better form of constitution than this one (...) thus it can be realized how the state succeeds in finding a remedy for the ills which afflict it, from within its own constitution" (Polybius, VI, 18, 1-6).

1.43 There is another aspect of Rome which Polybius notes and which has received too little attention from scholars on the subject: "In my opinion, in every state there are two elements by virtue of which its nature and its forms become either desirable or absolutely to be avoided – custom and laws. Now the desirable effects of these elements are those which render the private life of the citizens morally correct and characterized by moderation (...) while the effects to be avoided absolutely are the opposite ones" (Polybius, VI, 47, 1-2). On these two things, custom and laws, depends the good outcome of social life: – living together by individuals. Social life, something very different from what Aristotle thought of as "political life", *it is not something which comes about by nature. Human nature has need of laws and customs to give concrete form to what is perhaps only a tendency.* This was to become very clear in the writings of Cicero and also of Seneca, but Polybius had already succeeded in understanding in Rome that "only with the passage of time (...) does social life begin to mature" (Polybius, VI, 5, 10). *For the Romans, nature bestows nothing; everything is the fruit of laborious research.* The concept of perfect nature does not exist for them as it does for the Greeks, and we can understand that for them it was impossible to conceive of an ideal state rather than a possible one, like the one they had in effect attained. For this reason, in contrast to the philosophical "governors" of Plato, they never believed in the perfectibility of man so that (again, as Polybius writes): "No-one can hold a political office (in Rome) if he has not first completed ten years of military service" (Polybius, VI, 19, 4), or if he has not completed his *cursus honorum* in the civil sphere. No-one may dabble in politics if he is not trained to engage in it, even if he is predisposed to do so by nature.

1.44 To return to Cicero – it is easy for us to understand why it is wide of the mark to claim that Platonism plays a major role in his eclecticism. This judgment has not sufficed to give proper credit to Cicero and to the very real originality which his thought possesses, despite his many critics. Cicero's teaching would otherwise not have been for all those centuries at the basis of the humanistic and civic European renaissance, which from the birth of the autonomous communes until the modern state has characterized a great part of our civilization. Moreover, even a superficial reader who nevertheless pays some attention to the two "Republics" can hardly fail to see substantial differences between the two works. For instance, while in the Platonic Republic it is the philosophical Governors who rule, in the Ciceronian it is the laws themselves, and this is no small difference. However, it should be remembered that above all, "while Plato had philosophically achieved the Ideal State, Cicero idealized the real one" (Marchesi, 300). Nor can it be said that Cicero was unaware of this novelty, since he openly maintains that he has dedicated all his attention not, as Plato had, to "a tiny and unreal state (...) to a shadow or a ghost of a state, but to the most majestic Republic" (Cicero, DR, II, 30). The Republic of Plato and the Greeks in general was a closed political reality, a *civitas quam minima,* far from "the contacts and impelling necessities of large-scale social coexistence" (Marchesi, 301), where it is not merely principles which count, but laws and positive rules of government.

1.45 Because of this, in Cicero, in contrast to the Greeks, there is no illusion of creating a perfect or just society or state in its final form. Here too, we can find the awareness of being original in relation to the Greeks. For them, Cicero tells us, law, by its very name means giving to each what belongs to them; the Latin name, on the contrary, is derived from the word to choose. For the Greeks law has the significance of equity; for the Romans it is also the possibility of choice (cf. Cicero, DL, I, 6). Thus while in Plato we find the idea that a single expert or few (the Governors) can produce the rules for achievement of a just *polis,* the Roman Republic had arisen, as we have seen, not from the work of one single individual or one generation, but in the course of several ages, and by virtue of many men. Our notion, Cicero states, is centred around the life of a people: "*in populari ratione omnis nostra versatur oratio*" (Cicero, DL, I, 6).

1.46 Those who perform political actions in relation to this people (tribunes, quaestors, aediles, senators, censors, praetors, consuls, etc.) must be examples for all. Within the context of the laws, they must be examples of rectitude and virtue. In Cicero's opinion there is no political reform, and we cannot believe that by 'moral' he merely means the carrying out of abstract principles. It is a matter of being living examples of the institutions, as Montesquieu was to repeat (and not just by chance); because there is no Republic, as the writer of *L'Ésprit des Lois* reminds us, which can stand without the virtue of its component members. When this civic education is lacking, there is no law which can remain in force. Not even the punishments provided for by the law, however useful they may be, can keep men from crimes (cf. Cicero, DL, I, 14). Thus the Platonic claim to create a just society cannot even rest on just principles. Cicero is very specific on this point: "Among the most absurd things is the idea of considering all the principles sanctioned in the institutions and the laws of the people as just" (Cicero, DL, I, 15).

1.47 Virtue, or moral renewal, can only be obtained by a long labour of education and discipline (cf. Cicero, DL, III, 13). But this must begin from a particular class. In Cicero's eyes the Roman Republic is (to use Montesquieu's terminology again) an aristocratic republic, where the virtue of the individual and the honour of the *optimati* must be equivalent. I think, writes Cicero, that by changing the tenor of life of the *optimati,* the customs of the city are also changed. In fact only a few, very few, persons noted for their honour and glory are needed to corrupt or to correct the customs of the city (cf. Cicero, DL, III, 14). Bad examples cause more harm than bad theories. Political immorality, according to Cicero, should not be combated with theories on the Just State, as conceived utopistically by Plato, but by a practical life to be lived out by the most sensitive spirits for the purpose of convincing many others little by little. Thus it is not only good and bad laws which make a state good or bad, but those who devise the laws and conform to them. The truth is not given by Wise Men, as in Plato's Republic; the truth of laws, like their goodness, is the fruit of a slow search. The laws are the product of tradition and history because it is only through history that truth is sighted and sought. *"Intellego (...) in historia leges (...) ad veritatem"* (Cicero, DL, I, 1).

1.48 It is clearly not a question of merely tending towards a definitive truth, as Plato desired in his Republic, but of a continuous improvement of the laws, and hence of society. For Cicero, the analysis of the laws is a way of knowing reality. Laws have a genuine gnoseological value. *"Ignorance of law, rather than its knowledge, is the cause of dispute"* (Cicero, DL, I, 6). This is why for the Roman, *ignorantia legis non excusat.* It is not tolerable that a citizen should not know the fundamental instrument of his civic life. It is clear how far away this is from the Greek mentality. Ignorance is not only the worst of the ills: to say this is not enough, and may even become a convenient excuse for many. In civil matters, ignorance is an unpardonable evil. It would be like claiming to be a mathematician while being ignorant of numbers. Ignorance of the basic laws is inadmissible for anyone wishing to be free.

1.49 The measure of a society's maturity is the degree to which this awareness is present. Indeed, for such a society to exist at all (the concept itself was foreign to the Greeks because it was so different from the *polis,* and conceived in its full dynamism), it is not only necessary to possess the conviction of having laws in common, but also rights (cf. Cicero, DL, I, 7). Everyone is *"ad civilem societatem natum"* (Cicero, DL, I, 24), where the world *ad* indicates a tension, a conquest to be gained, and not a datum already acquired. The *societas* is in fact the result of a journey. It is a matter of a numbers of individuals, indeed, of "associates" (*socii*), who are of one mind in creating the indispensable conditions for a happy and peaceful coexistence: *"vitamque hominum quietam et beatam inventas esse leges"* (Cicero, DL, II, 5). These laws are not the end of society, they are its means. This aspect of the subject was quite clearly understood by mediaeval thinkers of the age of the Communes, and even by those who would reach the point of justifying tyrannicide.

1.50 The ultimate end of society, of which the laws are the means, is therefore peaceful coexistence between individuals. Only when life is lived in peace can all individuals, no longer under the pressures of fear and violence, fully realize themselves. This general aim must be set before all particular aims. The latter are not to be excluded, by any means: without personal utility it is impossible to conceive of human actions. But if we seek solely and exclusively our utility, even altering the rules of peaceful coexistence, we must be considered cunning citizens rather than good ones: *"callidi sumus, non boni"* (Cicero, DL, I, 14). This is why, along with positive rights determined by historical circumstances, certain inalienable rights must also exist. These cannot depend solely on agreements. Cicero is very clear in maintaining that not everything concerning rights can be founded in the decrees of the people and the deliberations of the governors. If this were so, who could prevent the majority from approving a right to rob, to falsify, etc.? (cf. Cicero, DL, I, 16). In short, there exist basic laws which ordinary laws cannot annul. This is the principle of the modern juridical state: in certain subjects, even a *Referendum* is not permitted. The basic principles are accepted in and for themselves, independently of any profit or advantage (cf. Cicero, DL, I, 18).

1.51 If we turn for a moment to the alleged eclecticism of Cicero: we have already seen how different his way of conceiving the Republic is from Plato's. The same can be said with regard to Stoicism. In Rome, this movement acquired particular connotations which distinguished it from the way it was defined elsewhere. Cicero is fully aware of this: "The ancient Stoics carried on theoretical discussions about the state, with great acumen indeed, but not in a practical manner for the utility of the state and the people" (Cicero, DL, III, 6). The same goes for the idea of cosmopolitanism, which the Stoics could only develop theoretically, since a state of world dimensions was only just beginning to take form, over and above all forms of theory, and it had the capacity to permit a citizen to say that he enjoyed the same rights whether he was in Athens or Jerusalem or Alexandria or Rome.

1.52 We can see how right Cicero's affirmation that the Stoics only thought "theoretically" about the state was from the care which he takes, for instance in the third volume of *De Legibus,* to search out in great detail even the practical mechanisms which can aid the functioning of the various institutions. Anyone who thinks that the oratory of the

Senators is infected with unhealthy logorrhea should think again, in the knowledge that in the Senate "three precepts must be observed: to take part, to speak when it is one's turn, and not to be prolix. The first because the discussion is more serious when the greatest number of those present take part in it; the second bans speaking when one is interpellating, and the third recommends restraint in speaking, because conciseness is the greatest possible virtue" (Cicero, DL, III, 3). Apart from the competence and the perceptiveness of the magistrate and the politician, there is here all the experience of the advocate. And then what of the fact that politicians should never be absent without valid reason when they should be exercising their proper functions, and must be considered blameworthy if they absent themselves in their own interests? Their work must also be meticulous, and senators must never bring more than one proposed law under discussion at the same time (cf. Cicero, DL, III, 4).

1.53 In Rome, politics is the laboratory of action, not a dream or an illusion. Even the great issues like cosmopolitanism are a proof of this. If we remember that Cicero himself said: "I will not deny that Arpinum is my homeland, though that other land, from which all men whatever their place of origin receive their rights of citizenship, is greater still" (Cicero, DL, II, 2). He said the same of Cato. Roman cosmopolitanism was no abstraction; it was what we might today call the better side of pluralism in universal citizenship: not a denial of one's place of origin, but something which gives it a new dimension which respects different cultures. Here cosmopolitanism is genuine pluralism.

2. The apogee of the principality and the long crisis.

A) Cicero once again is witness to an era of transition.

2.1 Cicero was not only the great theorist and defender of republican ideals and institutions; he was also the most informed analyst of their crisis. A few weeks after the death of Caesar he wrote with great farsightedness to Cassius: "what has been done up to now, it seems to me, has freed us from the tyrant but not from the tyranny: with the tyrant dead, we all become executors of his will. Nor is this all: so many dispositions that he would not have made, were he alive, we are ratifying as presumed expressions of his will. Nor do I see where we are going to end up with this step" (Cicero, Ad f., III, 18-20). Cicero had a bitter conclusion in mind: the force of arms was about to be substituted for the force of the institutions. He observed with some bitterness to a friend: "But no-one who thinks freely of the Republic can act without danger to day, in the midst of so many armed men secure in their impunity, and it does not seem to me to be consonant with my dignity to talk of affairs of state where the closest and most attentive listeners are the soldiers rather than the senators" (Cicero, Ad f., III, 56-58). Once again: "The situation of the republic is such – if we can speak of a republic at all when we live in the midst of soldiers" (Cicero, Ad f., III, 66-68). Cicero, who had never been a defender of Caesar, knew that the situation had deteriorated gravely with his death. The clemency of which Caesar had given adequate proof came to an end, especially because after the death of Pompey, he made an effort to pose as the defender of the institutions even more than as the man who had defended and extended the boundaries of the state. Cicero was well aware of this, and in numerous letters to Atticus he showed that he was worried about a possible victory by Pompey which would have meant the reopening of the list of prescriptions (cf. Cicero, *Ad Atticum*, the letters of the first half of the year 49).

2.2 Cicero had the honesty to admit the undeniable and rare qualities of his political adversary, held to be a veritable prodigy of speed, dedication and acumen. However, he also knew that these very capacities could not draw him back from his great projected aim of going to the Orient, in emulation of Alexander the Great, and he knew that such an undertaking, which would be enormously expensive, was not acceptable to the Roman aristocracy: so much so that it was to be one of the real causes of the death of Caesar. Thus he knew that, perhaps to gain consensus, Caesar showed himself to be bound by Republican legality. For him, the institutions, even though they might need updating in some cases, were untouchable. Even though the intention is clearly propagandistic, what Caesar says about his policy during the civil conflict witnesses that in the population the desire still lived on to keep republican ideals alive, and certainly for him it would have been counter-productive to attack them. Caesar wished in fact "to re-establish the tribunes of the people in their power (...) in order to feel himself free, along with the Roman people, from the tyranny of the factious few" (Caesar, DBC, I, 22, 5). Specifically declaring himself to be on the side of the *populares*, Caesar seeks to maintain this attitude in the military sphere as well (cf. Caesar, DBC, 1, 84, 2), frequently dealing with delicate questions before all his soldiers. It should not be forgotten that with the same respect for republican institutions, Caesar (nominated dictator in 49 B.C.), laid down this office when he was elected consul in 48. Even when the conflict with Pompey became more acute, he proposed several times to his rival that they should both submit to the decisions of the Senate and the people (cf. Caesar, DBC, III, 10, 8-10). By doing this he would have avoided spilling the blood of his soldiers uselessly and bringing inevitable harm to the Republic (cf. Caesar, DBC, III, 90, 2). We should also remember, in connection with this, that Caesar already felt anxiety about the demographic crisis to such an extent that on many occasions he sought to make life easier for larger families, even producing draft laws.

2.3 It was not likely that some liberal positions would be lacking in Caesar's policy. He was highly tolerant in matters of religion, and as a man of politics he was extremely open to the intellectual world. There are many testimonies to this, which Suetonius sums up in a succinct phrase: "Caesar conferred the right of citizenship on those who exercised the profession of medicine, or on those who taught the liberal arts in Rome, both to bind them to their place of residence and to attract others there" (Suetonius, De Vita C, Caesar, 42). It is clear that this kind of initiative was also welcomed by the aristocracy. Although they were opposed to him on the political plane, they were responsive to culture and acted as protectors to a fair number of intellectuals. This openness on the part of Caesar was the basic motive for his dream of heading for the Orient; the need he felt was not only a military one. His nature, we would say today, was typically Roman, and typically "western". He had not borrowed from the Greeks the Hellenistic mentality which looks towards a divinisation of power (even though such attempts were made in the Orient). In him, personal glory and that of Rome were inextricably linked, and it was from this that the need arose to express it by carrying "Romanitas" to the world at large. Such an enterprise was regarded by the Roman upper classes, who would have had to bear the burden of the costs, as too expensive and useless. In this sense it is possible to concur with the judgment of many historians, like F. E. Adcock, for instance, who maintain that Caesar was a victim and martyr of his own genius.

2.4 The political climate at Rome was thus quite difficult. Despite the killing of the tyrant, it was not all that clear who could reinstate the ancient republican guarantees, or how. It is noteworthy that in this situation Cicero is again far-sighted in looking into the future. In the young Octavian, whose praises he sings, he perceived the real rival of Antony whose coming to power would otherwise have been quite fatal to the motherland (cf. Cicero, Ad f., III, 114). Octavian is seen as a possible restorer, the one who will be capable of bringing back law and liberty and who will finally put an end to the civil wars. Octavian himself was well aware of this task, and of the expectations of the Romans. It should not be forgotten, for example, that in the thirties he did not make any mention of a conflict against Antony. The declaration of war was made against Cleopatra. The civil wars had been declared ended for a long time, and public opinion felt united against a foreign enemy who could threaten the recovered stability which had brought back security in commerce and tranquillity in farming. The population had in fact returned to its civilian occupations, or to work in the fields, and it is certainly not a coincidence that in these same years Varro composed his treatise on agriculture, Iginus wrote practical manuals for farmers, and above all, Virgil composed the *Georgics*.

2.5 Over the years Octavian accepted various titles, but he never accepted one which would lead, even remotely, to the thought that he was the head of a State deprived of liberty. The novelties were all integrated into the continuing pattern. Suetonius records that Augustus stated in one of his Edicts: "We hope that the State will be kept safe and prosperous, so that I may receive the reward which I seek: in other words that I will be remembered as the founder of the happiest of regimes, and can take away on my deathbed the hope that the bases of the state will always be truly solid, as I have established them" (Suetonius, De Vita C, Aug., 28). It was only in this relation between tradition and novelty, in which the latter finds a place for itself in the former, that Augustus could acquire that *auctoritas* whose significance was very clear to any Roman. We are not yet in the period when *auctoritas,* progressively breaking away from the cultural and "sociological" environment in which it had emerged, began to indicate a personalisation of power. Augustus' *Auctoritas* rests on the strength of the institutions which are embodied from time to time in more or less capable individuals. The actual title of *Princeps civitatis,* which he accepted with a good grace, was very clearly present in the tradition, and even in the writings of a fierce defender of Republican tradition like Cicero. The title itself, *Princeps,* reveals that his powers, especially the legislative ones, derive from the fact that Augustus had received the *Imperium* from the people by means of the famous *lex de imperio* (cf. *Digesta*, 1, 4.1). Here too Cicero declaims: "*Senatus censuit, populusque jussit*" (Cicero, Pro Plancio, XVII, 42). The people express their sovereignty and the Senate manifests their resolutions; for a long time various emperors, at the most critical moments, referred back to these criteria. With the passing of time, the burden of the resolutions was imposed by force of arms, but it is strange that, even when the will of the Legions was imposed on the Senate, the search went on basically, and even unconsciously, for the assurance of consensus. One need only mention Nero who, although he had received the imperial acclamation from the Praetorians, declared that "their ancient functions remain to the Senate" (Tacitus, Ann., XIII, 4).

2.6 The Senate was the basic institution of the Roman tradition. It is symptomatic that the duality of tradition and novelty which forms part of this whole phase should be manifested in the Senate more than any other institution. Augustus could concede the *latus clavus*, i.e. could open the possibility of becoming a Senator to those who were not so by birth. The senatorial dimension was opened to new and special classes. This was to be a novelty which in the West would be taken up in England, where, with the passage of time, it became possible to enter the House of Lords because of particular merit. Certainly these nominations and the respect for the Senate would allow Augustus to have considerable influence on the legislative system, since he himself had refused on many occasions the power to promulgate all the laws which he considered useful. Another way of intervening in public life was put into effect by Augustus, when he instituted new responsibilities in order to introduce new officials into the administration of the Republic.

2.7 Despite this, the novelty was apparent in all its clarity. The dimensions of the city-state, from which a real institutional miracle had emerged, were becoming confused with the whole known world, and it was certainly not possible to pretend that without a transformation, primarily of the administrative system, but not only of that, the ancient structure could have continued to exist. Tradition, which had never interfered in religious matters, soon found itself face to face with the numerous cults originating in every corner of the Empire. Again thanks to the strong impulse provided by the communication routes, the process of reciprocal osmosis, give and take, typical of the Roman mentality, was very soon under way. While a slow path towards Romanization was initiated, it is also true that Rome, by absorbing the most varied tendencies, showed itself to be a genuinely universal city. Only this reciprocal osmosis could guarantee the *Pax Romana* of which all made use. Spontaneous development was encouraged everywhere, and the progressive consolidation of the many diverse attitudes, along with that *laisser-faire* policy which was so important in the western tradition also prospered (as we shall see at a later stage). With regard to the reform of the administrative system, it should be remembered that the governor could be called to answer accusations by the provincials. When a governor was brought to justice, as a rule, the penal procedure began with the *concilium* of the province. The institution of these *concilia* must have made a substantial contribution to spreading confidence in the operation of the Roman administration in the most important of the provinces (cf. Stevenson, 86).

B) *The guarantee of legal rights and its role in social osmosis.*

2.8 Over and above the technical advantages of private law, its basic merit, which can certainly be described as philosophical in that it implies a precise vision of man in relation to political power, is to have provided a guarantee of liberty in the face of absolutism, especially absolutism of a monarchical-theocratic character. "The determining element, however, was very probably constituted by the new relations of landownership, previously indivisible, and the collective possession of the village: in other words, the preponderance of private property relations is the necessary postulate for the establishment of a genuine aristocracy, whose existence is attested both on the economic and ideological planes, by the necropoleis of the late Iron Age" (Coarelli, 86). In its ancient period, Rome was thus aware of the importance of property safeguarded by law, which substituted the war of words for the cruel struggle (cf. Coarelli, 91), and gave a new impulse to civilisation in this way. The guarantee of the laws constituted a genuine appeal for neighbouring populations, which confirms that Rome was the result of the unification of a number of villages, a number of populations and differing cultures. Law was the root of tolerance and is surely the reason which explains, more than any other, how Rome passed from a small village to a universal empire – a unique event – leaving as an inheritance to all the democracies concepts of citizenship, property, individual freedom and its relationships with other components of the state, which even though often revised and amplified, remain in substance irreplaceable.

2.9 The Roman Republic has been described as aristocratic, both by ancient and modern writers, and perhaps a true republic, if we view it honestly, always is a little aristocratic, even in our own days (I will take up this theme again when dealing with Montesquieu). If the Roman Republic was not egalitarian, at least it knew how to protect the liberty of its citizens against abuses of power. "Liberty is in the laws; in the voluntary acceptance of rules established by common agreement" (Gaudemet, 172). Since it had to defend this common agreement, the freedom of the individual, property, citizenship, etc., *Roman Law was immediately presented as the work of man.* This is an aspect of unbounded historical significance. In contrast to legislations which had gone before, and for a very long time to those that followed, Roman Law did not hand on the will of gods or epic ancestral legislators. For this reason, it always remained flexible, subject to improvement and easily adaptable, except for certain basic principles such as property. This explains why the Romans were always simultaneously respectful of the past and capable of adaption to the present. In short, they were capable of renewal in continuity. All this seems to be "the result of the combination which Roman genius was able to achieve between very concrete attention to practical needs and to the insertion of law into a context of doctrinal thought" (Gaudemet, 175-176). Latin jurists never began with the individual in the abstract; they saw man in action, and by his action, creating rules. We should beware, however: law did not merely follow behind action in an attempt to regularise it, which would have meant chaos. It drew up legislation for all those actions which came within the models of its own civilisation, models which future history has often judged, and found to be universal. We need only think of the heritage of vocabulary, or rather of concepts, which Roman law has left to posterity. But rather than making a list of terms which would be long and incomplete, it will be sufficient to point out that the basic requisite of very many juridical issues is consensus between the parties. The exchange and manifestation of consensus is at the basis of the notion of *"Romanitas"* and of the whole world which has a real claim to be democratic.

2.10 During the Republic and the golden age of the Empire, everything had to remain within the bounds of legality, even the use of arms. The army, for instance, had to be subject to legitimate institutions, even for the most inoffensive actions. In the case of a triumph, it was the Senate's privilege to grant approval for it. It should be remembered that the triumphant victor was obliged to remain outside the *pomerium* (outside the territory of the citizens) in order not to constrain the free will of the Senate and people. If he entered the city on his own initiative, he would have lost the *imperium*, in other words the supreme power of command in warfare and presidency over the execution of the laws. Hence, the triumphant military leader must submit, even with the force of arms, to the juridical rules laid down for the performance of triumphs, on pain of the loss of his rights. It will be remembered that when the German legions invited Germanicus to usurp the *imperium* (on the meaning of this word see Appendix 1), he refused, and fortified by tradition and the law, he succeeded in bringing back discipline to the army (cf. Velleius Paterculus, II, 125, 1-3). Something very different was to happen in the time of Ammianus Marcellinus. But as the centuries passed, the concept of *imperium* had already collapsed. The same thing happened to the institution of the *dictator,* which in the republican epoch had been institutionalised (cf. pt. 1.38). The Romans were aware of the usefulness of this office, but despite the limits established by law, they did not abuse it when they had recourse to it. Only in the time of Silla do we find a degeneration of this kind of power, to which, however, the Romans did not resort for one hundred and twenty years (cf. Velleius Paterculus, II, 28, 2). Cicero himself, when he expounded the idea of the *Princeps* capable of governing the Republic, was thinking of an authority which could oppose the advancing tyranny of Caesar, and others who were already destroying the ancient Republic.

2.11 This ancient Republic had been built up on the strength of law, both internally and in its dealings with other neighbouring or allied populations. It should be remembered that for quite a few historians, the strength of the Romano-Italic combination lay precisely in its law, which was able to bind differing peoples together in a community of interests. There can be no doubt that "the contemporary extension of the right of citizenship and the development of the prestige of Rome consequent upon the extension of that right to a common one" (Velleius Paterculus, I, 14, 1) marked a period of great prosperity resulting from stability and juridical certainty.

2.12 The strength of law, which often granted even defeated slaves the possibility of entering into civil life, was not merely boasted of by the Romans but also admired by the Greek historians who had never witnessed anything similar in their own country. Dionysius of Halicarnassus admired Rome for the possibility, for anyone who needed it, to receive asylum, for the granting of citizenship to the defeated or to slaves, and the absence of contempt towards other social classes, because everyone could prove himself to be useful to the community (cf. Dionysius of Halicarnassus, I, 9, 4). These were no transient achievements, but were of such durability that they were codified so that Roman legislation (again according to Dionysius) had been wiser than and superior to Greek legislation ever since the days of the Twelve Tables (cf. Dionysius of Halicarnassus, XI, 44, 5). As far as asylum and acceptance into civil life were concerned, ever since the earliest days, Rome "realising that many cities of Italy were ruled by malignant tyrannies and oligarchies, sought to welcome and attract to itself fugitives from these cities (...) without distinguishing between their differing misadventures and fortunes" (Dionysius of Halicarnassus, II, 15, 3). When Rome exercised its supremacy over these cities, in the vast majority of cases it did so by leaving them the possibility of governing themselves as far as their own internal matters were concerned, by their own laws, and even in many cases with their ancient forms of government (cf. Dionysius of Halicarnassus, III, 60, 3-4).

2.13 A further achievement for the dignity of the individual person in the early days of Rome was that of establishing by law that, in contracting debts, one could not offer as guarantee the physical person of free men. Creditors thus could only make good their losses from the property of the contracting person (cf. Dionysius of Halicarnassus, IV, 9, 7). They could not inflict physical punishments or violence (cf. Dionysius of Halicarnassus, XVI, 4, 1-3; 5, 1-3), and for political crimes, the guilt of the fathers could not be visited on their children, something which caused the Greeks amazement (cf. Dionysius of Halicarnassus, VIII, 80, 1-3). On private questions, it was with one's goods that one answered. Furthermore, even in very ancient times, judges were appointed who were to deal with cases involving private affairs. This contributed more than might be believed to the political stability of Rome, because it not only placed the decisions of private individuals under juridical tutelage, but by giving value and defence to contracts, it also contributed to the security and harmony between citizens which provided faith in the institutions (cf. Dionysius of Halicarnassus, VI, 28, 2). Contract also guaranteed the certainty and selfsufficiency of one's own goods; it established limits in relation to third parties and the state. Again, the limitations of possessions were fixed by law. These limits *(termines)* had a sacred value for the Romans, and they could not be arbitrarily challenged. Religious festivals were dedicated to the *termines;* the famous *terminalia* (cf. Dionysius of Halicarnassus, II, 74, 2-4).

2.14 It was also in the earliest days that certain embryonic forms of popular rights made their appearance, to be gradually perfected as time went on. For instance, peoples could freely choose, through elections, whether or not to be annexed to the Roman state (cf. Dionysius of Halicarnassus, XI, 52, 4). Slaves, once freed and participating in the rights of citizenship, could if they wished return to their own city of origin. Then there was the fact that the person of an ambassador, even if he were a spy, was to be inviolable (cf. Dionysius of Halicarnassus, VI, 16, 3; 17, 1): this is something which even today in the 20th century remains obscure and foreign to quite a number of states and cultures.

2.15 Rome contributed all the components of the Republic to the rich juridical heritage; for this very reason the republic was an institution destined to endure for so many years. Moreover, as Cicero confirms, it was precisely the varied components with their differing roles and weights which made it possible to speak of an aristocratic republic in which even in the earliest times the people had the capacity to ratify basic decisions – and the role was exercised (cf. Dionysius of Halicarnassus, VI, 66, 3-4), while the Senate, after bitter struggles, began to accept forms of control which were capable of imposing limits on its operation (cf. Dionysius of Halicarnassus, VII, 55, 5). The Senate, in turn, imposed such limits on the consuls (cf. Dionysius of Halicarnassus, VIII, 69, 2). A system of mutual controls was thus instituted which was to have great importance in the western tradition.

C) *Law, institutions and the army: towards the Principate*.

2.16 At the time of the origin of the Republic, the army was completely a citizen army, and was called to arms whenever circumstances required. At the end of the Roman world this was no longer the case. Soldiering had become a profession in which money played a very important role, to the extent that the various commanders could buy the loyalty of the army. This was also the case because the soldiers, once demobbed, were entirely at the mercy of the providence of their leaders if they owned no land. Historians of the crisis provide various examples. However this may be, the army was for centuries the element which more than any other spread many elements of Roman culture, including the ideal of urban life. This should not mislead us into mistaken notions about the Roman political system. The army, despite the extension of the Empire, never had more than thirty legions (cf. Wacher, I, 5-6). This makes it clear that the bond which held the Roman Empire on its feet was provided by a different strength, which was not a military one. The connecting element in the whole system of the provinces was the strength of the Law (cf. Wacher, I, 10). If this was so within the boundaries, the force of law and of treaties went much further. Based on the right of peoples, and anticipating the principle that *"pacta sunt servanda"*, Rome concluded treaties with neighbouring peoples, or with distant dynasties, and even in wartime often preferred the diplomatic way to direct conquest (cf. Maxfield, I, 208).

2.17 It was law itself which guaranteed an incredible social mobility: the non-citizen aspired to citizenship, the slave to liberty, the son of the freedman could be a free man, and thus enjoy many things which had been denied to his father (cf. Wacher, I, 14). Furthermore, as Wacher once again summarises well, the society which made up the Empire was quite varied and cosmopolitan, multi-lingual and given to travel. Those who lived in the provinces made use of the existence of local laws alongside the laws of Rome. The heterogeneous mixture of races and doctrines bears witness to the security of a pluralistic social life, guaranteed by the law. It seems paradoxical, but the peoples which did not integrate or which constantly rebelled were the most backward and distant from Mediterranean civilisation: in other words those which were unable to enjoy the security of trade, the benefits of law and of the civilisation built on citizenship continued to live a nomadic existence, incapable of appreciating a stable way of life. They would never learn to understand, and thus make use of, the kind of "commercial law" by which the Romans provided legal protection to foreign merchants (cf. Branigan, I, 55).

2.18 The greatness of Rome, which as I sought to show in Chapter 1, begins with its monarchical period, depends on the fact that the various traditions and cultures with which it came into contact were absorbed in all matters which were considered useful, and in all cases respected, leaving usages, customs and laws to the individual peoples which they had always had. However, this did not cancel out the Roman tradition; indeed it enriched it. Even when Rome came into contact with the Greek philosophical schools it did not merely submit passively to them, (the example of Seneca is a case in point, and we shall return to it later). It re-processed and "digested" them, adapting them to its own political ideas and reinforcing its own traditions. The preponderance of tradition in Roman society is a warning to any historian tempted to view Roman history in terms of separate upheavals and periods. The persistent attachment to tradition is a source of continuity even within the general framework of change. In other words, while the terms Republic and Principate suggest separation and change, we find that we are faced with a continuity which mitigates and to some degree negates such change. The Republic, in other words, not only conditioned the Principate, but continued into the Principate (cf. Braund, I, 62-63). This is a further confirmation that in Rome there existed a constant osmosis between continuity and novelty which is shown in that social mobility which I referred to above. Although this mobility never got as far as giving rise to genuine political parties, it did produce something like genuine pressure-groups. From time to time, and for specific purposes, temporary alliances were formed, which then later dissolved and there were sometimes bitter struggles, embryos of the civil wars which produced the Principate (cf. Braund, I, 63-64).

2.19 Anyone seeking an example of the foregoing could find it in the contrast between Octavian and Mark Anthony. The former was very soon presented not as the head of a faction in a civil war searching for personal power, but as the defender of tradition. For this reason he financed some senators, to allow them to maintain their social position; he put himself forward as the defender and restorer of the *mores* (ancient customs), and finally he recognised all the functions of the Senate and people, as we can see from the *Res Gestae* (cf. Braund, I, 75). Augustus had restored the Republic but *Res Publica* – literally public affairs – did not denote republic in the modern sense, but something nearer to the state (cf. Braund, I, 76). This claim may be somewhat debatable, but it is an undoubted fact that Augustus was in the end the guarantor of that *Pax Romana* which is the connoting title not only of a civilisation but also of the whole western tradition. He was first citizen rather than Emperor, and this was how the Romans conceived the *princeps* for a considerable time. This is witnessed by the fact that the problem of the succession was for a long period a special one which could not be allowed to depend entirely upon the sovereign. Touchard sums up this important problem in the following way: "It is nevertheless indicative that the principle of dynastic inheritance of the oriental kind never managed to establish itself, at least as a theoretical generalisation. The Empire is not a transferable property. It should be added that in contrast to Xerxes and Alexander and the Ptolemies, the Roman emperors were never able to dispose of the wide-scattered imperial domains as if they were their personal property, which could be divided, alienated or used at their discretion. They were merely the depositories of a heritage belonging to the *populus romanus*" (Touchard, I, 79): here were no examples of alienation or fusion of territories as a result of marriage. There were rare attempts, which always failed – Caracalla, for instance, attempted to unite the Roman world with the Iranian by a marriage. But with Caracalla, the empire was already well on its way to an orientalisation of power.

2.20 Returning to Augustus, we could say that he constituted the peak of a pyramid in his capacity as supreme magistrate. He certainly had the same *potestas* as other magistrates, but he knew no rivals as far as *auctoritas* was concerned (cf. Augustus, RG, 34, 3). It was really thanks to the latter that he could guarantee the *Pax Romana* which was so highly regarded by various strands of the population, to which it certainly proved useful. It was from this that Augustus obtained the consent which led everyone to believe that the institutional changes were included and installed in tradition. And the basis of tradition was in fact consent. Even so, the novelties were in fact substantial.

2.21 The *Res Gestae* were all written in the first person – a sign that something had changed, something which did not escape the ancient Roman historians. Florus, for instance, who wrote a substantial part of his famous *Epitome* by presenting the Roman people as protagonist, changes subject towards the end, with the exception of a few paragraphs. It was no longer the people, but the holder of *auctoritas* who was the protagonist now (cf. Florus, II, 22 ff). Florus too understood that the mania for glory of certain individuals could easily subvert the good sense of the people at a later stage, and he notes bitterly that "it is more difficult to preserve the provinces than to conquer them" (Florus, II, 30, 29). In this he shows a pacific and conservative mentality which Augustus had made his peculiar hallmark.

2.22 In view of this we may think one of Augustus' statements appears paradoxical. Even though he has no effective rivals, he maintains that he wishes to restore strength and credibility, as well as power, to the Senate and people of Rome (cf. Augustus, RG, 34, 1). By this he means to appear as an arbiter, even in international issues, pacifying all, and pardoning whole populations (cf. Augustus, RG, 3, 1-2). In a similar programme, he echoes the Virgilian dictum of *parcere victis et debellare superbos,* which summarises the policy of a whole era. On the institutional plane, however, an irreversible step has been taken; even the defenders of the mixed constitution and the republican institutions are aware of it. Cicero himself, in his *Somnium Scipionis,* sees Rome spreading itself in the form of an Empire. Subsequently Tacitus, the standard-bearer of liberty against the pretensions of an authoritarian principate, holds that the notion of a citizens' republic has already had its day, and he accepts the new system even though he condemns its defects. The Prince is already necessary, even though they wish him to be authoritative rather than authoritarian. This is not a play on words, because it is precisely here that the whole great issue of tyrannicide and regicide, which is at the basis of mediaeval and modern dissent, is centred.

2.23 This dissent was possible because the whole Western world adopted to itself the lapidary saying of Ulpianus, handed down from the *Digest*: "The will of the Emperor has the force of law because with the passage from the *lex regia* the people transfer to him their own power and their own authority" (*Digesta*, 1, 4, 1). This formula, on the basis of which the whole of western political thought is developed, translates the Ciceronian concession in which power derives from the people, who are its real depositary. The whole Mediterranean world made use of this principle; for this world the two concepts of *ius gentium and ius naturale*, as Sabine rightly stresses (cf. Chs. VIII-IX), combined more and more closely with each other in a fruitful way, and made possible in the thinking of the great jurists, the conviction of the existence of a law superior to particular experiences. However, the latter, as with the common law in England, would enrich the juridical process continually and vitally.

D) *Early theorists of the Principate.*

2.24 The Prince is the expression of the capacity to guarantee the universal law which could be disregarded unless there is a strong central power. Even though a certain nostalgia for the Republic may be preserved, the dimensions reached by the state render the old way of managing power impossible. There are quite a few thinkers who see it in this way, and not only political scientists, but also philosophers such as Seneca, writers like Pliny the Younger, poets like Lucan – apart, obviously from Tacitus and others whom we shall encounter shortly. Lucan himself, in his *Pharsalia,* speaks about the opportunity of reconciling the Principate with liberty. The Principate had been imposed as a result of the civil wars which, if taken to their extreme consequence, would have shipwrecked every institution and in the end, destroyed liberty itself. Destiny had found no other way but that of the Principate to save the Roman world (cf. in general terms the Proem of Book I). The balance within the republic had become precarious: concord, in complete disaccord, could already only endure for a few moments. The expression "*concordia discors*" (Lucan, I, 98) seems particularly appropriate; it brings to mind Kant's "social unsociability" which was to enjoy such popularity in our own times. *Concordia discors,* being unaware of any kind of rule, could not endure for very much longer. These rules were no longer recognised because the moral strength of the people who had given birth to them had failed. Here again the expression used is very specific: "*Nobilitas cum plebe perit*" (Lucan, II, 101), meaning that the desires of the people themselves were now quite different, and a force capable of guaranteeing them was necessary.

2.25 By the time of Pliny the Younger, the Principate was already consolidated and universally accepted. It enjoyed full consensus, which was shown in the context of the unifying principles of the Roman institutions. The adhesion to the figure of the Emperor depended on a whole series of guarantees which he gave to his citizens. The person who reaches the high point of government is the best-suited precisely because of the guarantees which he is able to give those who place maximum trust in him. If this does not happen, if the criterion of imposition is substituted for that of adoption, fear not only of the present but also of the past prevails. It should be noted that in the *Panegyric of Trajan,* we read that when the people are afraid to speak ill of a bad Prince of the past, it means that they are afraid of the malevolence of the present Prince (cf. Pliny, 53, 6). Because of this Pliny the Younger insists strongly not only on adoption but on a form of adoption which is not the consequence of civil war but the fruit of a peacetime confrontation (cf. Pliny, Chs., 5-9). The Emperor thus appears virtually to be elected, as the President is in a modern presidential democracy, and he governs by consent and not by force of arms. Pliny's essay, even though it might have been rather shorter in the first place, is very rich in such ideas, and it is really strange that it has been neglected for so long.

E) *Seneca.*

2.26 Seneca, like Lucan, also had Nero in mind. He helped and advised him, but he reminded him too that while he is indeed the first, he is so in the interests of the many: he is the safeguarder, not the master. He must guarantee and not impose; his strength is in relation to an order which otherwise would not exist. In *De Clementia,* similar ideas are expressed. Too much success renders people insatiable, and the passions themselves prove to have no rules at all (cf. Seneca, DC, I, 7). The Roman people had already embarked on this road, and the Prince must use his capacities to mitigate, rule, correct, etc. It is from this that clemency derives: in the opinion of Seneca it needs severity and strength, otherwise it is mere complicity which no longer governs, but drags all down into the chaos of civil war. In short, order is characteristic of good imperial government, just as it was in the past the hallmark of the Republic.

Concetto Marchesi says of Lucius Annaeus **Seneca** that he was one of the most modern writers of Latin literature; it could probably be said rather that he was one the most modern figures of the whole ancient world. The son of a writer, Annaeus Seneca, author of a work which provides us with knowledge of Roman oratory at the time of Augustus, he devoted his time to studies of the most varied kind, from philosophy to poetry and theatre to letter-writing, as well as oratory and what we would today call existential reflections. He was born around the time of the birth of Christ, at Cordova, and he often took part as an active protagonist as well as a witness in the events which saw the definitive establishment of the principate in the first century. Among his works, special mention should be made of the *Dialogorum libri,* the *De clementia,* the *De beneficiis,* the *Naturales quaestiones,* the nine tragedies and the famous *Ad Lucilium epistolarum moralium libri;* there are also numerous fragments of works which have not survived. Accused by Nero of being party to a conspiracy, he committed suicide in 65 A.D., showing, as he had always claimed, that he was able to face death with serenity.

2.27 Seneca's opinion is quite unusual, not only for his own time, but because it would appear to anticipate some of the themes of more recent political thought on the state of nature, while giving it new, and at that time original, consequences. Original happiness, if there really was such a thing, was for Seneca due not to the goodness of human beings, but to their ignorance. It was the latter "which rendered them innocent: there is a great difference between not wanting to do harm and not recognising it. They lacked justice, prudence, temperance and fortitude, yet their lives in the crude state had something similar to these virtues. Only an educated and cultured soul could possess virtue – a soul which had reached it by constant commitment to perfection" (Seneca, Ad L, 90). Nobody is born virtuous, not even those we call the better class of men; all must strive in order to obtain virtue. "It is not nature which gives virtue; there is an art in becoming good" (Seneca, Ad L, 90). 'Art' here is understood as a slow and difficult journey, leading us to emerge from that original innocence which, precisely because it is not acquired, is similar to ignorance. "I do not believe that this philosophy existed in that crude era when the arts had not even been invented and the usefulness of things was learned directly from their use" (Seneca, Ad L, 90). Reasoned use led to the sense of limitation, and brought into being the first conception of property (cf. Seneca, Ad L, 90). To sum up, for Seneca, a social life worthy of man needs a cultural backing; it is the fruit of constant improvement, and it cannot be either a gift of the gods or a utopian return to the remote past of the state of nature.

2.28 The task of philosophy is to aid this process of cultural improvement. In a typically Roman view of things, philosophy resolves itself in action. Seneca's expressions on the subject could not be clearer: "Philosophy is not an art which serves to show off in front of people: it does not consist of words, but of actions" (Seneca, Ad L, 16). Seneca knows that the whole of Roman morality is expressed in this, so different from the Hellenic concept that he advises the reading of writers who, like Sextus Quintus, wrote in Greek but presented Roman moral norms (cf. Seneca, Ad L, 59). The latter are founded above all on the free action of the single individual, so that for Seneca "What is not free cannot be honest: fear is a sign of slavery" (Seneca, Ad L, 66). Free action may honestly pursue its own interests; indeed if it respects the rules of the game it must pursue its own interests, because in this case "the private interest is intimately linked to the public, so that the praiseworthy and the desirable are indistinguishable from each other" (Seneca, Ad L, 66).

2.29 The philosophy of action, however, must not be understood as a mere constant trailing after the deed. Political action must allow pauses for meditation and reflection, without which action becomes sterile. "We Stoics do not want our followers to participate in every government, in every occurrence, and without a break" (Seneca, Ad L, 68).

There must be alternation, so that those who govern may ensure peace and legality to allow everyone to pursue his or her own objectives or reflections.

2.30 There is alternation between theoretical and practical phases not only in political life, but also in moral life. "Virtue derives both from doctrine and from practice. We first have to learn, then confirm through our own behaviour what we have learned" (Seneca, Ad L, 94). This passage from the theoretical to the practical is not always easy, and for this reason there is a need for laws which not only advise us but also succeed in inducing us to fulfil our duty. The laws themselves, however, become devoid of sense if there is no moral tension between human beings. The laws are not abstractions. As in the whole Roman juridical conception, there is the conviction that "in the city where there are bad laws, customs too will be bad" (Seneca, Ad L, 94). It is here that Seneca becomes the interpreter of the crisis not only in the institutions but in those moral principles which had made the Republic great. When the sense of honesty itself fails, then every kind of disgrace is permitted. "Man, and what is sacred to man, is now destroyed simply for amusement" (Seneca, Ad L, 95).

2.31 Mutual respect between men is, for Seneca, the basic condition of civil life: "we are born to live in society. Our society is very similar to a stone vault; it would fall if the stones did not support each other, thus holding the whole vault in place" (Seneca, Ad L, 95). This is the reason that being together is called 'society', *a term which* – as we have seen in the previous chapter – *has the underlying meaning of that bond of solidarity without which everything decays and fragments.* All of this requires a constant commitment on the part of all, so that the social bond is never given and acquired once and for all. "Nothing is stable in private life as in public life" (Seneca, Ad L, 91). Prosperity itself must always be defended because it is constantly menaced (cf. in this context the whole of Letter 91). In connection with prosperity and the risk which it involves both for better and for worse, we should note that Seneca justifies interest paid on capital, if it is fair, as a legitimate thing: "while they pay interest as well as capital to the creditor, they should recall that the use of the benefit has been gratuitous. And the benefit grows with the passage of time: the longer the delay is, the more one must render back. The man who returns the original 'availment' without paying for its use is an ingrate: account must also be taken of this when the calculation is made of what has been received and what has been given" (Seneca, Ad L, 81).

2.32 Seneca lived at a very special moment of ancient history; a moment in which the necessities of the republic had passed away for good, while those of the Principate had not yet found their complete stability. This is the reason why Seneca ascribes great value to the moral quest; i.e. he intends to appeal to the conscience of everyone and of the whole of collective society, to the point where one can speak of social morality because, despite the disappointments arising from the Principate of Caligula, Claudius and Nero, Seneca had "always felt and believed that it was possible to ensure just and satisfying conditions of life, both interior and exterior, for mankind" (Viansino, XLIV). It is precisely this interior and exterior life that belongs to all human beings and renders them equally co-responsible for, and worthy of, the quest for liberty. Thus, despite its infinite contradictions, Seneca loved Rome as the first expression of a multi-racial and cosmopolitan city, where *the exercise of tolerance, for those who understand it, is a source of riches.*

2.33 In order to be truly free, it is necessary to preserve one's own individuality. Seneca is well aware that the crowd, often an expression of collectivist irrationalism, denies liberty because it cancels out the interior quest of the individual. But he is also aware that along with this danger, we should also fear the tyrannical degeneration which cancels all rules and all limits on the activity of power. Under tyranny, the ancient distinction between slave and free also disappears, because all are reduced to slavery, even though in different forms. "In substance, slavery ends up by becoming for Seneca the symbol of a system consisting of servility, fear and cowardice" (Viansino, LXIII). It is in this light that we can understand clearly what death means to Seneca. There is no irrational invitation to suicide in his writing, or worse, a nihilistic standpoint. In him there is only the conviction that "if we live in certain periods of history, we must learn to conquer the fear of death; we must learn to die" (Viansino, LXXI). The individual, in short, cannot be completely fulfilled in the state – a grandiose novelty for the ancient world – and for this reason there is a right to combat it and to reject it along with its slavery.

2.34 Suicide is an extreme case, when everything seems lost and one arrives at the final attempt which may, perhaps, rouse consciences. But before this, one may not give up on the moral commitment, a long and exhausting journey. The philosopher's words in relation to this are extremely lucid: "Tiredness claims the best: the Senate frequently holds audience for a whole day, while in the meantime the scum of the city or the fields are indulging their idleness, or sitting in the shade of the inn, or spending their time in some chattering group. The same thing happens in this great state: the best sort of people tire themselves out, consume their own resources and are at the same time consumed, and this, moreover, is done voluntarily" (Seneca, DP, V, 4). These hardworking individuals, who exhaust themselves, belong to the whole human race, and in them there is a conviction that "it is not for fear but for mutual love that one adheres to a pact and to mutual assistance" (Seneca, DI, V, 3). When such individuals lose their faith in their moral commitment, all possibility of civil life collapses. The first symptom of all this is when the idea of not being to blame for what happens begins little by little to take hold of the hearts of everyone – or worse still, the idea that no blame exists (cf. Seneca, DI, II, IX, 1).

2.35 Existence should induce us to constant improvement: "Right up to the last confines of life we shall be in action: we will not cease to strive for the common good, to help individuals, to bring aid even to our enemies" (Seneca, DO, I, 4). Action, in the Roman view, is superior to contemplation as an end in itself. In order not to be misunderstood on a crucial point, Seneca says this: "Contemplation is accented by all; some direct themselves towards it; for us it is merely a stopping place, not a gateway" (Seneca, DO, VII, 4). It should not be forgotten that even for Cicero, *true immortality did not belong to philosophers who become lost in abstractions, but to honest administrators of the state. His famous Somnium is evidence of this.*

F) *Tacitus.*

2.36 Tacitus was the first within the western tradition to perceive that with the crisis in the republican institutions, the force of arms had replaced the force of law. (This aspect would appear again in the analysis of Ammianus Marcellinus). In Rome, law and tradition was no longer respected, and these were the two hinges on which the power of the state turned. But this power already depended on the condottieri who no longer received their authority from the people or from the Senate, but from their own soldiers (cf. Tacitus, Ann., I, 31). The writer asks, in astonishment, "if they were to contend with the Emperor, what other resources remained?" (Tacitus, Ann., I, 47). He remarks bitterly that a period had begun in which "concessions had been extorted by force which had never been obtained by normal means" (Tacitus, Ann., I, 19). There was an attempt to give some sort of legitimacy to the force of arms and to their commanders by conferring on them some quality of the sacred. This aspect was due to the Hellenization which was at this time encountering the Roman Empire. Like the oriental despots, the Emperors also moved to divinise themselves, and it is certainly important that even by the time of Augustus the Emperor had done everything to distance himself from such a notion, while the cult of his person had in fact developed in the orient even during his lifetime (cf. Suetonius, De Vita C, Aug., 52). This too was a sign of the times: the ancient liberty provided for by the laws and sanctioned by juridical right was progressively disappearing, and in the state "the more liberty was dressed up with a sumptuous apparel, the more headway was made towards a deadly slavery" (Tacitus, Ann., I, 81).

We know neither the first name, the place or the date of birth of Cornelius **Tacitus**, a writer and historian of unusual effectiveness and precision. Information about him begins to appear in 77 A.D., the year in which he became engaged to the daughter of one of the most notable figures of the time, Gaius Julius Agricola. In 88 he was praetor and quindecimvir; in 97 he was assistant consul, in 112-113 proconsul in Asia, and from the year after that we know only that he devoted himself to composing his *Annals*. Apart from this work he also wrote the *Histories*, the *Dialogus de oratoribus, Germania,* and the *De Vita Iulii Agricolae liber,* a biography of his father-in-law.

2.37 Periods in office for the magistrates lasted longer than in the past and "the laws which fixed time-limits for the activities allowed for the candidates to acquire titles of merit were violated" (Tacitus, Ann., II, 36). In this way the laws were subjected to force, and power went constantly beyond its specific limits. It was not only the certainty of the law that vanished, but also its clarity and hence its comprehension on the part of the citizenry. "And already the draft laws were not made for the common benefit, but against individual citizens; and the proliferation of laws corresponded to the increasing decadence of the state" (Tacitus, Ann., III, 27).

2.38 Tacitus laments the few but stable and clear laws of the golden age of the Republic. He is sceptical about whether such a degree of sickness which has entered into politics can be cured through laws. They cannot reform uses and customs which have become part of the so-called common morality. Laws and politics are a reflection of the moral life which, when it falls into decay, cannot be reactivated by legal means. The way in which Tacitus records a speech by Tiberius (cf. Tacitus, Ann., III, 53-54), is a demonstration of this. The historian is very clear on this matter: "The laws contemplate facts which have already happened; simply because we cannot know the future. The wisdom of the ancients held that first came the crime and then followed the punishment; and there is no reason to subvert principles which grew out of reason and were always accepted (...) the force of law diminishes gradually as the power is reinforced; nor does one have to resort to authority when one can proceed by law" (Tacitus, Ann., III, 69).

2.39 It was always law and not force of arms which united peoples: this was the characteristic of Rome which distinguished it from Greece. "What was the fatal error of Sparta and Athens? Powerful in arms, they held the conquered at a distance from them, as people of another race (...) They (the conquered) have already entered into our customs, our activities, into the links of familyhood (...) plebeian magistrates follow those from the patrician ranks, the Latins follow the plebs, and these in turn are followed by magistrates of the other peoples of Italy" (Tacitus, Ann., XI, 24). And so it goes on; there is only one purpose: the stability of the Republic. According to Tacitus, the Romans understood that in politics, where the certainty of law was missing, everything became momentary, uncertain and transitory. The principle of inserting the different peoples little by little into the various magisterial offices only met with difficulties in the case of certain specific peoples. In the east, for instance, the Armenians were always of uncertain reliability because, Tacitus claimed, never having known liberty they were more inclined to be subjects, now of one power and now of another. This also explains why at the time of the great conquests in the East, the major criteria for founding colonies proved unworkable. "It was not whole legions with their tribunes, centurions and soldiers of every order, who were destined to found colonies; they would have founded a community which originated in consensus and in bonds of affection. But it was soldiers who did not know each other, from scattered groups without a real head, without common sentiments, almost men of differing species thrown together casually" (Tacitus, Ann., XIV, 27). It should be noted that like Cicero before him, Tacitus speaks of *consensus,* without which it is not society but a mere multitude which is produced. *According to him, it is only where consensus is found that real strength exists; all the rest is vain.*

2.40 In Tacitus' opinion, in those very difficult years little or nothing was any longer understood of the state; it had become estranged from the majority (cf. Tacitus, His., I, 1), and even estranged from the citizens of a capital choked with military personnel beyond the normal limits (cf. Tacitus, His., I, 6). The fact that the institutions were alien to and remote from the citizens seems truly strange if we compare it with what Polybius had noted in Rome some time earlier (cf. pt. 1.39). By now, the civic sense of the people was in deep decay. Politicians were judged for their image rather than their effective capacity. Nero was admired for his exuberance: others admired for their good looks or their imposing physical presence (cf. Tacitus, His., I, 7). Adulation, flattery and petty personal utility took the place of a sense of the state and a rigorous policy. The Principate appeared inconvenient in certain ways to Tacitus, because adulatory assent was substituted for the consensus typical of the Republic (cf. Tacitus, His., I, 15). In contrast to what Hobbes was to say on the efficacy of the monarchiacal system in comparison with other systems, Tacitus maintains that the Principate is often not only more inefficient than other systems, but also surely risks becoming more corrupt still, because in advising a Prince one does everything to make one's self acceptable. Flattery extinguishes and kills the critical spirit; the fear which creeps in with it (though even the criterion for fear is different from that of Hobbes) does the rest.

2.41 And yet, despite his opposition, Tacitus defends the Principate. It is his realism (would we ever have had realist writers without Tacitus?) which leads him to accept it. Passages taken from a conversation with Galba confirm this (cf. Tacitus, His., I, 16). He states that even if we were really desirous of creating the Republic, present necessities would force us to choose differently. There is a constant state of civil war, and these wars are characterised by being moments in which "action counts for more than meditation" (Tacitus, His., I, 62), and moments in which madness and fury necessitate a secure strength capable of control. Otherwise, in absolute indifference to good and evil, society will end in the most absolute state of impunity (cf. Tacitus, His., I, 72). The certainty of law guarantees life to the institutions, but when they begin to be stable in their insecurity so that they would not possess any credibility in time of peace (cf. Tacitus, His., I, 88), it means that the moment has come in which the force of law has been taken over by brute force, by arbitrary will, and the return of any form of security will be accepted with relief.

2.42 This is the origin of the constantly growing importance of the armed forces, which ended by imposing their leaders. Even if the phenomenon did not appear until late on, they were seen by the troops thirsty for novelty as favoured by the gods (cf. Tacitus, His., II, 33). This is the first step towards that "sacralisation" of the *Princeps* which the first Emperors had refused. Even though it was an eastern-tending and ridiculous idea, the leaders could not always straightforwardly reject it without running into clamorous opposition from their own soldiers, for at the human level, these had lost all respect for authority (cf. Tacitus, His., II, 56). These are aspects that no politician can ignore, because for anyone aspiring "to the Empire, there is no middle way between the peak and the precipice" (Tacitus, His., II, 74) – in sharp contrast to what applies to the lives of ordinary mortals. Arrogance and effrontery were to be found among men at arms (cf. Tacitus, His., III, 11-12), and a great deal of effort would be necessary to return everyone to his own role and bring back discipline and legality. Men pursued rank rather than responsibility, and in order to obtain it, there was no limit to the lies and crimes they would commit (cf. Tacitus, His., III, 49; there are numerous other passages, in which he even seems to prefigure Machiavelli). In this context there is one particularly important passage; a reflection on Eprius Marcellus, who had twice been consul: "He never forgot what sort of times they were in which he lived, what kind of a constitution their forefathers and ancestors had founded: but while he admired the past, he was closely attentive to the present. In his heart he wanted to have good emperors, but he was ready to submit to those whom fate produced (...) the worst emperors preferred a despotism without limits; thus the best, in whatever degree they happened to be so, wished for some degree of liberty" (Tacitus, His., IV, 8). This latter Principate is the kind that Tacitus admired, since the return of republican freedom, in which liberty was established by laws, was already impossible. One could speak of the Principate within a legal framework capable of giving back to Rome at least an appearance of its customary aspect: the strength of the laws and the correct function of the magistrates (cf. Tacitus, His., IV, 39). In short, a Principate which would bring an end to the civil wars and would be in a position to put victors and vanquished on the same level, bringing back peace to the provinces and prosperity to the state.

2.43 From what has been argued above, the criticisms of a "moralistic" kind which have often been levelled against the work of Tacitus seem quite meaningless. Vico very rightly speaks of him as an historian capable of examining men as they really are. Furthermore, it could be said that as someone with a profound knowledge of both past and present institutions, Tacitus finds, in comparative history, a motivation for reflection and analysis. In other words, he was a realist historian who would serve as a model and a "storehouse" of examples for all writers of political realism. The same could well be said of Ammianus Marcellinus, not so much because he himself claimed to be the successor of Tacitus, as because he analysed an even more difficult moment, when catastrophe was predicted. Like Tacitus he justified the Principate as driven by necessity, and like him he also refers back to that ancient Roman tradition full of *humanitas* which had characterised the senatorial aristocracy. It is certainly no coincidence that he often resorts to quotations from Cicero, who was the standard-bearer of the ideal of an aristocratic republic. His moralism, moreover, is typical of the ancient historians. Morality, even though it may be repudiated at frequent moments, is always held to be closely linked to politics, and thus, given these close links, to history.

2.44 It is precisely this reference back to a class which had made Rome great which leads Tacitus in contrast, as it would lead Ammianus, to see defects and vices in the present. This aspect is also highlighted in Roman satire, especially in Juvenal, but in Tacitus and Ammianus, the sense of the ridiculous proper to the genre of satire is often overwhelmed by the pessimism of the historian, who analyses the present with political eyes. There is certainly a distinct difference between Tacitus and Ammianus over questions of psychological insight into personality, and over style, but it should not be forgotten that Ammianus was a Greek who chose to write in Latin, reversing a custom and an opinion that was still too prevalent: *here in fact we have a Greek historian who took a Latin one as his model.* This is a clear sign that Rome had already created a world civilisation: of these two historians of the crisis – or rather of two differing crises – one came (possibly) from Belgic

Gaul, and the other from the Greek world. Both of them were admirers of a reality which no longer existed, what I have described as the first seedbed of the open society, and they both introduce us to it in a negative way, by criticising what they have before them and hoping that their intellectual strength may help to avert catastrophe.

G) *More on the Army*.

2.45 I have said several times that the army was never so great as the huge spread of the imperial territory demanded. This was due to the fact that the strength capable of uniting such diverse peoples and cultures was never that of arms, but of Law. This is undoubtedly true, but if the army was held within bounds, this was due to other reasons. The economic reason was by no means secondary, but political reasons were just as important. Augustus had already realised that an over-large army would be dangerous to him personally. Too many soldiers in a single province constituted a temptation for anyone who might wish to usurp his power in a period when civil strife was easy to foment (cf. Scott Anderson, I, 100-101). We can easily understand, as Suetonius says, why Augustus rushed so quickly to make pay and awards equal for the whole army, but above all was concerned to give economic help to the soldiers who wanted to return to civil life, without feeling any further nostalgia for arms (cf. Suetonius, De Vita C, Aug., 49). Moreover, when a soldier retired, apart from having the benefit of medical care, he also had the chance to enter civil life after having learned a trade. Many legionaries were experts in particular kinds of work and trades (...) there were printers, architects, nurses, smiths, dairy-manufacturers, plumbers, stonemasons and woodcarvers (cf. Scott Anderson, I, 108). The return to the civil state was also favoured because it allowed or legalised marriages.

2.46 All this lasted for well over two centuries. Beginning with Septimius Severus, and for the whole of the third century, the role of the military was progressively changing. It is certainly no mere chance that Septimius Severus himself was the first emperor to be elected by the Army. It was he who gave legal recognition to the marriage of soldiers, augmented their pay and privileges and increased the actual number of soldiers (as can be verified from the *Historia Augusta*). Not only the number of men, but also the amount of resources requested for military purposes was increased. The cities needed walls – we need only think of the Aurelian walls in Rome itself – a sign that Law and treaties were beginning to count for less and arms for more. The Emperor was more and more of a military chief and less and less a "*princeps civile*". The best generals came more and more to be chosen as his advisers – for instance, as in the famous *Tetrarchia* of Diocletian. We can undoubtedly state that the period which stretched from Septimius Severus and Caracalla to Aurelius and Diocletian represents the true 'Middle Ages' of the empire, the period in which it detached itself slowly from a phase which we might call civil, and moved closer and closer to a military one. The latter went on inexorably in the fourth century to the ultimate crisis in the institutions and laws as they had been understood not only in the republic, but also in a certain sense right up to the end of the second century of the Christian era. It is true that times had changed, and that Diocletian, and Constantine and Valentinian after him, are given the credit of having prolonged the life of the empire in the east, but it is also true that their military policy, which culminated eventually in the idea of a mobile army which would be moved around according to changing necessity, was to deal a mortal blow to Roman civilisation. The army had always been an element of stability, and hence of integration.

2.47 Another element of cultural and political stability was the city. With its traffic, its markets, the collection of taxes, the administration of justice and the expansion of building and architecture, it is the synthesis of what we mean by "Romanitas". The best aspects of local culture and the Latin world flowed together there, and were amalgamated. The harmony between building styles and local materials is a good example (cf. Drinkwater, II, 32). In the cities merchants and the native population helped the spontaneous spread of ideas, and along with them, tastes, fashions and the *modus vivendi* which found its finest expression in business guaranteed and safeguarded by law. In the city, people not only felt themselves to be citizens in their own right of the world state, but they also enjoyed maximum security. This is demonstrated by the fact that the greatest number of flourishing settlements in the west were open and without walls, a sign of the value and efficiency of Roman order (cf. Drinkwater, II, 54-56). It is in fact the city which helps us to understand how important to Roman culture was the relationship between civil society and law. In the Roman Empire, the distinction between the cities and the other types of civil settlements was clearly defined by law, and was never established merely on the basis of dimension or economic or social importance. It was Rome which granted its statute to a city, or which recognised its juridical status with a treaty (cf. Poulter, II, 69). And this status, like all law, was subject to transformation. Nothing was "crystallised", so that it was perfectly possible to witness a *vicus* obtaining the rank of a recognised city as time went by. In fact, on the subject of the *vicus,* it should be mentioned that it was often ruled by an evolved and liberal administration: two magistrates were elected, of whom one was a *peregrinus* (i.e. an inhabitant of the place and not a Roman citizen), while the other was a Roman citizen (cf. Poulter, II, 82).

In short, there was an attempt to integrate whatever was possible and convenient. In Egypt, for instance, where the administrative centre was the village, things continued in this way, and the cities never assumed significant roles or dimensions, apart from those which already existed.

2.48 Anyone who wished to could aspire to Roman citizenship, which naturally involved certain privileges, because such aspirations did not depend on one's ethnic origin. *This explains the general stability of an Empire which lasted so long, and which in contrast to the others, was not defeated by nationalisms, because the peoples who came into contact with Rome generally became integrated* (cf. Hassal, III, 166). The Roman Empire survived so long, longer than any other of the empires of history, because its strong point was government by means of consensus, supported in the last resort by an overwhelming military force. This means that the vast majority of the population was probably glad to be governed in this way, and drew advantages from the peace and protection ensured by the *Pax Romana* (cf. Wacher, III, 359). Wacher rightly speaks of military force as the last resort which Rome employed only against its more daring adversaries, to whom it dictated conditions to suit itself (cf. pt. 1.5 with regard to the *debellatio*). Otherwise, as many treaties translated into Greek which have come down to us as epigraphs show, the diplomatic way was always preferred.

2.49 *Rome probably had a stable government for a reason which is hard for us to understand today: it governed very little. The aims which it proposed to attain were limited.* Apart from the collection of taxes and the maintenance of public order, the rest was left to the self-government of the provinces or the city federations. This explains the substantial consensus which it encountered. There was also a strong sense of the state and of the need for the *pax Romana* among the governing classes because they came from the most prestigious social classes, the senatorial and knightly ranks. The governor was assisted by friends and counsellors whom he had personally chosen, and this not only prefigured the future "spoils system" so dear to the Americans, but also ensured stability and continuity at the same time (cf. Burton, II, 110-111). These administrators were few, if we compare them to the populations of those times, because they collaborated with the local civic authorities, to whom the majority of the administrative tasks were entrusted. The arrest and detention in custody of criminals, for instance, was the task of the local authorities, who not only brought the accusations, but also carried out all the investigations into most of the local common crimes. This explains why Roman penal law was not as complex and full of rules as civil law. At times it was even defective, as we can deduce from the fact that in the first two centuries, no laws condemning the Christians actually existed. It was the local authorities themselves and the governors who made decisions according to case and custom. The case of Pliny the Younger is a notable witness to this (cf. Carrara, 54-59). The only matter which concerned the central government was the fiscal issue, on which (somewhat like the present-day US government) it was intransigent, partly because it had the possibility of directing the resources of the richer provinces to the poorer or more needy ones in special cases: wars, epidemics, earthquakes and so on. Many cities were reconstructed after a calamity on the initiative of the central government and with its aid. The problem of taxes was one on which the central government, in the periods of real prosperity (i.e. until the mid third century) showed all its farsightedness. The passage from the *Codex*

Justinianus which follows (4.62.1), cited by Burton (cf. Burton, II, 125), is clear evidence of this: "The exaction of new taxes should not be conceded lightly, but if your city is so weak (in resources) that it needs extraordinary assistance, present to the governor of the province the data that you have gathered in this petition. The governor, after a close examination of the situation, and having taken into account the common interest, will pass on his conclusions to us. We will then adjudge whether and in what measure your request should be acceded to". We are here plainly faced with a central power which does not intervene with its citizens other than through the local authorities which could not only provide explanations, but could also act as a guarantee of that stability from which all profited for their business, trade, agriculture, and all those activities which stood in need of social order.

2.50 From what has been said, one conclusion can be drawn: as I have pointed out in the first chapter, law in Rome is above all the product of tradition. Tradition, however, was not only expressed in the Republic but also in the three centuries of Empire up to the period in which, thanks to the work of certain major jurists, this whole body began to be codified and unified. From this gathering together of materials, which were then amalgamated into the famous *Codex*, there emerges what is the basic tendency of the Romans: to improvise and to introduce new praxis alongside the old (cf. Green, II, 131). Once again, we observe that same criterion of continuity and novelty which is typical of the Roman world. The new praxis flanked the formal laws, the senatorial decrees, the precedents, the authority of the jurists, the edicts of the magistrates, and the customs, etc. – all of them forms which even in the time of Cicero constituted the various sources of law.

2.51 The connecting link of what has been said above is to be found in Augustus. It was he who was able to bind together the republic with the better part of what was to survive under the Empire. As I have stated, Augustus sought to modify and adapt the old to the new rather than to abolish it. The relations between the Senate and the Empire are evidence of this. Despite its modified constitution, the Senate continued to be jealous of its privileges, and if the close link with the Emperor undoubtedly increased its prestige, this link also increased the privileges of the Emperor: the benefit was mutual (cf. Green, II, 135). However, as time passed, and the *Princeps* gradually acquired increasing importance, what he decided was only modified with great reluctance by his successors, a sign that even the imperial rules became part of those juridical sources which were always on the increase and gave a sense of continuity to the Empire. Precedent, though not binding, was of maximum importance. This was so for all, if it is true (as has been authoritatively claimed by both ancient and modern historians) that interest in law was so great among the Romans that almost everyone possessed a substantial knowledge of it. It may be remembered that Polybius was astonished that even at a tender age children learned by memory passages of the *Laws of the Twelve Tables* (cf. pt. 1.39).

H) *Ammianus Marcellinus and Zosimus*.

2.52 Ammianus too, like Tacitus before him, was a realist more than a moralist, a writer living in the time of crisis. He wished to stand up to the disintegration, but he could not. He knew that this was already the era of brute force, and often of the irrational, where law and its limits had no meaning. It was the period in which the ostentation of showiness "is developing in more and more serious form, being favoured by impunity" (Ammianus, XIV, 2, 1). Impunity generates insecurity, above all because justice fails when only a few rich people can purchase it. "The poor, on the other hand, who had only modest means to protect themselves, or indeed lacked the means altogether, were condemned without the least consideration. Thus the truth was hidden by lies, and more than once the false passed for the true" (Ammianus, XV, 2, 9). Even the highest magistrates were subjected to aggression, a climate of fear spread everywhere, so that the people, in order not to reveal even their dreams, claimed not to have slept a wink (cf. Ammianus, XV, 3). There was constant fear for life and limb, but what offended good sense even more was that those who had faced exhaustion and grave risks for the state saw ignoble individuals promoted to the highest positions, which they had very often purchased (cf. Ammianus, XV, 5, 23 and 28). In this situation it was dangerous to speak to anyone at large, so most people preferred to talk only among their intimates (cf. Ammianus, XXVI, 6, 12) because otherwise it was possible that, "as happens in internecine strife, certain people emerged from the scum of the people, urged on by desperation or by blind ambition, while others, even though of very noble origin, were condemned to exile or even death from the highest positions" (Ammianus, XXVI, 7, 7). To this situation were added the evils of a constant state of war. Death was often a liberation in the face of external enemies and internal informers, ready to invent anything in order to curry favour with the Emperor and his officials (cf.Ammianus, XXVI, 10). The latter, and often even the Emperor himself, actually intervened in trials even when the judge was directing the hearing, provoking a sense of horror in everyone (cf. Ammianus, XXIX, 1, 27) because the certainty of law ended up by collapsing in what had been its real native land. Honest judges often witnessed truth being overturned before their very eyes, and when the madness exceeded all bounds, these executors of vengeance set fire to everything that stood in their way, whether it was judgments, debates, books or volumes of all kinds (cf. Ammianus, XXIX, 42), *demonstrating that barbarism is typical of every people which loses its sense of limits.*

A Greek from Antioch, **Ammianus Marcellinus** served for a long time in the *protectores domestici*, a real élite corps of the Roman army. Thanks to his activities there, he learned Latin, the knowledge of which he then perfected on the basis of well-established literary models. He was probably born around 335, and the last certain date of his life is 392, which we know about because of a letter of Libanius, a famous rhetorician and fellow-citizen of Ammianus. The latter mentions a success enjoyed in that same year by a public reading of the *Histories*, which was probably held in Rome by the author himself. He died around 400. His work *Rerum gestarum libri XXXI* must have begun where the *Histories* of Tacitus leave off; however, only the last eighteen books have survived. they recount the tragic events of his own times, which the author almost always experienced in person.

2.53 It is clear that in such a state of disaster, it was even natural for an historian to make comparisons with the past. When it became known that a debtor, oppressed by his poverty and unable to repay anything, had been put to death (cf. Ammianus, XXVII, 7, 7), it came to mind automatically that the physical integrity of the debtor was counted sacred in the earliest days of the Republic (cf. pt. 2.13). Similarly, when it was seen how corruption was spreading so widely, it came spontaneously to mind that the Empire – according to what Cicero himself had said – was nothing else than concern for the welfare of others (cf. Ammianus, XXIX, 2, 18). But there was no need to delve so far back into the past. When a decree was issued – in a fashion which at the very least could be called intolerant – prohibiting the teaching of rhetoric and grammar to masters who were Christians, (cf. Ammianus, XXV, 4, 20), there must have been regret for the Edict of Constantine, which provided freedom of religion for all. There was also regret for the fact that whereas Constantine had instituted the "*concilia*" in the various provinces – i.e. the assemblies which were supposed to keep the Emperor informed on the state of affairs in the province and keep a check on the governor – they were by this time moribund and not taken into account.

2.54 This crisis was the failure of a tradition. The people failed to recognise itself in its own past, and did not even remember it; thus it had no yearning for the future. It was completely absorbed in the present, in a mania for entertainment, of the cruellest kind. Ammianus is desolate, to say the least. "The few things which had been rendered illustrious in the past because of the severe pursuit of studies, were now prey to a dull indolence which is worthy of scorn (...) instead of the philosopher, it was the singer who was invited, and in place of the orator, the grave-master (...) and it is indeed strange to see a countless multitude in prey to a form of madness, following the chariot-races with rapt attention and bated breath. Matters of this kind mean that it is impossible to do anything serious or worthy of record in Rome" (Ammianus, XIV, 7, 18 and 26). This is the moment when "liberty of speech is confused with arrogance" (Ammianus, XIV, 9, 6): the moment in which even the leaders prefer to be exalted by "zealous and sophisticated praises" (Ammianus, XV, 1, 3). Eating habits were geared to waste: meats of every kind were sought, and there was nothing but bitterness in the reminders of the writings of Tacitus or even Caesar that soldiers should only turn to meat if they were deprived of corn. Shame scarcely existed any longer, and in contrast vainglory was triumphant; heroism consisted in the telling of jokes (cf. Ammianus, XXVIII, 4, 9 and 12). Such was the profound idleness of some people that they considered it exhausting even to read a book, while telling travellers' tales was seen as equalling the achievements of Alexander the Great or Caesar (cf. Ammianus, XXVIII, 4, 14 and 18). Even friendship no longer existed, in the mutual suspicion which was added to that deriving from shady motives or gambling games. In this context, Ammianus recalls even more bitterly a passage from Cicero's *De Amicitia*, in which he states that, apart from interest, those individuals who like the animals only love those from whom they can gain advantage, know nothing at all (cf. Ammianus, XXVIII, 4, 26). In all this, what dominates is ignorance – especially of those who having broken off their mainly juridical studies, have not even an idea of what Law signifies, and pass judgment, believing themselves to be in the right (cf. Ammianus, XXX, 4, 14 and 18). Frequently, they get away with it. They buy everything with money, even curses. It is a rare case when one meets with the temperance of the elders, uncorrupted by the luxuries of life, and not too licentious, who do not seek to have ambitious positions and shameful gains: only these are ready to make sacrifices on behalf of the state and the good of all (cf. Ammianus, XXXI, 6, 14).

2.55 This state of crisis and disorder was manifested in a fairly serious fashion especially in the army. The passages from Ammianus which could be cited would be too numerous, in which the historian bemoans the state of mind of the troops who placed their leaders and the gains that they could ensure before the good of the state. Most often, it is enough to read the speech of Julianus Augustus to his soldiers; they stooped to secret intrigues to obtain rewards reserved to the brave, or curried favour or, even worse, sought to rise to high rank without merit (cf. Ammianus,

XX, 5, 3-7). Bad habits had thus taken hold among the legions, which could only be held in check by lavish promises or by extraordinary commanders. Very often, the military were arbiters of political events, and when this did not occur, it was a matter of surprise. Ammianus himself expresses astonishment when, speaking of Constans Augustus, he writes: "he never allowed the soldiers to exalt their leaders too highly. Under him, no general was elevated to the dignity of *clarissimus* (...) Nor did a provincial governor clash with a cavalry general, nor did he permit the latter to meddle in civil affairs. But all the military and civil authorities always treated the Praetorian prefect with the traditional respect, as the highest rank in the hierarchy" (Ammianus, XXI, 16, 2). It is easy to see in this quotation the contrast between the former institutions and the present confusion. The various authorities, outside their own limits, acted in different contexts from those intended, and the only law at this juncture was the law of prevarication. Without discipline, the soldiers were ruthless where they had no need to be, and sought comforts and entertainments such as they had never enjoyed: feather-beds in place of pallets, expensive crockery instead of earthenware, and effeminate songs instead of military marches (cf. Ammianus, XXII, 4, 6-7). Like Tacitus, Ammianus set his hopes in this state of things – Machiavelli was to come to much the same conclusion in yet another period of crisis – on a *Princeps* who would at least bring the soldiers back to order. Such a prince, it seemed to him, was Julianus Augustus (Julian), who although devoid of talent was free of vices and fear, and for this reason was also admired by the soldiers. At his death, the dream was finally smashed. The election of his successor provided new proof that in moments of crisis the most riotous (*tumultuantibus*) designate the successor (cf. Ammianus, XXV, 5, 4). Those who were concerned about such a state of things, prefiguring Hobbes, "sought a leader of long and rigorous experience" (Ammianus, XXI, 1, 3), confirming that security is a prerogative first and foremost of democratic institutions, and when it is lost sight of, these institutions can no longer survive. However, the search was in vain, because the leaders were by now in a position to offer a price for the Empire (cf. Ammianus, XXVI, 6, 14); thus they had to pay their soldiers more than the others. These leaders felt themselves urged on to commit every kind of infamy, so that it was extraordinary in these circumstances if there was anyone who managed to avoid having his hands stained with blood.

2.56 The Empire had thus entered into an irrevocable crisis. This was also, as Zosimus pointed out, because the aristocratic class was progressively declining. Previously its moral strength and example had guided the common people when they competed with the nobles in civil advancement. Zosimus is not an historian of the stature of Tacitus or even of Ammianus. He indulges in curiosity and fictional speculations too often, but even in his work can be found the conviction that the Principate, seen as a necessity, survived as long as it had the moral and civil support of the "aristocratic republic". When this collapsed, and the figure of the ruler acquired more and more oriental features, then the Principate too collapsed. Zosimus is clear on this point: "As long as the aristocracy controlled power (...) the Consuls competed in acts of valour (...). Then the Romans abandoned the aristocracy, and chose Octavian as their monarch, allowing him to administer everything according to his own wishes, without realising that they were consigning the hopes of everyone to fate, and the risks of too great a power to the initiative and authority of one single individual" (Zosimus, I, 5, 1-2). Then began the system of flattery which as time went on discouraged the virtuous, exalted the mediocre and deadened the enthusiasm of the soldiery (cf. Zosimus, I, 5, 4). The Senate progressively lost prestige and power, and even the capacity to confer the imperial authority, which first occasionally and then regularly became the prerogative of the soldiers (cf. Zosimus, I, 7, 2). Rome, which at first was scandalised, gradually got used to the system.

Very little is known about the life of **Zosimus**, and even his birthplace and the period in which he lived are unknown. From the very sketchy material available to us, and also from certain deductions that can be made from his work, it may be supposed that when the Empire was already in decline, he held offices of a certain importance, and that this work *Historía néa* (the *New history*) was composed between 507 and 518.

2.57 Like the other historians mentioned above, Zosimus is a pagan, and ascribes one of the basic causes of the crisis to the loss of traditional religion. Because of this he indulges in details of oracles, ceremonies and forewarnings which seem amusing to us today; however, behind these descriptions there emerges the portrait of a state which had lost a common civic basis, that common bond of morality and tolerance which had cemented its greatness for centuries. From this came the lack of respect among Roman citizens themselves which gradually showed itself even from the material point of view, in the increasing impoverishment of families and cities which had once been prosperous (cf. Zosimus, II, 38, 4). On the political level, the conflicts were no longer resolved in civil fashion. Fratricidal wars were already a matter of habit, and when they were rejected it was only because a greater danger could be seen threatening the state from the outside (cf. Zosimus, II, 51, 1).

2.58 In the Republic, the continuity of the state was based on the institutions and on individuals. In the late Empire, everything rested on the latter, and Zosimus recalls with some bitterness, in speaking of Julian: "the death of one single man provoked such a substantial change in the affairs of the State" (Zosimus, III, 34, 2). The fall of a man meant the ruin of many, who were removed from their offices (cf. Zosimus, IV, 2, 3); friendships and recommendations came to count for more than continuity and experience. It was not that the former were absent at other times, but by now they had become the only criteria. In the court, and especially in Constantinople, the eunuchs possessed a certain role, thus introducing an oriental practice which was completely foreign to the merits of the aristocratic republic praised by Cicero. While many peoples, such as the Egyptians, asked to be enabled to go on living according to the Roman laws, the most prominent citizens flouted such laws, allowing usurers to buy positions, offices, magistracies and often judgments (cf. Zosimus, IV, 28, 4 and 30, 5). "Everything that contributed to corrupting character and life was widespread" (Zosimus, IV, 33, 4). Anyone who sought to oppose this, armed only with honesty, was physically eliminated. Quite a large number of magistrates who did their duty, and many very high officials who only had the safety of the state at heart, were killed (cf. Zosimus, V, 32, 4 and 47, 2). Without top-ranking officials, as happened in Iran during the eighties of the last century, the army knew no bounds. With leading commanders killed or exiled, the legions were sometimes assigned to men who had never seen a battlefield, and the defeats that followed were thus quite predictable.

2.59 To all this was added the phenomenon of the *Principes pueri* – described thus because they were emperors without *seniores* for colleagues. This was the case with the sons of Theodosius, entrusted to the semi-barbarian Stilicone, who had to bring up the two boys, and at the same time watch over the unity of the Empire. This must still have been conceived as a common *imperium divisis tantum sedibus* (a single empire divided only in its capitals). The work of Stilicone was wrecked, as is confirmed by the fact that by the end of the fourth century or beginning of the fifth, there were already two empires (cf. Mazzarino, IR, 794-795). Especially in the east, the "court" was assuming a notable importance and authority, to the extent that officials and bureaucrats ended up with a decisive power. Fortunately in the West, a certain tradition, even though it had fallen into decline, remained as a substratum, still capable of fascinating thinkers during the future centuries; it thus made its own contribution to civilising the barbarians. It was for this reason that the West remained a basically open society, capable of assimilating foreign elements rather than eliminating them as Islam was to do (cf. Boissier, 7). And it is for this reason that even in one of the moments of greatest crisis for the West, when Roman authority had almost entirely disappeared, Boethius could remind the barbarians that liberty consisted in being governed by laws (cf. Boethius, I, 5).

3. The beginning of the conflict and dilemma between religion and politics: Eusebius of Caesarea, Augustine of Hippo.

3.1 The relationship between Christianity and politics is certainly one of the most conflict-ridden in western history, and it is no wonder that so many completely disparate judgments have been made about it. To give an example of the extremes, we may remember on the one hand those who credit the Christian religion with the merit of having bestowed on western civilisation the presuppositions of liberty and equality, characteristic of the liberalism and democracy of the future, while on the other hand there are those who see religion as the sustainer of power, and hence identify Christianity with the justification of the *status quo* of many absolutisms, or at least of self-perpetuating power structures. Between these two extremes, there is a whole variegated world of positions, which makes it clear that it would be difficult to reach a definitive conclusion. Probably, historical reality could in fact to some extent give its backing to any of them, given that in any era, including the initial one, the different positions were all present. Already by the end of the fourth century or the beginning of the fifth, a careful reading of Eusebius of Caesarea and of Augustine of Hippo provides an accurate confirmation of what has been said above. Moreover, it seems clear to me that in Popper's work too, elements may emerge favouring the view that in the Judaeo-Christian tradition some of the presuppositions are to be found (on this, see Appendix III from point 3 to point 6).

3.2 In Rome, the religious problem was conceived in such a way that it always ended by being in harmony with the fundamentals of civic life. Moreover there was tolerance towards every type of religious belief, because religion was basically held to be a private matter. "The only rules to be observed are those which refer to the maintenance of public order and respect for morality. For the rest, the State should not concern itself with anything, and should not intervene in a question considered to belong to the private domain" (Bardy, 22). Anyone seeking proof of this need only consider the institution of property, one of the cardinal points of Roman political and juridical reflection. "The greatest protection that can be guaranteed to property or to legal right was that of the divinity. The most effective way of ensuring respect for these things lay in investing them with a sort of sacred character: *sancire autem,* Servius states, *propriae est sanctum aliquod, id est consecratum facere fuso sanguine hostiae, et dictum quasi sanguine consecratum.* Whatever one may think about the etymology of this, it makes it possible for us to grasp the religious element inseparable from the term *sanctus* understood in the juridical sense of what must be safeguarded inviolably" (Bardy, 40). This long quotation throws light on the preceding one, and shows the sacrality of rights over things, as well as the civil function of religion as it was conceived, in conditions of maximum tolerance, in Rome. When it appeared as a simple private fact, it had its own law which protected it: the *jus privatum,* in fact. Tolerance and civil and political stability were closely connected, and this pair of notions, as many people have written, always succeeded in overcoming the many particular and contingent difficulties. We only have to think of the fact that the Jews often obtained permission to show their loyalty to authority in different ways from those demanded of the pagans. And many Romans, either for liberal reasons or because of opportunism, held Judaism in some esteem. The incident may be remembered when the Jews themselves said to Christ about a Roman centurion, "He loves our nation and has built us a synagogue" (Luke, VII, 5).

3.3 It could be said that, despite misunderstandings of various kinds, Christianity spread in the Roman world because – in sharp contrast to the way in which Islam was later to behave – Rome never sought, or indeed was able, to assimilate elements which were alien to it, and thus resolved the confrontation with other civilisations and cultures in open fashion (cf. Boissier, 7). On both sides, certain basic rules were accepted which guaranteed common coexistence and civil development. The latter were the two elements which really concerned the Romans, who in their strong pragmatism prepared their children for civic life not with the texts of Plato and Aristotle, but by making them attend the sittings of the Senate and public debates from their early years. "At twenty years", according to Cicero, "a man who had followed the law court as his school and experience as his teacher, and who had taken part in a battle and had heard some great orators speak, was maturely ready for public life" (Boissier, 84). This firmly realistic attitude was to remain typical in the first centuries of Christianity, even among fathers of the western Church, who unlike the orientals, never made use of abstract general characteristics of a philosophical type, but always took the real human being as their main point of reference, viewing him or her in specific contexts and in the light of contingent difficulties (cf. Boissier, 120-121). In Rome and in the west in general, writers made every effort to present the neophytes as normal people who carried out common activities and useful professions. New converts were not presented as isolated or misanthropic persons, so that even monasticism as it developed in the west acquired very different characteristics, even on the social plain, from that of the eastern type.

3.4 Even in a moment of crisis like the fourth century, the sense of openness which seeks to assimilate peoples and cultures was in fact preserved. In the first lines of the so-called Edict of Milan, it is asserted that "nothing would be more useful to our peoples", and the use of the plural is certainly intentional. Freedom of worship was not only granted to Christians, but to anyone who had his own religious faith to manifest. "The principle of religious tolerance was officially proclaimed (...) and this is the first time that the world heard such language" (Boissier, 33). Constantine was the guarantor of this tolerance. Some have claimed that apart from purely civil motives, there were others of a more pragmatic kind. Religion was united to certain claims of a national character, and to apply the principle of tolerance was to some extent a way of saving the unity of the empire. This may be said by those who forget that the former republic had already invented the federation, which preserved diversity in unity. This criterion was very willingly accepted by diverse peoples. Those who "wished to become Gauls or Spaniards but did not intend to cease being Romans (...) indeed, I can believe that (...) they preconditioned their own independence without compromising the unity of the Empire (...); all this meant that they wished to affirm that they were Romans and wanted to continue as such" (Boissier, 218 and 225).

3.5 It should also be remembered that not only Constantine, but also the emperors who had been quite zealous in showing a faith of their own, had never had any hesitation about using the services of persons who professed different faiths for the good of the state. Even on the institutional plain, Roman society was in fact such an open one that Rutilius Namantianus, who was of Gallic origins, could say "The Senate does not close its own sanctuary to outsiders; indeed it accepts into its bosom all those who deserve this high honour" (Boissier, 243). These remarks about institutions need not be seen as artificial: can anything in Rome be thought of as outside the law? This civil and religious tolerance was itself given sacred status by the laws. The Edict of Milan is only the last example of this, and it would permit Rome also to take "to its own service the barbarians who merited the title of Romans. The time was to come – Ozanam says – when Rome would forget the fine art of victory, but it would never forget the art of government" (Boissier, 333). On the basis of this structure, the Church would slowly take its place, with the disputes I mentioned at the beginning of the chapter. These arguments would show the bitter dissension existing between what today we would call closed societies and open societies. Eusebius of Caesarea could be described as a good exemplar of the former.

There is little documentation of the life of **Eusebius**, Bishop of Caesarea. He was born some time between 258 and 265. He studied at the biblical school of Panphilius, which belonged to the tradition of Origen. He was a witness of the persecutions against the Christians, and he welcomed the seizure of power by Constantine enthusiastically, for in his eyes he seemed to embody the celestial monarchy. He had a fundamental role in the definition of the Nicene creed. He died a little after Constantine, in 337. The most outstanding of his works is the *Historia Ecclesiastica*.

3.6 Eusebius, a witness of the last persecutions, lived just at the moment when Christianity was officially recognised by Constantine. This event enthused him greatly, but it also led him to misunderstand the actual nature of the Empire and of Christianity. In his opinion, the universal political monarchy would eventually coincide with the theological monarchy. Under Constantine, the *Pax Romana* was no longer a stage of preparation for the *Pax Christiana*, but instead, both coincided. Constantine appears as the sole head, willed by God, who, once discords and divisions were overcome, would succeed in uniting the Empire right to the far ends of the cardinal points of the compass (cf. Eusebius, X, 9, 6). Speaking of political-teleological theories, it is certainly important to recall that Eusebius belonged to the eastern Church, that he wrote in Greek and shows quite a few affinities with those Greeks who from Polybius to Plutarch contributed to shaping the myth of Rome and of peace which was eventually to be seen as a kind of ideal state on earth. The Empire of Constantine seemed to Eusebius a culminating moment in history, a moment which took on itself political and religious dimensions and reconciled all their possible conflicts: this was a typical feature of the future Byzantine, and therefore eastern, situation.

3.7 Constantine's imperial dignity is made clear by the fact that since he had God Almighty as his ally, he eliminated all rivals and tyrants, reconquering lost liberties for the Romans (cf. Eusebius, IX, 9, 2). This is why Eusebius tends to point out that his is not an isolated position, at least in the East, because after the Edict of Milan "every one of the Church's rulers present, according to his ability, delivered a panegyrical oration, inspiring the assembly" (Eusebius, X, 3, 4). Indeed it could hardly be otherwise, since the Emperors described as "the most exalted on earth" (Eusebius, X, 4, 16) are considered not only most dear to God, because they purify the whole world of tyrants, but also dear because

God himself chose their souls (cf. Eusebius, X, 4, 60) and through them purified the whole world and restored it to peace.

3.8 Eusebius did not content himself with generalities. He was convinced that the greatness of Constantine was not only political. In the Emperor the political and religious dimensions coincide, to such an extent that he gives orders for a Council to be held at Rome for the union and concord of the Churches (cf. Eusebius, X, 5, 18-20). He also intervened in the practical aspects of civil and religious life: "It is the custom of our Benevolence, that we will that whatsoever appertains by right to another should not only not suffer harm, but should also be restored" (Eusebius, X, 5, 15); thus he defended the property of Christians and restored to them the full dignity of Roman citizens. Because of this, "God was Friend, Protector and Guardian of Constantine" (Eusebius, X, 8, 6), to such an extent that his Empire corresponded in everything and for everyone to divine intentions, and the emperor can be described as a representative of Christ on earth. In fact it should not be forgotten that Constantine strengthened the position of the bishops on every occasion, recognising them as heads of the local Churches and thus accelerating the process by which "Caesarism was transformed into Caesaropapism, since the Emperor was claiming to regulate the inner life of the Church" (D'Addio, 136).

3.9 A diametrically opposed opinion is that of Augustine of Hippo. Quite apart from the theological motives which inspired what many call his "theology of history", Augustine's political thought has a major characteristic which fits into the context of that slow and difficult route leading to the open societies: Augustine's intention, in fact, is to safeguard the independence of the spiritual order in relation to the temporal, and their reciprocal autonomy. From this arises a reflection in sharp contrast to that of Eusebius, and thus contrary to every utopian dream which aims at the realisation of a perfect society on earth. Augustine is decidedly hostile to every type of perfectionist claim: justice and peace, for instance, as absolute values, only belong to the heavenly City, which uniquely possesses metahistorical characteristics. This does not mean that the political dimension must live in a sort of state of resignation; on the contrary, everyone should feel obliged to do his best to achieve the maximum possible justice and peace in any given historical moment, but no-one may lay claim to having achieved the perfect and ideal state.

It is not easy in a few lines to give a portrait of such a rich experience, especially at the interior level, as that of **Saint Augustine**. It is even more difficult to summarise his monumental activity as a writer, which ranges over the most varied possible areas of knowledge. As well as the *Confessions*, mention should be made here of the *De Trinitate*, and most especially the *De Civitate Dei*. He lived between 354 and 430, in one of the most troubled periods of the western civilisation. Among the personalities who had the greatest influence on forming his personality, and on his conversion, were his mother, Monica, and the Bishop of Milan, Ambrose.

3.10 In contrast to what was believed for too long, Augustine had no sympathy for political thought of the neo-Platonic type. His constant reference is the Roman state, seen in its real condition and, by this time, in its moment of crisis. The state thus rediscovers its own basis in the individual: in every political society there exists a will which puts into effect a real process of unification of individuals (cf. D'Addio, 144). Political society and the order which corresponds to it do not possess a static reality because everything, in the political dimension, is seen in a constant dynamism in which human beings are manifested with their complex existential realities, vices and virtues included. This is why peace and justice are always constantly under threat, and this is also "why the political order must be continually willed (...) order thus de-assembles itself from within, hence the processes of decadence of a political society mature in its own deepest levels, and are not immediately discernable" (D'Addio, 144). To use a Kantian phrase, there is a sort of social unsociableness. *The individual aspires to the collective life because he perceives its advantages, but at the same time he perceives the disadvantages for which it is partly responsible.*

3.11 Augustine is extremely clear on this issue. When he speaks of the two cities and of the distant future in which they will realise their eschatological dimensions, he says explicitly: "this is their epilogue" (Aug., DCD, XV, 1). Over and beyond this context, every claim to realise perfect societies is destined to shipwreck. The attempt had already been classed in the Jewish tradition as an act of senseless pride, made evident "in the building of a tower up to the skies, symbol of an ungodly exaltation" (Aug., DCD, XVI, 10). It is this state of exaltation which leads to the search for presumptuous adventures, which then go on even to the point of de-naturing human beings. On the contrary, in order to improve its social life, humanity has only one way: that of moral rigour, not to be confounded with facile moralism. Here too the expressions used by the Bishop of Hippo are unambiguous. With regard to the crisis of the Roman state, he writes that if "virtue had grown and flourished in prudent care for the city, liberty would have endured in correspondence to virtue" (Aug., DCD, I, 31). How near these ideas are to modern ones we may learn from Montesquieu, who saw virtue as the foundation of any republic. The Roman Empire, and before that the Republic itself, had, in Augustine's view, enjoyed an effortless growth and development because the support which the citizens ensured to the state and its laws was equally great.

3.12 Augustine reminds us that the *Twelve Tables* were the moral as well as the legal basis of the sturdy growth of the Republic. According to these presuppositions, life must be submitted to the judgment of the magistrates and the legal process, and not to the arbitrary will of the players or adventurers (cf. Aug., DCD, II, 9). In other words, and with a specific reference to Cicero's classic exposition, the Bishop of Hippo holds that the certainty of law has broken down because the moral support of the law has been irremediably shipwrecked, and hence their spirit has collapsed. What is the result of this? "No summons to a court save for those who impugn their neighbours or damage their goods – their homes, their health; as for the rest, everyone does as he thinks best (...) who in his right mind would dare to compare this republic – not, I would say, with the Roman Empire, but with the Palace of Sardanapalus?" (Aug., DCD, II, 20). In confirmation of this statement, Augustine himself reports the comments of Cicero, in whose opinion, already in his own time, the Roman state had begun that emptying of republican institutions in such a way that one could no longer really speak of a republic (cf. Aug., DCD, II, 21). Thus we find a typical paradox of epochs in crisis: "bad action calls everyone to contemplate it; good advice finds few to listen to it, as if one should be ashamed of honesty, and boast of dishonesty" (Aug., DCD, II, 26). Dishonesty is a degeneration of the glory which made Rome great, because while the latter led people to put the good of the state and the citizenry before their own, exactly the opposite happens with dishonesty, and the state, before yielding to external pressure, caves in from within, because the citizens no longer uphold it.

3.13 Here too, in contradiction of what has been stated for too long, Augustine is not appealing to a millenary mentality current at the end of the Empire among quite a number of Christian or heretical writers, but using Roman and pagan authors to demonstrate that the crisis of the state depends on causes which are profound and hard to eliminate. Sallust and the specific conclusions of Cato, as well as Cicero and Tacitus, these are the authors who provide constant reference points for Augustine. A statement which becomes crucial for the whole of the *De Civitate Dei*, in fact, derives from the first of these. With regard to the ancient Romans, it should be said that "other things made them great, which today we are completely lacking; capacity for work at home, justice in their authority abroad; a free spirit in their assemblies, non-subjection to criminal passions. In place of this, we have luxury and greed, a poor state and private wealth (...) the rewards due to virtue are all enjoyed by intrigue. Nobody should wonder: each of you thinks only of himself" (Aug., DCD, V, 12). Subordinating the interests of all to one's own is the most obvious sign of the disintegration of civil society (cf. Aug., DCD, V, 15), and the demonstration that the laws have already lost their *raison d'être*, to such a point that an attempt is made to twist them, and the greatest fortune is considered to be the ability to get round obstacles by licentious means (cf. Aug., DCD, V, 26).

3.14 From what has been said so far, it is clear that in Augustine's view, politics is closely connected with the existential reality of individuals who alone, by their choices, concur to make it possible for states to develop or degenerate. Each individual is "unique and singular" (Aug., DCD, XII, 22) and is completely directed towards "unity in plurality" (Aug., DCD, XII, 23). I mentioned earlier that in Augustine, there is a sort of "sociable unsociability" and this conclusion does not seem to be out of place if we remember that the individual, in relation to his peers, lives in the existential uncertainty of improving himself and others or of worsening himself and worsening others also. "One is never vicious by nature, but one is always vicious by corruption" (Aug., DCD, XIV, 6). *This is why states, like the Roman state, for example, do not depend for their prosperity or their decadence on the gods. Politics is a concrete matter, not a theological one.* Even the Christian religion cannot claim to achieve lasting political models, because its perspectives are metahistorical, since it is convinced that nothing static, and thus lasting, can exist in social life (cf. Aug., DCD, IV, 28 and 30). The unacceptability of Eusebius' conclusions now appears fully evident.

3.15 The man does not exist who acts in a political manner in his public life and then divides himself in two in his private life. It is inconceivable that the manner of acting will become uniform, and this is true for all. According to Augustine, all men – the "great" just as much as the "obscure", the "good" just as much as the "evil" – end by showing the same tendencies. "When all is said and done, will, caution and happiness belong to the good as well as to the evil: or in other words, the good as well as the evil desire, fear, enjoy, but the former in a good way and the latter in an evil one, what is the will of humankind, correct or distorted" (Aug., DCD, XIV, 8). This will shows the freedom of everyone to realise one type of life rather than another, and it also shows how social life is from time to time willed and constructed on the basis of their desires and expectations. For Augustine, human beings are all equal in their sentiments so that there is no-one who "with vanity as inhuman as it is exceptional, without ever exalting himself or becoming emotionally stirred for any sentiment, without ever giving in, divests himself of all humanity (...) to be firm does not mean to be right, and to be inert does not mean to be healthy" (Aug., DCD, XIV, 9). It could hardly be otherwise since, in contrast to the Graeco-Platonic vision with which he is often and erroneously associated, Augustine maintains that *nature is an imperfect cause of sin* (cf. Aug., DCD, XIV, 10) *and every dream of perfection is pure utopia. Only constant improvement, but at the cost of hard work, is conceded to men in their social life.*

3.16 Sin, conceived as a possibility of choice and as an inclination to evil, is the confirmation that God too is respectful of the limits of mankind which are synonymous with its precarious state and its exertions. "Who, in fact, would think or say that the avoidance of the fall of both the angels and man was not within the power of God? But He preferred not to remove choice from their dominion" (Aug., DCD, XIV, 27). Choice not only means liberty, but witnesses, in creating social life, constant adjustments, continuous corrections to a way of life which can never be conclusive or definitive. To speak of choice, for Augustine, does not however mean exhausting the problem of will. The latter implies a spring, an intrinsic *raison d'être*, which acts on the will and determines it both in good and evil. This spring is love. The two cities imply two differing types of love: *love for oneself, and love for God* (cf. Aug., DCD, XIV, 28). Every human being is, most of the time, a mixture of the two, and above all the second, in the absolute state, is impossible to realise in the earthly political terrain.

3.17 If this were so, mankind would be diminished by it. The choice of God – and here Augustine is surely thinking of his own existential experience – is a fact which arises from within, and is the product of freedom. It matters little whether there is a political system upheld by men of faith. Augustine knows, in open polemic with the followers of Eusebius, that it is difficult if not impossible to enter into the hearts of men, even more so if they are politicians, in order to assess the genuineness of their faith. He knows that power can put on any clothes to serve its own convenience. He writes clearly elsewhere: "Much more wisely now, kings do not seek to kill him, as Herod did, instead they voluntarily worship him" (Aug., S., 200, 2). But he is also aware that it is equally impossible to enter into the hearts of simple ordinary citizens. The *amor Dei* cannot be imposed, it can only be presented, but in order to be genuine it must possess free allegiance. Allegiance which is also valid in the political sphere, as well as the religious. In fact, for the Bishop of Hippo, power cannot assume the connotations of what was in the future to be Caesaropapism, because it is founded on the consensus of those associated – St Augustine uses various formulae to indicate this consensus. The people is defined as the association of a multitude not of beasts but of rational creatures; a multitude associated in the harmonious communion of the things that they love; the observation that men are not beasts but rational creatures is meant to stress that the dominion of man over man no longer exists, while the terms of association and of agreed communion refer, although only implicitly, to the consensual nature of these (cf. D'Addio, 146). From the consensus the social contract springs, and from the latter, as Cicero insisted, the laws as expression of agreement and hence of the tradition of the consociates.

3.18 The decadence of states is the result of an internal process of disintegration because the laws, which are the expression of what the consociates love, become devoid of content and no longer express the desires and sentiments of the citizens (cf. D'Addio, 148). This disintegration results in the onset of conflicts which are no longer resolved, like their predecessors, within the context of the laws. In this way a climate of disorder is created, which makes associative life impossible. That free will which through its decisions guarantees the progress of the human race, (cf. Aug., DCD, XV, 22) no longer has the security to act as it would wish, and as in fact it does act in time of peace. The Christian, with extreme realism, knows that without a juridical order, it is not possible to attain that common good which is at the origin of *Civitas* (cf. Barbero, 27); a common good which is the product of the union of harmonised wills regulated by law. This guarantees that temporal peace which is the instrument and presupposition for any action by fully moral man (cf. Aug., DCD, XIX, 17), which means first of all responsible action because it is carried out in full freedom and in the security of the juridical guarantees. If all of this is lacking, the state ends by becoming a band of robbers or pirates which only guarantees to a few – the dishonest – the possibility of attaining their aims. Hence the importance of power which is not only seen as a form of service, but also as one of the toughest forms of discipline. Power, in fact, "is the force which respects the rights of subjects; domination, on the other hand, enslaves the subjects in everything and for everything to the aims of those who possess it" (D'Addio, 146). The person holding power has the task of containing those elements which could cause a betrayal which would render men suspicious of one another, and would force them to retreat into their own selfishness. Because of this, the basic task of power is to be vigilant (cf. Aug., DCD, XIX, 16) against every seed of disintegration.

3.19 Because of this, Augustine showed admiration for the Roman state of times past, about which he says unhesitatingly: if "'people' is the aggregation of many rational beings bound together by a common agreement on the objects of their love (...) according to our definition, the Roman people are 'a people', and their state is a republic" (Aug., DCD, XIX, 24). What has changed, on the other hand, is the object of the love of the earliest times, which implied very different moral conditions (cf. Aug., DCD, XIX, 24). What has been said about the Roman people also goes for all peoples, because human nature, setting aside various historical contingencies, has the same way of thinking, and hence the reasons for the progress or disintegration of a civilisation can be subjected to the same analytical method.

3.20 This is probably the reason why there has been talk of a *philosophy of history* in Augustine. In his opinion, however, *there is no type of determinism which underlies human action.* History is the product of the free concourse of human action, and if anyone sought to see in it a kind of theological itinerary, this should be seen outside traditional schemes, in a distinctly modern fashion. In anticipating the themes of modern existentialism, Augustine arrives at a conclusion very close to that of Kierkegaard. It is in fact the people who believe in God who, by acting, make Him enter into history. When this happens, when the infinite breaks forth into the finite, all is transfigured and assumes different meanings. The very life of the individual is overturned by this, and the more the individual lives this new experience, the more he is transformed and also those around him.

Augustine had been through all these experiences himself, and thus it was very easy for him to talk about them.

3.21 Anyone can undergo this experience, provided that he wishes to. The message is valid for all civilisations and for all latitudes, because this liberty of conscience knows no limits of space and time. It can be realised anywhere, as the advent of the new novel was clearly showing. Only those devoid of sense could accuse Christianity of bringing the empire to the point of crisis. Its message, if lived out adequately, would have given new vital substance to a structure which was in itself incurably in crisis. It is possible to understand now why the Augustinian classic shows a clear apologetic purpose. If it had been understood, by a world already in prey to its own self-love, the Empire would have emerged from it regenerated, and would have had new vital energies. But this did not happen, and an ancient world headed irrevocably for disintegration.

3.22 All this is a source of great regret for Augustine. Rome had become reduced to a kind of Babylon, making it clear in advance what its end would be. Rome, with its history, is compared to other empires, but Rome always remains the earthly city which has guaranteed the ordinary people a common law, a stable and durable peace never before seen, and as a consequence stability and progress. But above all, Rome had spread a universal way of feeling which seems to be a useful premise for the diffusion of the new message. This is why, on the fall of Rome, a kind of panic overtook the world as a whole. "Augustine says that the entire universe lamented, and the emotion was carried to the most remote parts of the Orient" (Boissier, 294). And it could hardly be otherwise, for Augustine knew very well that the disintegration of a rational order based on tradition meant chaos, within which irrationality would end up by justifying every kind of folly.

3.23 Disintegration is a cause of disunion in society, and even before that in human conscience, and its consequences are not only disorder but constant conflict beyond any kind of rule. At this point political institutions *de facto* no longer exist, even if they continue nominally in being. "The state, the republic, exists as long as the individual puts order into practice, so that the political order is realised by all the individuals who compose society" (D'Addio, 143). Peace and order are thus a fraught search on the part of humankind; they do not fall from the skies, nor can they be imposed. They are an existential need of human beings who, in order to obtain them, unite with other human beings in order to enjoy the benefits of peace along with them. The *tranquillitas ordinis* (cf. Aug., DCD, XIX, 12) acquires a particular significance in the political thought of Augustine: "order becomes the presupposition of every political institution which is intended to guarantee and maintain peace" (D'Addio, 143). The presupposition is hard to seek out and even harder to maintain, and for this reason human history acquires dramatic colours and sometimes tragic ones, because order is continually undermined, and can never be taken for granted. It is from this that the great message of Christianity is derived, for Augustine: while it gives secure and definitive order a metahistorical significance, it nevertheless invites the will of man to measure itself against that order. From here too come the providentialist interpretations of history, understood not in the sense that God takes the place of man in his actions, (it will be remembered that in politics nothing can be seen as descending from on high, but must spring from below and be based on consensus), but considered in relation to a transcendent order which, even though it is impossible to achieve, cannot be set aside on pain of the loss of the most elementary social sense.

3.24 Augustine therefore has a political notion which is far from being an alienating one. We could describe it as rigorous, but certainly not aimed at considering politics as a last resort for a Christian who has nothing else left to do. It is a difficult and exacting task, to which one must dedicate oneself with the best intentions. In a famous letter he does not hide his disappointment about those Christians who do not prove themselves to be capable administrators of the state. "If you really want me to tell you the whole truth, there is only one thing which I find it difficult to tolerate, and that is that (...) you want to go on being a catechumen, as if baptised Christians were not capable of administering public affairs more faithfully and better to the degree that they themselves are faithful and good. What purpose do you intend to achieve among so many anxieties and efforts other than the good of the citizens? If in fact you are not aiming at this end, it would be better to sleep night and day rather than carry on wakefully the fatigues imposed by the state, if these are not intended to bring any benefits to the citizens" (Aug., Epist., 151, 14). Politics and its institutions for the good of the weakest: this is how we should understand the bitter regret of Augustine for the fall of Latinised and Christianised Africa, and the sadness of seeing "the whole world slain in one single city" (Pincherle, 319 and 441).

3.25 If these conclusions leave us a little baffled, we should remember that the era in which Augustine lived is an era of maximum insecurity, in which everything seemed to be vague and transitory. The Bishop of Hippo gives meaning back to life, security to tomorrow, a will to re-start and begin living. This explains the great success which the *De Civitate Dei* was to have for so many centuries in the middle ages and even beyond, because it brought with it the great secret and mystery of hope (cf. Boissier, 313). This hope the ancient world, which identified itself with that of Rome, had already lost. Augustine transfigured the best contents of that world in a new way. His *Civitas* is not in fact surrounded by walls and frontiers; it is open to all those who observed the same laws, recognise only one God, have the same hopes. A community which extends to all the corners of the earth, like the Empire itself, because it has common links, since its objectives too are common: those of guaranteeing a civil life which the disintegration of the world seemed not to be able to guarantee any longer. This was to be, or, (if we are to remain faithful to Augustinian language), would seek to be, the *Christian Republic*.

3.26 It is precisely this ideal of the republic that at the end of these reflections enables us to return to the prologue, that is to the bases of Augustine's political ideas. Augustine transforms the republican ideal from Cicero "the most admired and principal writer, and indeed perhaps for Augustine the only master and model" (Pincherle, 19 and cf. Aug., Conf., III, 4, 7). It was in fact the *Hortensius* in which Cicero "demonstrates the aims and the limits of the various sciences" (Pincherle, 20), and in which he asks himself questions about the meaning of happiness (which in a typically Roman conception cannot be derived from this or that philosophy, all at war with each other, but from taking what is best in all philosophies), which played a key role in the life of Augustine. According to what is said in the *Hortensius*, happiness can never be gained as long as one lives in a state of real uncertainty and insecurity. Augustine was to give to this state of heart not only a civil and moral meaning, but also one which we could call existential, since as we have seen it is external order and tranquillity which is the reflection of what is generated in interior fashion. Because of this, peace is connected to another typically Ciceronian aspect which we mentioned earlier: limitation. This means the participation of all in the context of the laws. It should not be forgotten that – thanks specifically to Augustine – the daily rhythm of the monastery where he lived witnessed the participation of all, in turn, in the administration (cf. Pincherle, 239), according to a genuinely democratic principle which may seem strange only to those who are ignorant of the real history of the ancient world.

4. The rebirth of dissent: John of Salisbury.

4.1 The Middle Ages has been described for too long as a "closed" period from the political point of view; closed, that is, to any hypothesis which sought to challenge preconstituted authority. The latter was considered to be the will of God, and to disobey it could mean committing an act of sacrilege. In reality, the many scholars who sought to demonstrate the contrary were not even acknowledged by many "intellectuals" who were propagators of particular ideologies, rather than being serious researchers. While the Mediaeval period did have a reverence for authority – as it certainly did in its early phases – this was due to a menacing insecurity which was far from being a brief interval, but lasted for several centuries, from the fifth to the tenth. As a result of the repeated transmigrations of invading peoples, a need arose for defence which only strong government could guarantee. Clearly all this had repercussions in every area of human life, including economics. This aspect, too, should be re-examined with less prejudice, and it will be found that after the tenth century, once the problems of internal stability had been resolved and the incursions eliminated, the foundations were laid in Europe for the future liberal society, by taking up again those elements from the Roman world which had been set aside, but certainly not eliminated.

4.2 If there is one writer who clearly demonstrates this passage from the need for an authority which can guarantee stability at all costs to another kind of authority which, even though necessary, must have special prerogatives but also elementary, specific limits, that writer is John of Salisbury. Like all those who live in moments of transition, but with their gaze turned profoundly towards the future, John shows the characteristics of the man of tradition, but also the man of innovation. It will be worth taking a look at the former first of all, after which we shall point out the novelty of the latter.

The historical range of the *Polycraticus* is very notable. In this work, **John of Salisbury**, diplomat, philosopher and churchman of the twelfth century, dealt for the first time since Roman antiquity with the subject of the legitimacy of tyrannicide. The author's objective is that of discrediting the squalid life of the court of Henry II Plantagenet of England, at whose instigation the famous murder in Canterbury Cathedral of Thomas à Beckett would later be committed. The purpose of the work is to restore truth to a political struggle dominated by various kinds of vice, which debased social life and all its initiatives.

4.3 Around 1085, Manegold of Lautembach, although an upholder of the independence of the Church and supporter of the legitimacy of the excommunication which had been imposed by Gregory VII on the Emperor Henry IV, put forward an important new notion in political thought, which can be seen within the framework of a resumption of the Roman tradition. "The ideas put forward by Manegold presuppose the distinction between authority and power: the first represents the principles and values on which the political order is founded, and thus expresses the criterion which gives them legitimacy, while the second is related to the exercise of the activity of government" (D'Addio, 160). This is the line of thought also followed by John of Salisbury (1110-1180), who lived at a moment when the typically mediaeval conflict between the spiritual and temporal powers was being fought out in all its dramatic fierceness, with the murder in Canterbury Cathedral of Archbishop Thomas à Beckett. Between the two orders, as an ecclesiastic, he favours the religious side, even though at the same time he criticises its arrogance and immorality. This aspect shows John as a man of transition, as we have mentioned. He attacks the court jurists, and ecclesiastics who do not do their duty, referring to Roman Law, and reopening the discussion about the limitation of power which had been interrupted in the early middle ages. But when it is a question of judging the clergy, he is clearly contrary to secular jurisdiction, reserving for the clerical world a space of its own in which to regulate its own justice, even in matters concerning land (cf. Carlyle, 541-542). It is incredible to him that the Church should be "judged by men" (Carlyle, 550).

4.4 Equally typical of the period is the judgment of the political authority as not only inferior in dignity to, but also dependent on, the religious authority. "The prince receives his sword, which is a sword of blood, from the Church, even though the latter, properly speaking does not possess it (...) the prince is thus a sort of minister of sacerdotal power: it is he who exercises that part of the sacred office which is held to be unworthy of the priesthood" (John of Salisbury, IV, 3). Similarly understandable are some reflections which refer directly to the Fathers, and to Augustine in particular. But it is not only the historical and political thought of the Bishop of Hippo that is referred to, but also what could be called his more theological and existential thinking, even though this is a prelude, in his considerations, to his political notions. It is in fact in Augustinian terms that John stresses how "the love of oneself is not so much congenital in all as innate; and it becomes blameworthy if it exceeds its limits" (John of Salisbury, III, 3). Again: "Cupidity is the source of all evils, and according to the definition of the Fathers, it is the love of those things which one may lose against one's will" (John of Salisbury, VII, 17). In the same way, he considers tyrants as ministers of God because – indirectly, and without wishing to – they do his will by punishing the wicked (cf. John of Salisbury, VIII, 18).

4.5 Equally mediaeval is the need to see politics as strictly linked to morality. This coupling, of which some sort of a revival is being sought today, was, as is well known, completely repudiated by the theorists of *raison d'État*, led by Machiavelli. It is truly surprising to meet with passages and positions in the *Polycraticus* which are later to be taken up and contradicted by the author of *Il Principe*. John writes unambiguously: "The Prince (...) should concern himself with being loved more than with being feared, and should give such an image of himself that his subjects, out of devotion, prefer his life to their own and consider his safety vital to the public good" (John of Salisbury, III, 4) These statements should not lead us to the conclusion that our author is illuded. What he has in common with the future author of *Il Principe*, as a shared inheritance from Roman law, is the conviction that without force, it is impossible to govern. "Since without the employment of force, kingdoms cannot be conquered, and without justice they cannot be preserved" (John of Salisbury, IV, 11). Employment of force is justified, then, but for it to be exercised, it must be used justly within the context of legality. It is in this that John of Salisbury is open to novelty, anticipating (if only in embryo) certain themes relating to the limitations of power.

4.6 It is in this light that we can understand the difference between king and tyrant, to which John gave a better theoretical definition than any other writer of his time. It is here that he shows that capacity to look beyond his own times, thanks to which political thought was able to make a further step forward. King and tyrant are distinguished not on the basis of humane qualities or exclusively moral criteria. What distinguishes them is their relationship with the law. This fact also shows that in England too there was that renewed interest in the rediscovery of Roman law and the common law on which the authors of the first struggles against the excessive power of monarchs based their case. The right of which John speaks, as Cicero had taught, is a right which emerges in practical terms from human experience as history has handed it down to us. It is in fact "from history that it emerges clearly that it is just to kill public tyrants, and free the people so that they can serve God" (Carlyle, 161). Law and history proceed in step with each other, demonstrating that the law is an expression of a concrete reason; by not obeying it, we give rise to an illogical and unnatural system. No-one can have the right to authority if he or she does not recognise that it "is an expression of justice and reason" (Carlyle, 159).

4.7 In John's day there was a renewed ferment over the analysis of authority. The word *auctoritas* itself, with its corresponding term *autenticus*, was accepted into mediaeval language with all the weight of its past associations, thanks to the revaluation of private law which saw in the *auctor* the person who took the initiative in certain acts (cf. Chenu, 383). With the passage of time, authority came to designate the person who possesses the capacity for initiative at certain moments. It should not be forgotten that the rise of a new mercantile society gave back to private law, to the notaries, and in general to all those operating in the economic sphere, that active role in society which rendered them full agents in their own right and thus juridical figures capable of taking initiatives. Once these initiatives were recognised, both obligations and rights would eventually spring.

4.8 The temporal power would draw from these figures, such as doctors of law, attorneys, notaries, scholars in Roman law, etc., the strengths which would enable it to produce political works, booklets, polemical texts, epistles and dissertations through which the independence of the political power from the ecclesiastical power received a theoretical justification. As Sabine has shown, the discussion of trade, taxation, judicial procedure, relations between the government and commerce began slowly but surely to take on a new profile in European intellectual life – that of the educated and professionally trained layman (cf. Sabine, 204). And it is precisely to them that we owe the fact that *sacerdotium* and *imperium* began to be seen as two independent powers. John has also much to tell us of these and of their professional status, especially with regard to the figure of the magistrate. He states that "in the exercise of his functions, he must possess the following qualities: to have a good knowledge of the law; to be disposed towards the good; to have sufficient power; to be bound to the laws by an irrevocable oath, because he must know that he absolutely cannot depart from their scrupulous observance" (John of Salisbury, V, 11).

4.9 The aim of political power, as the classic authors had clearly shown, and as the moderns were to do after them, is the public welfare: in other words the wellbeing of both the individual and the community (cf. John of Salisbury, III, 1). This quest for public wellbeing must not, however, sacrifice the basic requirements of civil life. In other words, for the author of the *Polycraticus*, wellbeing cannot justify any act of tyranny. In contrast to what Hobbes was to say later, no

Leviathan can be justified in exchange for security, also because the latter, if guaranteed by a tyrant, may only be momentary – for what security can be offered or maintained by one who takes no account of the laws and seeks to elevate himself into the supreme law? Public wellbeing rests on the knowledge of truth, and (we seem already to hear the voice of Montesquieu) on the pursuit of virtue (cf. John of Salisbury, III, 1). Anyone who rejects all this certainly does not govern according to justice, and by consent. "Against people of this kind, all law and all justice cry out; against them every creature should arm himself as against an enemy of the public good" (John of Salisbury, III, 3).

4.10 It is always necessary to be on guard against the rise of tyrants. If a system produces them, this is certainly not due to chance. In politics, changes come when certain conditions are created rather than others, because previously determined facts have disposed events in one way rather than another. In the political struggle (to paraphrase Cato), we should not call Fortune blind, for she is not (cf. John of Salisbury, III, 8). As Machiavelli was later to show clearly, fortune depends on the capacity and long-sightedness of the Prince, just as misfortune depends on his evil disposition. But for John of Salisbury the prime virtue is that of keeping a distance from the means used by the tyrant, because the latter, even if he succeeds in assuring himself of momentary success, will sooner or later fall into disaster, especially in relation to those he governs; they will do all they can to free themselves, by resisting his commands more and more firmly.

4.11 In justifying resistance to a tyrant, which in certain circumstances may even lead to tyrannicide, John finds support among the great authors of antiquity, and above all in Cicero. "Even pagan literature warns that it is one thing to live with a friend, and quite another to live under a tyrant. In fact it is not licit to flatter a friend, while it is licit to soften the ears of a tyrant, since it is legitimate to flatter those who it is also legitimate to kill, and to kill a tyrant is not only licit, but just and right" (John of Salisbury, III, 15). The direct appeal to Cicero has been mentioned before. There is a clear reference to the Ciceronian conviction according to which anyone who acts to bring benefit to human society does not merit any kind of condemnation if he acts against tyrants. This is also because he is acting according to the natural law which seeks to assure the common good. There is no element in common between those who pursue this end and tyrants; indeed, there is an unbridgeable abyss. Killing tyrants is like amputating a gangrenous limb; it is therefore an honest action aimed at eliminating this rascal race from the earth (cf. Cicero, DO, III, 6). How could it be otherwise when the tyrant "buries every right, by submitting the law to his own will"? (John of Salisbury, III, 15). Tyrannicide is thus seen as an attempt to bring politics back within the context of legality, in that it not only punishes the crimes of the tyrant but prevents the latter from giving rise to other even worse ones.

4.12 "Among the many crimes which those who hold power may commit, none is graver than that committed against the body of justice itself. Thus tyranny is not only a public crime, but, if this were possible, even more than a public one (...). It is certain that no-one will rise up to avenge a public enemy: those who do not combat against them commit a sin against themselves and the whole body of the city" (John of Salisbury, III, 15). The nature of tyranny is clear at this point: it is a matter of that type of government which "does everything to make the laws vain and reduce the people to slavery" (John of Salisbury, VIII, 17). How can such a form of government be tolerated? Its author should be killed without mercy, because he is an image of evil-doing. To this, our author adds a reflection which is really unusual for his time. Tyranny is not solely the prerogative of individuals as everything seems to imply, it is also a characteristic of groups: "even among private individuals there are many tyrants, who make use of their power for illicit aims" (John of Salisbury, VIII, 17). Among these "private individuals" not a few are ecclesiastics, against whom John of Salisbury intends to warn the Pope, Hadrian IV. In fact, the latter was already well aware of cases of simony, against which he was taking action. But equally well-known are the feudal disputes of those who were seeking to achieve little "realms" within the greater realm, and who adopted every available means for their purposes. All this seemed to John to be a mere search for power for its own sake, without further consideration of the notable burdens which it involves if it is used, as it should be, for the common good. In the past, or in antiquity, when to become a bishop meant as often as not to end up a martyr, only those who were most forgetful of their own interests could have certain aspirations. "I do not know how it has come about, but today the situation has been reversed: All aspire to become bishops, but when they do become so, they rot in idleness" (John of Salisbury, VIII, 17). Who has the good of the faithful at heart? All this is a sign that even within the Church, there are many of those groups which operate with the sole intention of asserting their power: such people are groups of tyrants, and as such they must be eliminated.

4.13 From what has been said above, another point about tyranny emerges. "The latter consists in the abuse of power granted by God to man" (John of Salisbury, III, 18). To struggle against tyranny is thus to struggle against a terrible abuse, and for this reason anyone who puts an end to it is extremely praiseworthy, since he has no ties of fidelity to the tyrant (cf. John of Salisbury, VIII, 20). In this case, not only do undertakings entered into come to nothing, but can the person who was until a little earlier an accomplice of the tyrant give real guarantees of redemption? The people must be on their guard against such men who may, in their turn, become tyrants themselves.

4.14 It is interesting to note that John of Salisbury not only points out the characteristics of the tyrant, but also seeks to draw a profile of what should be the nature of the real prince, to distinguish him from the tyrant. Here too, the departure point is juridical. The sovereign must be the guarantor of the law, and can never replace it with himself. He must remember that "he is superior to others in the sense that while they, as private individuals, are held responsible only for their private affairs; he assumes the burden of the problems of all" (John of Salisbury, IV, 1). Here we find for the first time a notion of political responsibility, even if expressed in a fleeting manner, which was to become one of the cornerstones of modern constitutionalism.

4.15 Among the other functions of the political power which acts in legal fashion is the need to harmonise the various members of the body politic itself, with the aim of guiding them naturally – i.e. without rough handling – towards a real and progressive pursuit of the common good. This need (cf. John of Salisbury, IV, 1) to harmonise the various components of the State, shows an organic conception, always present in western culture, which has led to spirited discussion about the concept of the unity of the State itself. The unity which the *Polycraticus* puts before us has nothing to do with the rigid and sclerotic unity of Platonic thought which has been taken up by not a few modern utopias. Instead, it is a question of harmonic unity, typical of Roman federalism, which from then onwards was to find precise formulation in political thinkers who would open new paths of enquiry. In this author there is already a notion of unity guaranteed by the laws which prevent any attempt to dissolve it, and also any abuse by the central power, which must itself be subject to the same laws. It is not hard to see how this concept is derived from Roman Law. "The prince must recognise that he is bound by the laws: this, according to a great emperor, is a maxim truly worthy of the majesty of a ruler. Since his authority depends on the authority of the laws, the submission of his government to them is something greater than mere command, and hence he will not hold himself to be free to do anything which is in contrast with the equity of justice" (John of Salisbury, IV, 1). The political community (and it is noteworthy that John uses this statement in speaking of subjects) is instituted and guaranteed by the laws: here we find fully restated the classical Ciceronian concept of *societas*, which shows quite clearly how the law is an expression of an intrinsic rationality. We can conclude with some justice that "the prince is thus a minister of public utility, and servant of equity" (John of Salisbury, IV, 2). A kind of *primus inter pares*, in fact: what we would today define as a President with full powers.

4.16 If these premises are accepted, we can understand clearly enough why our author asks himself a very significant question: what sense is there in talking of a free manifestation of the political will of the prince if he is not allowed to will anything which the law has not already laid down? The question (cf. John of Salisbury, IV, 2) shows that the prince's function is above all one of control as long as he does not distance himself from what the law wills – i.e. the pursuit of the common good; subsequently it is also a function of judgment, to exercise the principle of equity. The prince is thus a genuine administrator. He cannot dispose at pleasure of the goods which he administers, "nor dispose at pleasure of the income from taxation, which is public property. And there is nothing strange in this, since the sovereign is not even master of himself, but belongs to his subjects" (John of Salisbury, IV, 5). A prince who behaves in this way will have nothing to fear; he may tour round his state with equanimity, without making use of the escorts of which only tyrants have need (cf. John of Salisbury, IV, 4). In this connection it should be said that there are many counsels given to the prince which one can read in the *Polycraticus*, and many of these, as we have mentioned, are taken up and deliberately contradicted by Machiavelli.

4.17 It is not only to the prince that advice about good government is directed, but also to the magistrates, because in a state based on Law, their activities cannot be replaced. Here too there is an anticipation of certain themes typical of Montesquieu, and John writes, in reference to the magistracy: "Each (magistrate) should keep intact the honour conferred on him without injuring the dignity of others; he should assert his own dignity without offending the public power" (John of Salisbury, IV, 7). Also within the context of Roman law, we can see the reawakening here of the need to limit and circumscribe the powers with the intention of guaranteeing the real functioning of the organs of the state, and indeed of the Church. Citing Justinian, the need is stressed to exclude men of the court and officials from ecclesiastical honours (cf. John of Salisbury, VII, 20), in order to avoid the confusion of offices which leads to corruption and does not assist the pursuit of the public good. When the distinction of roles within the state is missing, there is a failure of the critical function which ensures real social development, and everything levels out to the pursuit of personal interests. John has derived this conviction too from history. Rome was great and attained an unrivalled strength because before taking a decision, it listened to all the possible criticisms, even those of its enemies (cf. John of Salisbury, VII, 25). To listen to criticism is a sign of extreme tolerance, which cannot be divorced from respect for liberty, from the respect for justice and from fidelity to agreements stipulated with other peoples, with whom it is necessary to keep friendship on every occasion. This was what made Rome great (cf. John of Salisbury, V, 7).

4.18 With further reference to the distinction of powers, we should note that our author recognises the state organism as possessing two hands, one armed and the other unarmed, and he adds that "for both specific regulation is needed, because their tendency to degenerate is well-known" (John of Salisbury, VI, 1). The duties of these two hands are different, and "it is necessary that their functions are carried out by different categories of persons" (John of Salisbury, VI, 1). Here we can find a sort of first draft of the recovery of the separation of powers so dear to the Roman world.

4.19 We spoke a little way back of the honour which the prince and the magistrates must maintain, but on what does this honour depend, if it is to arouse the admiration of the governed? The reply is very clear: "the devotion of subjects is due to dignity of behaviour" (John of Salisbury, IV, 8) on the part of those who exercise the functions of government. Here too it is easy to draw a parallel with

Montesquieu's reflections concerning the stability and the good functioning of the monarchical system. John of Salisbury, however, warns us that here the moral force of a state passes from the summit to the base and vice-versa in a continuous osmosis, almost as if to remind us that the health of the body corporate depends on all the components of a political system. "The crimes of the lesser harm the reputation of a good prince, while the sins of the greater give the subjects the pretext and justification for their crimes (...). When the people is honest, the prince is mild, and when the prince is honest, the people do not rebel" (John of Salisbury, VI, 29).

4.20 Even this reflection on the honesty of the prince need not lead us to think of the usual moralism of a mediaeval kind. Our author draws it from tradition. Reshaping an example from Roman history, he writes clearly: "The power of the prince does not depend on blood, but on merits; the man reigns in vain who, although born a king, does not have the merits of one" (John of Salisbury, IV, 11). In fact, there were few occasions in Rome before the Empire became orientalised, that a sovereign left the power in heredity to his son (cf. John of Salisbury, IV, 12). The civil conscience still present at the highest point of the Empire made it clear to all that an incapable sovereign was an evil for everyone, and would soon end in ruin. John demonstrates all his realism at this point. Against the anarchic fashions present in almost every era, but also against Utopias, he maintains that "where there is no government the people will go to ruin" (John of Salisbury, V, 7). This is a biblical admonition, and John frequently makes reference to biblical wisdom, certainly not to indulge in facile moralism, but to show the wisdom of the examples of the past without which we lose ourselves in the pursuit of absurd chimeras.

4.21 The realisation of a perfect society in fact requires a genuine mutation of the species (cf. John of Salisbury, V, 3), because it is like adhering clearly and completely to the truth which, in this terrestrial domain, is practically impossible. Men can always improve themselves, but they cannot claim to be divinities, and John stresses this quite strongly when he says: "I do not posit a man who is just in absolute terms, but one who is just in relation to others" (John of Salisbury, V, 9), and he goes on to write that not even the stars, which are in the sight of God, are immaculate. Claims to achieve a perfect society simplify the complex social relationships which, on the contrary, it seems clear that no one has even been able to place into precise categories without impoverishing them (cf. John of Salisbury, VI, 20). Civil society has such richness of expression and of function that every Utopia tends to reduce it and render it inoperative. "In any case, the general principle is valid for all, by which everyone should concern himself with not passing beyond the limits established by the law, and must refer constantly to public utility" (John of Salisbury, VI, 21). Because of these observations, which sum up a great part of his work, John of Salisbury has been held to be not only the greatest English writer of his century, but the one who sought to define how far the behaviour of a politician could be held to be correct and just (cf. Acton, HF, 45). In any case, it is certainly true that in him, after the attempt of the ancients, there is a resumption of the analysis of the meaning of authority in relation to the limits which it must encounter in its exercise.

4.22 It would be an error to think that the *Polycraticus* should be thought of as a purely English work of politics. Thanks to the universality of the Latin tongue and the phenomenon of the birth of the universities, there was an almost unique cultural osmosis throughout the continent of Europe in that era. The themes dealt with are common everywhere when they have, as in the case of the *Polycraticus*, a universal bearing on dealing with the issue of authority, its nature and its limits. The birth of a mercantile economy, the rediscovered security in travel and the new juridical guarantees at the basis of the commercial activity brought to birth that distinction between the sphere of the public and that of the private which would be at the basis of the political reflection of the modern age. "In effect, Roman Law, the product of a civilization which had developed to the highest degree its social and economic relations, represented a highly valid instrument for combating the hard feudal hierarchy" (D'Addio, 164-165). To this should be added the birth of communal institutions, which were drawing up statutes and the first rudimentary constitutions in the conviction, sustained here by the leading scholars of Roman Law, that from the people, equally with the emperor or the legislative power in general, may emanate laws which are an expression of their own will.

5. Between secularism and theocracy.
Aquinas *versus* the theorists of papal supremacy.

5.1 In discussion of the thought of Aquinas, stress has often been laid on the need to recognise the autonomy of reason and to seek at the same time to harmonise it with the demands of faith. This is undoubtedly true, and finds specific reference at the level of the political situation at the time when Thomas' political notions were to be formulated. For Aquinas, the political dimension is that of actual humanity, it is the dimension in which all those who seek in the secular dimension to realise their own rationality, their talents and their aims, must live their lives. In assessing political action, in short, there is the conviction that by exclusively following the Franciscan spirituality then in vogue, "the risk of the exaltation of the perfect Christian life informed by humility and poverty was that of expressing an ideal which was certainly valid for a minority of the elect, but which would have ended up with a denial of the real common humanity of mankind" (D'Addio, 171). Everyday life was lived out, for Thomas, in the context of the complexity of social relations through which humans seek their own happiness. Out of this comes for the first time in mediaeval thinking, a "secular" way of understanding politics with a specific autonomy in relation to religious experience.

Aquinas was born around 1226, in the castle of Roccasecca. He was educated for the ecclesiastical life in the monastery of Monte Cassino, and studied theology in the University of Naples. Against the wishes of his family and against the prospects for his ecclesiastical career, he entered the Dominican Order. He continued his studies in Paris and Cologne, with

Albertus Magnus. He returned to Italy to take up a certain position in Rome, and then taught once again in Paris and Naples. In 1274, sent by Clement X to the Council of Lyon, he was taken ill, and died during the journey, at the Abbey of Fossanova. His literary output was enormous; in this context, apart from the *Summa theologica* and the *Summa contra gentiles* mention should also be made of his *De regimine principum* and the uncompleted *In libros Politicorum expositio.*

5.2 This conception is at one and the same time the recovery of the Aristotelian conception of the autonomy of political science seen as an "architectonic" science (in relation to this, see Aristotle's *Commentary on Politics*), and its surpassing, because there is no political situation which can fully satisfy mankind and completely realise its nature. It follows that there is no political power which can completely bind human beings to itself to the point not only of fulfilling them in their social existence, but of declaring itself superior to them to the extent of incorporating into itself all intellectual and economic activities, to say nothing of affections and private life in general.

5.3 The social nature of man is not only a natural characteristic, but it is also the fruit of a slow conquest, which little by little refines what nature reveals instinctively, and renders it more rational. Rationality finds expression in the laws which express a genuine path of civilisation for human nature. "The law is a kind of norm or measure of actions by virtue of which a person is induced to act, or is dissuaded from acting. The term "law" in fact derives from *legare* because it obliges, binds, us to act" (Thomas, ST, I. II., q. 90, a. 1). Law measures the degree of civilisation which a people has reached, in the sense that it regulates its life. Because of this, a people which wishes to lay claim to genuine participation in the life of its state must know the laws which govern its existence, and must demand that these always be made known. "This is the reason for which promulgation is necessary, so that the law has its own vigour" (Thomas, ST, I. II., q. 90, a. 4). Without promulgation, the law has no moral force; it does not possess the virtue of law. Promulgation, in short, is not only a *conditio sine qua non* of law, but it is a substantial requisite of law itself; it is its essence (cf. Soria, 31-32). Without this, it is a mere pretext to believe that the law can aim for justice or any other purpose, because it offends the basic characteristic of man himself: consciousness. To know the rules of his civil life is, for the citizen, a fundamental duty in order for this life to be genuinely civil. The knowledge of the laws once again highlights man's intrinsic rationality. The rectitude of human actions and of the laws in fact depends on their intrinsic nature. This is guided by reason. In Thomas, everything is dominated by an ineluctable rationality. The divine law itself orders things according to reason (Thomas, SCG, III, 121). Humankind's own activities, if well ordered, are subordinated to reason; and the activity of lawmaking is one of the highest practical activities of humans, who when they behave as social animals, reveal the best of themselves precisely in the laws.

5.4 This law, known as positive law, issues from a legislative hierarchy which for Thomas presupposes the eternal law, the divine law, according to an intrinsic natural order: it assumes the law of nature which "is manifested in the spontaneous inclination of man to rational ends. By law of nature, man is in a position to appreciate the distinction between good and evil, to have an awareness of what is just, and thus to define the precepts relative to natural justice" (D'Addio, 175). This conception should not lead us to suppose that Thomas considers law, and hence political activity, in a static fashion. From the hierarchy of the laws, and from those of nature in particular, there come general indications which, according to time, place and circumstance, gradually attain concrete form in what human beings hold to be the best way to follow: this explains why law is an expression of rationality. "Thus", Aquinas reminds us, "Cicero writes: the beginning of law came from nature; subsequently other elements useful to nature became customs" (Thomas, ST, I. II., q. 91, a. 3).

5.5 In Thomas we can find a virtual exaltation of imperfection on the social plane, favouring the dynamism without which the life of socio-political organisms would not be possible. Natural law, with its principles, is virtually an itinerary, a disposition, a premise which, however, entirely awaits further development. Principles are in fact abstractions, while the concrete fact of existence needs a positive quality which only human laws can give. "From this point of view, nothing prevents a change in the natural law to which, both by divine law and by human laws, much has been added for the promotion of human existence" (Thomas, ST, I. II., q. 94, a. 5). In this summary definition, two cardinal concepts of western juridical tradition are present, and the liberalism of the future was to develop in the light of them. On the one hand the laws are not mere abstractions, but are the product of a civilisation's "historical becoming", and they can always be enriched; on the other, human advancement depends on the free action of individuals in the pursuit of their own wellbeing. Aquinas is very clear on this point: "Now the aim of positive law is the wellbeing of men, as the (Roman) jurists also teach" (Thomas, ST, I. II., q. 95, a. 3); their authority is expressed through the Digest. The actual attainment of wellbeing has, from time to time, changed the natural law itself. For example, the institute of property, absent in the state of nature, where all is held in common: "in fact the division of property, like slavery, is not a product of nature but of mankind's reasoning to improve its existence" (Thomas, ST, I. II., q. 94, a. 5 ad 3um). It is certainly worth remembering that in Europe the new mercantile society was beginning to assert itself, a society which made property the presupposition of its civic character. But this was a very broad concept of property which went beyond traditional landed property, and stressed the kind of commercial property which as a new security in transaction, was progressively making headway. This justification depends: "First, on the need for the seller to acquire means of livelihood or appeal to charity; secondly, on the demand for the provision of a service; thirdly, on the improvements brought about by the goods sold, fourthly on the difference of price in space and time, and finally, in the fifth case on the risks run by the seller" (James, 32-33). These concepts can be deduced from the famous letter to Fra Giacomo of Viterbo, in which a distinction is made between gain, which exploits the just increase of prices, and usury – a question which exercised the minds of all mediaeval theorists.

5.6 "Another just cause to change the law derives from men, as a result of the change in their conditions, since in different situations different norms are needed" (Thomas, ST, I. II., q. 97, a. 1). Law serves to accompany the actual development of life, but all this should not lead us to think that laws suffer from intrinsic weakness because not all pretexts and occasions to change them are good; it is necessary that the whole community draws effective advantages from it. In other words, the common good must really be improved for all, or for a great part of the community, from any change in the law. "Consequently, the positive law must never be changed other than for a reason which compensates – in favour of the common good – for the disadvantage which the change brings with it" (Thomas, ST, I. II., q. 97, a. 2). The legal system, therefore, cannot live by improvisation, since the damage which would derive from this would endanger the certainty of law itself, and everything would be dragged into the most absurd demagoguery. The most profitable situation for the prosperity of a state is one which is achieved when the people genuinely and spontaneously observe what the laws and customs demand: in a word, when the community shows its own consent to the laws which regulate its own civil life.

5.7 The problem of consensus in the *Summa Theologica* is one which immediately brings us back to that of the form of government. Here, without a shadow of doubt, Thomas intends to favour the mixed form of government, judged to be the best because in it each social party contributes to the formation of the laws (cf. Thomas, ST, I. II., q. 95, a. 4), even though such a system requires a high degree of civic virtue on the part of the citizens. *It remains a fact, however, that the mixed form is the best because it involves all.* "This is the best political order, in which there is a wise mixture of monarchy, in that there is one who commands, and of aristocracy, in that many participate in power according to virtue, and of democracy, that is, popular power, in that the governors can be elected among the people, to whom the election of the governing body belongs" (Thomas, ST, I. II., q. 105, a. 1).

5.8 One of the key concepts in Thomist political thought is the resumption of the classic conviction clearly expressed by Cicero and Seneca that man is a social animal. This conception, which differs substantially from the rather more restrictive Aristotelian one of a political animal, is clearly expressed from the outset of *De Regimine Principum*. The social nature of man is not merely a necessity, but is also a consequence of human rationality which, in its search for the better, finds that living together proves to be more useful and advantageous for all (cf. Thomas, DRP, I, 1, 3). Social existence is thus a consequence of a practical rationality, also acquired through experience. Out of this comes the conviction that in order to satisfy certain needs, which without mutual help could not be satisfied, human beings decide to live together in more and more articulated forms of society (cf. Thomas, DRP, I, 2, 4). By its very nature, social existence is thus an indicator of plurality, which in itself postulates the need for a unifying principle (cf. Thomas, DRP, I, 1, 5), without which the political community would simply disintegrate. This principle, which is identified with the government, must be understood as an organ intended above all to coordinate the activities which are carried on within the context of its sovereignty, and to check that everything takes place according to the prescribed rules – in other words, according to the laws.

5.9 It is easy enough to see why the political problem is joined to the moral one, and thus it should not surprise us that, as has been widely shown, Thomas places strong emphasis on the moral doctrine of Cicero's teaching (cf. Vansteenkiste, 378), because of the close links which it shows with his political ideas.

5.10 For this reason, those who govern must take account of the fact that they exercise their functions over free men, who are always seeking to improve their own life in order to augment what Thomas refers to as the common good. It follows that "if the government is directed not at the common good of society, but at the private interests of those who command, an unjust and corrupt *régime* will be established"

(Thomas, DRP, I, 2, 1). This unjust *régime*, described as a tyranny, can, as the classics demonstrate, be exercised by an individual, by a more or less restricted class and even by the multitude: "in this situation, the whole population constitutes a single tyrant" (Thomas, DRP, I, 2, 2).

5.11 Unjust *régimes* are such because they have lost sight of the purpose for which the organs of government were instituted. The eminent purpose of government "is that of realising unity in peace; if this is lacking, then the advantages of social life cease to exist" (Thomas, DPR, I, 3, 1). *But peace must never be understood as an end in itself, because there could be régimes which, with the excuse of safeguarding peace, put obstacles in the way of other aspirations of humankind.* For example, "tyranny may not compromise peace, but it creates barriers to the specific good of single individuals" (Thomas, DRP, I, 6, 1). This is a statement which seems to be a criticism of Hobbes in advance, were it not for the fact that it was already a tried conviction of the Middle Ages that only nineteenth-century utopianisms have made us forget.

5.12 There has been much debate about whether Thomas prefers monarchical or mixed forms of government. The texts seem to indicate preference for one at some points and the other at different moments, but what is certain is that Thomas is more interested in the guarantees that the forms of government can give to the governed, and in the dangerous degenerations which these forms can assume. When Thomas points to the advantage of monarchy, he does so because it guarantees better than other forms the unity of the state, and reaches decisions of general interest with greater ease. This does not mean, however, that Thomas does not see the numerous dangers inherent in the monarchical system, and not only because of the possible degenerations which may lead to tyranny, but also because of the psychological limits, and hence the impediments to development, which it can show. "It happens most often that the subjects of a monarch possess less stimulus for the common good, because they form the idea that their efforts towards social wellbeing do not work to their advantage, but benefit another whose power also includes the common good. On the other hand, when they do not consider the common good as comprehended in the power of a person, they promote the common good not as something belonging to someone else, but as if it were their own. For this reason, experience shows that a city ruled by governors who stay in power for a year is sometimes more prosperous that those cities, or even three or four cities united with each other, governed by a king, and the people find modest burdens imposed by a king harder to bear than even heavy taxes requested by the mass of the citizens" (Thomas, DRP, I, 5, 1). If this is so when there is a just system of monarchy, how much more so when this degenerates into tyranny? In other words, when the tyrants not only use their strength to do harm, but fear that power, prosperity and riches of their subjects will turn to their disadvantage (cf. Thomas, DRP, I, 4, 6). In this case, anticipating Montesquieu, Thomas shows how tyranny is based on the power which causes subjects to flee tyrants as cruel beasts (cf. Thomas, DRP, I, 4, 7).

5.13 It could, then, be said about the system of monarchy described by Thomas that it may be compared, without a shadow of doubt, to a modern presidential system with an efficient executive. The long quotation which follows certainly goes to back up such a conviction. "1. It is necessary above all that the citizens, to whom the task of electing the king belongs, should choose a person equipped with gifts which offer the moral certainty that he will not slide into tyranny (...). 2. Subsequently, they must move on to elaborate a structure for the monarchical *régime* so that the king, once elected, is deprived of the opportunity for tyranny. 3. At the same time, limits must be placed on his power, with the aim of making it difficult for him to slide into tyranny (...). 4. Finally, if they allow the hypothesis that the king *does* transform himself into a tyrant, appropriate remedies must be sought" (Thomas, DRP I, 7, 1). The first observation that needs to be made is that the citizens have an active role both before electing the king (cf. point 1) and after the election, when they must draw up a political structure capable of not degenerating into tyranny. In short, as was the case in ancient Rome, the people-to whom Thomas constantly refers – remain the real destinees and actors in political activity.

5.14 There are many other very interesting observations to make. The king is not such by birth or heredity; he is elected, and those who elect him maintain constant control on him, because "the society which has made him king may legitimately remove him, or place limits on his power" (Thomas, DRP, I, 7, 4). The action of substitution of those in office, which does not affect only those at the top level of government (cf. Thomas, DRP, I, 16, 6), is for Thomas the most just and the most "natural" of political actions, because it indicates the renewal and growth of the body politic.

5.15 Another crucial point in Thomist political thinking is that of the limits which must be placed on power to prevent it from degenerating. It is possible for anyone to fall in a difficult and trap-ridden terrain like that of politics, partly because "basically there is no individual who begins to behave dishonestly unless seized by the urge to attain some advantage which he earnestly desires" (Thomas, DRP, I, 12, 1), so that, when this power degenerates, it is not very easy to bring it back inside its limits by peaceful means. This is the moment in which the people, in order to eliminate exploitation and vexations, may back some revolutionary spirit, even to see that justice is done (cf. Thomas, DRP, I, 11, 5). This is the point at which the fear which characterises tyrannical *régimes* is generated, or at any rate periods of great insecurity, moments in which "when one is seized by the desperation of no longer being able to save oneself, and led on by one's own audacity to every kind of extremism" (Thomas, DRP, I, 11, 6).

5.16 In this light it is easy to see why Thomas puts so much stress on the problem of peace, which is the first condition for attaining that unity of the state which is so much desired. From peace comes the possibility of acting well, and achieving specific aims, among which the first, from which many others spring, is that by which the sovereign acts so that everyone "has available, in necessary quantity, the requisites of a good life" (Thomas, DRP, I, 16, 4). This idea of the requisites of a good life is very broad, and one need only turn to the first four chapters of the second book to see that it extends from concerns which today we would call ecological, such as the health of the environment, to the opportunity and the places for entertainment, and the need to find employment for all.

5.17 From what has been said it becomes clear that for Thomas, state and the authority which springs from it are values which are positive in themselves. This is also true for those states which are not yet inspired by Christian values, but which express a fully justified authority in terms of human and natural law (cf. Passerin D'E., 12). The state, which although it can never fully absorb in itself the life of the individual, seems completely justified insofar as it helps in the pursuit of that common good which is superior to the good of individuals (cf. Passerin D'E., 14-15). The latter sometimes need to be coordinated in order to be more efficient. Because of this, obedience is owed to authority, though certainly not unconditional obedience, because it is exercised by free individuals. Thomas makes an appropriate distinction between the *subiectio servilis* and the *subiectio civilis*, and he stresses that the first is contrary to nature, while the second is necessary in any society in order to have that needful cohesion without which no kind of civil life is possible (cf. Passerin D'E., 19). This does not mean that such civil obedience should not encounter precise limits, and Thomas, as we have seen, "recognises and affirms not only the right but also the precise duty to resist unjust political power" (Passerin D'E., 22).

5.18 For Thomas, injustice should not be measured merely on the juridical or political plain, but can also be moral, or even fiscal. We have only to consider that on the one hand there is an obligation for the citizens to maintain those who act for the public good, while on the other is the duty of the governors not to demand taxes which surpass the established limits or are insupportable for the people. Aquinas' words on this score are again very clear: whoever may be "operating for the common good has the right to live at the expense of the community and can carry out his ordinary tasks with the funds allocated; if these are lacking or insufficient, he may have recourse to the contributions of individuals. The same criterion is valid for exceptional cases of emergency, in which it is necessary to request greater sums (...). On the other hand it is absolutely immoral for governments to demand taxes superior to the agreed limits, simply for greed or gain, or to abandon themselves to unjustifiable and exaggerated expenditure" (Thomas, DRJ, 408). The firmest kind of action should be taken against administrators of this kind, to prevent others in the future from behaving in the same way, encouraged by the impunity of their predecessors (cf. Ibidem).

5.19 After the foregoing, it is not hard to understand why the political thought of Aquinas can be described as the first exposition of the Whig theory on revolution (cf. Acton, HF, 37). It could hardly be otherwise, given that from a careful reading of Thomas' works emerged all those aspects, such as limited and elective monarchy, an aristocracy of merit, consensus, participation in the management of power at different levels, the right of rebellion and deposition of tyrants which, when expounded for the first time were to be at the basis of the English "Glorious Revolution". Thomas had reached a similar series of notions because he was one of the most open spirits of the western world. Certain elements were decisive in the formation of his thought. He had read the Fathers of the Church, and had also read the classical texts of the Greek and Roman world, but also the Jewish writers and the Arab thinkers (cf. Acton, LMH, 86). Moreover, Acton asks, if Thomas had not had substantial elements of liberalism in his thinking, how would he have acquired various followers among the liberals themselves?

5.20 To speak of consensus, of capacity to elect and depose, means to say that the whole community carries out a basic role, and that it virtually demonstrates the capacity for self-government (cf. Fasnacht, 26). Thomas also made great steps forward in the theorisation of liberal principles because he was the first to present the theory of liberty of conscience; it is from this, in fact, that true liberty springs (cf. Fasnacht, 34). From these observations comes the conviction of quite a number of scholars that it is precisely from the thought of Aquinas and a few of his contemporaries that those elements which were to be at the basis of future representative governments actually sprang.

5.21 If we were seeking for real liberal thought, we could find it by putting together the thought of Thomas with that of Marsilio of Padua. The two thinkers, who seem poles apart, in fact complement each other in many aspects (cf. Fasnacht, 187, note 8). Basically both have handed down to the modern age two requisites which have become basic to it: liberty of conscience and government based on consent. Aristotle seems so far away as only to be a pretext for the thought of Thomas. The idea of mixed government itself, so enthusiastically put forward by Aquinas, is the first mediaeval form of the Whiggism which was to enjoy such success in the modern age (cf. Fasnacht, 195).

5.22 The modernism of Thomas is also seen in the fact that he does not leave the legislators with the freedom to formulate the laws in arbitrary fashion, but on the contrary establishes general principles within which the legislator must move (cf. Balmes, 345). At this point the law becomes a means of civil power because it expresses a rationality of its own, a *rationis ordinatio* which excludes any possibility of arbitrary conduct. The latter, on the other hand, is typical of tyranny, because – incapable of showing such rationality – it replaces the force of law with violence. Because of this, the law, as it is sanctioned by the will of the legislator, becomes an aid to the reason which has manifested it, an instrument of that reason. And thus the sanctions which are brought into play by failure to observe it are amply justified because they themselves derive from the very same will which has produced the law. This delicate and basic relationship is absent in despotism, which for that very reason will never possess its own legitimisation (cf. Balmes, 349). But often, even in other systems, although they have their legitimisation in law, the case of civil disobedience may occur. When in conscience the laws appear unjust because they do not express the rationality which should lead to the common good, or because they are the expression of a legislator who goes far beyond his own responsibilities, or otherwise, for other motives which are easy to discern, civil disobedience is an obligation. With regard to the way it should be applied, prudence may from time to time suggest the most appropriate way which circumstances and the various political systems to be dealt with impose (cf. Balmes 433).

5.23 It has been said that Thomas was able to gather from the best in the western tradition, the links existing between morality, law and politics. This explains why his reflection, synthesising Aristotle, the Roman jurists, St Augustine, the Fathers and the previous Scholastic tradition, was so useful to the school of Salamanca, and particularly to Vitoria, when it was a matter of defending the most elementary (and thus natural) rights of the inhabitants of the New World (cf. Soria, 10).

5.24 We should add, however, that the political notions of Aquinas did not receive an immediate welcome in ecclesiastical circles. We need only recall that in the last year of the thirteenth century and the beginning of the fourteenth, a number of works came from the various religious orders defending the theocratic position, though with new insights and motivations. Among these, Aegidius Romanus, general of the Augustinians, played a major role. With his *De Regimine Principum* (1285). And above all in *De Ecclesiastica (sive de Summi Pontificis) Potestate* (1301) he reasserted the supremacy of the Church over temporal orders. For this writer, man is led by an *impetus naturalis* to live in a political dimension. It follows from this that power, arising in a natural way, belongs to the temporal order, but precisely because of this genesis, it is founded on imposition and violence. "The only way to confer on power the baptism of legitimacy is that of instituting it on the basis of the principles of justice; now this may be done only by the supreme spiritual authority. Thus the power of the Emperor and of the king derives, and thus depends, on the *plenitude potestatis* of the Pope" (D'Addio, 186). Various studies were to appear in opposition to the assertion, many of them being published anonymously. Among those whose authors are known, the *De Recuperatione Terrae Sanctae*, and more especially the *De Potestate Regia et Papali* are deserving of note. In the first, written in 1313 by Pierre Dubois (who ascribes a real primacy to the French nation over other European peoples), he maintains that to bring peace back to the human consciousness it is necessary to free the Church from the weighty conditioning of worldly affairs. In the second work, (1302) by Jean de Paris, in line with Thomism, the distinction of powers is maintained by demonstrating that the spiritual power cannot manifest its jurisdiction in the temporal sphere.

5.25 Giacomo da Viterbo seems to follow the same line as Aegidius in his *De Regimine Christiano* (1301-1302). For him, "the Church is the one sole *regnum* existing, in fact giving to the term (...) a universal acceptance" (Chevallier, 319). It is logical, therefore, to go beyond the polemic on the separation of power since the Church, by virtue of a series of characteristics shown in the first part of the work, has its own unique character to which the temporal kingdom cannot even aspire. Even though in certain aspects, there may be concordance in the way of understanding power, " there is always a difference in the way of exercising it, since the temporal power applies to men from a natural standpoint, whereas the spiritual power applies to them from the point of view of divine grace, from which it derives" (Rizzacasa, 62). It has also been observed that the work of Giacomo da Viterbo has more of an ecclesiological aim than a political one, but it is beyond dispute that such conclusions had a notable effect on the political debate of his times, and were another key point in the supremacy of the spiritual power over the temporal, even for matters involving conflicts which merely concerned land.

6. Dante. The problem of peace in the conflict between universal authority and local autonomy.

6.1 "We need to free Dante's political teaching from all subsequent superstructures, reducing it to its precise historic significance" (Gramsci, II, 758). Despite this judgment, which seems to fix Dante exclusively in his own turbulent century and render him incapable of offering us any useful suggestions for the continuation of western political reflection, Gramsci nevertheless maintains elsewhere that Dante's work is all "political par excellence" (cf. Gramsci, I, 522) because even Dante's existential experience is permeated by political passion.

Dante Alighieri was born in Florence in 1265, of a family which in the past had played a very important political role. Little is known of his cultural upbringing; the first definitive information we possess is that he enrolled in the guild of doctors and herbalists, and that from then onward he played an active part in the political events of his city. During his absence from Florence, on an embassy to Boniface VIII in Rome, a political upheaval in the political leadership in Florence forced Dante into exile in order to avoid not only the confiscation of his goods, but the death penalty itself. Troubled and difficult years followed, during which Dante served a number of lords of northern Italy, among them in particular Cangrande della Scala. He died in Ravenna in 1321. Among his notable literary output, apart from some of the cantos of the *Divina Commedia*, we should mention in the present context the *De Monarchia*, where he enquires into the content and basis of political authority.

6.2 The basic aim of Dante's political thought seems to be that of understanding the basis of authority seen as an expression of "unity of directives to coordinate the activity of individuals" (D'Addio, 190). In this sense every form of human aggregation which seeks to merit the term "civilized" must possess its own expression of authority, which must of course also be legitimate. This can be observed in the family, the village, the city, the kingdom and the empire (cf. D'Addio, 190). This almost pyramidal structure points to the presence in Dante of a conviction that the unity of the human race is not in fact to be understood in a rigid and ossified sense, but on the contrary in harmonic fashion, respecting all those differences and autonomies which contribute to the cultural enrichment of the human race. It could be said that Dante's conception of the Empire anticipates the need for a supranational body (of which the need is felt so strongly today). Such a body will ensure peace because, according to the poet, this is the essential condition for the complete development of humanity and the collective whole. The Empire, in other words, is seen as "the necessary coordination of all types of minor communities; each of them autonomous and independent in its own proper sphere" (D'Addio, 190).

6.3 In the *Commedia,* this idea of harmonic unity already emerges clearly in all three of the sixth cantos of the three canticles. The conviction also emerges that when the various autonomies produce political bodies which are not capable of guaranteeing peace, we find the vices – we might almost say the decay of civil morality – which produce a climate of insecurity and political crisis, causing everyone to live by expedients, and in an extemporized and improvised way. In the sixth canto of the Inferno, he deals with civic autonomy: and it is Florence that he has in mind. The corruption of the city already rules out the hope of anything good emerging from it. The very few honest citizens – for Dante, in fact, they have been reduced to two, so rare have they become – are no longer listened to:

> *Two righteous men there are, whom none will heed;*
> *Three sparks from Hell – Avarice, Envy, Pride –*
> *In all men's bosoms sowed the fiery seed.*
> (Hell. VI, 73-75).

The moral crisis of the Commune, warns Dante, is such that the city is no longer able to emerge from the crisis on its own. The failure of the legitimate authority of its citizens requires greater and more authoritative force in order to resolve the crisis. The poet does not foresee it, but the democracy of the commune, having had its day, is heading towards the *Signoria,* since it does not have in itself the moral strength to survive.

6.4 The same goes for the Kingdom – a kingdom or state which does not in fact exist: Italy. Municipal corruption affects the entire peninsula, and prevents it from remembering the role played in the past, and the potential of the present:

> *O house of grief! O bond-slave Italy!*
> *Ship without pilot in, a raging gale!*
> *No mistress-province, but a stews and sty!*
> (Purg., VI, 76-78)
> ....
> *Search, wretched! search thy seas and coasts around;*
> *Then, search thy bosom, see if thou canst hit*
> *On any nook where pleasant peace is found.*
> (Purg., VI, 85-87).

The dramatic consequence which has arisen out of this disorder is evident: the absence of peace. From this comes the insecurity not only of private life, but also of trade and the economy, which was causing the decline of Italian civic life, and making the moral situation even worse. Insecurity in the cities, but even on the seas and the internal routes; the hard-won progress of the communes and of mercantile life had suffered a notable setback, which on the institutional plane was almost irreparable. This was the cause of the servile state in which the peninsula found itself *(serva Italia)*, because it was subject to tyranny and at the mercy of arbitrary governments devoid of any rules and lacking specific objectives (cf. Sapegno, II, 65). This view of the situation was not caused merely by Dante's anguish as a result of his exile from Florence, but is also shared by other great minds of the time, such as Petrarch, even though they may have different solutions in mind.

6.5 In the corresponding canto of the *Paradiso,* hope for a solution is vested in the last institution capable, because of its prestige, strength and authority, of restoring peace universally, and in particular in the *Bel Paese* (Italy). This institution is the Empire. It was not as if the events of Dante's time encouraged too many hopes even from this type of government, but the poet is convinced that only a government above parties can regain the credibility which the local governments, like the kings, have now finally lost. The task of defending the role of this universal authority is allotted to Justinian. Why to Justinian? The information which Dante possessed about this emperor was limited, and there were many gaps in it; perhaps it was also too laudatory (cf. Sapegno, III, 70); it had been rendered thus by a tradition with a strong inclination to hagiography. But it is certain that the merit which Dante recognises in Justinian is that of having gathered together and passed on the best of the juridical experience of Rome. This single fact is already a guarantee that it should be used for a peace which, if divorced from Law, appears to be completely unobtainable.

> *Caesar I was, and am Justinian,*
> *Who from the Laws – urged by that Primal Love*
> *Which now I feel – winnowed the dust and bran.*
> (Par. VI, 10-12).

It should be noted that since he no longer holds any institutional post, Justinian is a soul like any other *(Caesar I was, and am Justinian)*, but when he was alive, it was only by virtue of the imperial authority that he could take on the task of systematising the Law, and removing from it *the dust and bran*. All this was certainly not done in arbitrary fashion, because Justinian made use of an aristocratic intelligentsia presided over by an able official, Tribonianus, while military questions and what we would now call foreign affairs were entrusted to Belisarius:

> *...whom Heaven's right hand so befriended,*
> *'Twas token clear I should withdraw me thus.*
> (Par., VI, 26-27).

It hardly matters that this does not correspond to historical reality; what interests us is that in Dante's political conception, the imperial authority is what it is because he delegates certain of his functions, and coordinates his best collaborators, in subjection to the laws. And to the authority of the laws, even the Emperor must submit.

6.6 In modern terms, the power of the Emperor takes on the connotations of that of a President. In other words, it is a question of a strong executive power controlled by an effective *Corpus* of Laws: a government which has the basic function of guaranteeing peace, without which no other activity is possible. The Romans succeeded in this intention, for with the Empire they made peace a possibility, and with it the development of the ancient world. This is what Dante states in his treatise on Monarchy, the objective of which is to revitalise the only institution capable of bringing Europe out of the state of insecurity into which had fallen.

6.7 From the opening words of the treatise, Dante points out that the basic task of an imperial power is not to impose itself, but to coordinate the various aims of all the lesser institutions. The Empire has in common with these institutions the basic aim of any society: peace; without which it is not even conceivable to think about the realisation of Justice and possible liberties. The Empire, in short, has a coordinating function and has the same aim as other political formations (such as communes, kingdoms and so on) "because it would be madness to think that a purpose exists for one society or another, but that there is no purpose valid for all societies" (Dante, Mon., I, 2). This statement clearly refers to the basic purpose, which is peace, within which there can and should develop all the diversities of intention which justify other forms of authority. These diversities can only enjoy development if there is peace, and a peace that someone can guarantee, obviously making use of the help of particular princes who must coordinate with the emperor. The latter, to make use of an analogy drawn from medieval logic, is compared to the speculative intellect, while the individual princes are likened to the practical intellect (cf. Dante, Mon., I, 14).

6.8 Peace, for Dante, is not the final purpose of a society, but it constitutes the precondition for one. Only where peace is stable and lasting can man fully realise himself on the practical level – "arts and trade" – for which peace is an irreplaceable guarantee, and on the intellectual plane, because study and extended knowledge require a tranquillity of soul which only peace can guarantee. In fact, "it is evident that in the quiet or tranquillity of peace, the human race realises itself freely and easily in its proper activity (...). Hence it is clear that universal peace is the best of things which are ordered in our beatitude" (Dante, Mon., I, 4). The need of a single body which can guarantee peace derives from the fact that the human race in its most crucial and characteristic attitudes, "is absolutely one" (Dante, Mon., I, 8), and this is specifically demonstrated by the fact that the need for peace brings together all upright men, who may differ only on the ways to attain it, to render it stable and lasting. For Dante this can only be the peace which will seek to realise the maximum possible justice (cf. Dante, Mon., I, 11), because the more injustices grow and become evident, the more political stability is weakened.

6.9 The ideal of justice, like that of peace, is not a Utopian dream, but shows its concrete character when it succeeds in giving real value to the liberty of humankind. Only thanks to freedom "are we on earth happy as human beings, and in heaven as Gods" (Dante, Mon., I, 12), and it is certainly no accident that precisely to defend liberty, men are ready to sacrifice everything, even their lives. The *Commedia* itself is permeated by this conviction, which Dante sums up in splendid fashion in the invitation which Virgil offers to Cato before entering Purgatory:

> *Be gracious to his coming, I entreat;*
> *'Tis liberty he seeks – how dear a thing*
> *That is, they know who give their lives for it.*
> (Purg., I, 70-72).

Liberty is elsewhere described as the greatest gift God has given to humankind (cf. Par., V, 19-24); it is understood in the broadest sense, above all as moral liberty which is the basis of all the others, including political (cf. Sapegno, II, 8). Political action, according to the classical notion. takes place within the framework of the moral dimension.

6.10 Freedom, moreover, must be assured not only by the good intentions of the monarch, but also by the laws. Law, the real glory of the Roman people, reveals the wisdom of the path of liberty and its efforts to establish and defend itself. For Dante, as for Cicero, law is the expression of the history of a civilisation in all its different aspects. *To study law is virtually to undertake a hermeneutic task in order to understand the motives which have conditioned the development of a state and also its decadence.* In Dante's opinion, "anyone who aims at the benefit of the state aims at the purpose of law. The proof of this is as follows: Law is a real and personal relationship between man and man which, if it is upheld, maintains human society, and if it is corrupted, corrupts it – in fact the definition of the *Digest* does not explain the essence of the Law, but describes it in practical terms" (Dante, Mon., II, 5). Practicality is very close to Dante's heart, perhaps because his existential experience prevented him from indulging in vague and utopian dreams.

6.11 Law must guarantee the relations between individuals within a state as well as what we would today call international relations. Within a political community, law guarantees that the debate and healthy competition will take place without prevarication. As Cicero writes in the Third Book of *De Officiis:* "anyone who runs on the track must make the effort to extend himself as far as possible in order to win: but he must not under any circumstances cause the competitor against whom he is racing to fall" (Dante, Mon., II, 7). In other words, outside the rules there is no such thing as a race, or at least the race is always irregular. No less important is the problem raised in going beyond the boundaries of one's own state. What law, and what authority will guarantee in this instance that everything will take place within the context of legality? Before accepting that everything is beyond repair, and reaching the point of war, it is necessary to proceed like a medical scientist who before operating attempts every other kind of cure (cf. Dante, Mon., II, 9). But when every effort to avoid war proves useless, it seems clear that the need for an universal authority is shown to be the only way to return everything to within the framework of legality, and hence of peace.

6.12 This authority must be absolutely secular. As Gilson states, Dante has not followed "any of the genuinely philosophical notions of Averroism; to the best of our knowledge at present, however, he is the first to have made use of Averroès' dualism (...) because he distinguishes between two ultimate purposes in humanity" (Gilson, 690-691). Without venturing into the notions of Averroès, we may safely affirm that Dante became the protagonist of the dualism which, in politics, was always the greatest achievement of western thought, from the Roman juridical experience with its distinction between the public and private spheres to Christian thought with its two dimensions, natural and supernatural.

6.13 The separation of the religious from the political power (and here we must agree with Gilson) comes in fact from a cultural conviction, i.e. that theology and philosophy, though they exist in a context of mutual collaboration, have distinct fields of investigation, and thus enjoy mutual autonomy. In reality, this distinction means that earthly society, inasmuch as it is *naturaliter* human, has its own ends, which it must reach with its own means. As far as Dante is concerned, it is not the immutable principles of science which apply to politics, but the flexible capacity to act, though within the rules which govern civil life. He is very precise on this point: "since everything political is subject to our power, it is clear that the present subject has as its aim not theory but practice" (Dante, Mon., I, 2). If politics is subject to our power, this means that not only its aims but even its institutions depend on our will. This is still the dualism, that of God and Caesar, which assures differing authorities with differing tasks, and with autonomies which neither of the two powers may in any way arrogate the right to impair, because in this case rather than exercising a right, it would be committing the most absurd of wrongs.

7. Marsilio of Padua. William of Ockham.
The difficult search for consensus guaranteed by law.

7.1 It may seem somewhat artificial to align the political thought of Marsilio and that of Ockham, but in fact both of them, given the extremely close links by which they tie political experience to religious experience, end up by following the same path to such an extent that one of them (Ockham) can be considered the continuer of the thought of the other (Marsilio). The latter has sometimes been considered a contradictory thinker because he found it impossible to disentangle the religious question from the political one, as Ockham did succeed in doing. He was able to see religious experience as having its own individual value and to safeguard it from the claims of the *universitas fidelium*, which risked dragging everything along the perilous path of future totalitarian democracies.

7.2 Gilson amply demonstrated that in the political and religious dualism which appeared in European culture in the thirteenth and fourteenth centuries, there is influence from the political creed of Averroès, of which the work of Marsilio was to be the most perfect example. In his *Defensor Pacis*, beginning "from the classical distinction of the two purposes of man, Marsilio distinguishes two corresponding ways of life; the temporal life, which the princes regulate according to the teachings of philosophy, and the eternal life, to which the priests guide man with the aid of revelation" (Gilson, 829). These are two ways of life which, still according to Gilson, carry the implication of two different kinds of needs: various categories ranging from artisans to officials entrusted with power see to the earthly concerns, while heavenly matters are dealt with by the religious. Marsilio, however, seems to think that philosophers have never found a way of demonstrating the role of the latter in the city (cf. Gilson, 829). It is significant that Gilson, in pointing out the Averroistic dualism, stresses the fact that "its origin lies in the classical distinction between the two purposes of man", which calls to mind the Augustinian dualism of the two cities, and the juridical dualism of the Romans. With the recovery of the Aristotelian pattern of thought, both these elements converge fully in Marsilio's analysis.

The date of birth of **Marsilio** may be placed around 1275, in Padua. As he was the son of a notary, he took an interest in legal studies, but he also explored the realms of natural philosophy and medicine. He studied at the University of Padua, and then in Paris. After serving Matteo Visconti for some years, he returned to Paris, where he finished writing his *Defensor Pacis.* This work brought him a certain amount of trouble with the Church authorities, and he was forced to take refuge with Ludwig of Bavaria. From then onward, he became the inspirer of imperial policy, which was seeking for its own autonomy. Before he died, around 1343, he wrote other works, among them the *Defensor minor* and the *Tractatus de translatione imperii.*

7.3 In relation to the two differing purposes, we can unquestionably say that Marsilio's great merit is to have shown very clearly the complete autonomy of the natural and worldly dimension of man as it was being portrayed in his period. It was no coincidence that this was the period which witnessed the revival of Roman law, precisely because the Communes had felt the need to appeal to a consolidated juridical experience on which to build rules for the present – both for their own institutions and also for their commercial activities. It is on this need for rules that the design for peace is based; he had become aware of the need both in his native Padua and in Paris. The Venetian city had experienced all the dramas of conflicts between factions which had already brought an end to the experiment of the Communes, and the French capital was witnessing the birth of a national monarchy whose future fortune Marsilio completely perceived. On the one hand an economic prosperity which had no structures and institutions capable of defending itself and fostering further development, and on the other, a rising power which guaranteed stability and all types of development.

7.4 Thus for Marsilio peace assumes substantially different connotations from those outlined by Dante. There is no moral necessity or intellectual design which is the prelude to the complete development of intelligences. Peace is referred to prosperity, to the "well-being" of the bourgeois and mercantile society. It is the ultimate aim of the citizen of the community who turns to the institutions of his city for guarantees capable of preserving the tranquillity needed for the conduct of his affairs and his trade (cf. D'Addio, 195).

7.5 It has been said that Marsilio, when speaking of peace and political order, recalls the analysis carried on in the fifth book of Aristotle's *Politics*. But this reflection seems insufficient in itself, unless it is integrated with the major dissension which affected the fourteenth century – i.e. the conflict between the Church and the Empire. It is only in this way that we can understand why Marsilio favours the civil power, because he sees in the Emperor the guarantor of peace, the *Defensor Pacis*. The Emperor must, even by force if necessary, prevent any religious authority from exercising any form of command over against other governing powers or individual citizens (cf. Marsilio, DP,

II, 18, 8). Once again, a clear Augustinian strain of thought can be seen in this standpoint. We have only to remember that for Marsilio the state, as in the *De Civitate Dei*, is considered a positive ordinance, aimed at the realisation of order and temporal peace (cf. Vasoli, 21).

7.6 Because of this the State, like politics itself, is based on rigorous presuppositions of human science (the advance signals later taken up by Machiavelli are very clear here). Human science is distinguished from revelation, and thus from all the problems related to faith. This drastic distinction also derives from the ascetic necessities of Christian perfection, which can only be realised when the ecclesiastical power withdraws from civil life and concentrates on its religious purposes (cf. Vasoli, 24-25). The need for the separation of the temporal from the spiritual power thus arises from a precise methodological conviction, because only when there is a clear distinction between them can the two powers fulfil their purposes and realise their aims. The distinction between two "orders" arises from the fact that for Marsilio "two orders of truth exist – that of human reason and that which is related to faith: they are two orders of considerations which must be conducted in complete autonomy, without claiming that there can exist between them a connection which systematically coordinates reason and faith" (D'Addio, 196). We are a long way from the Thomistic notions which attempted a coordination between reason and faith, and thus between Politics and religion.

7.7 This is why, from the opening lines of the *Defensor Pacis*, there is much insistence on the fact that political society owes its formation to a natural process (cf. Marsilio, DP, I, 1, 1). From the most elementary forms of association, society passes through the more complex ones to the state itself. In this context there is a very clear citation from the *De Officiis* of Cicero, which Marsilio inserts into the first chapter of his work: "as the Stoics like to assert, all the things which are generated on this earth are created for the use of mankind, but mankind is generated solely for the care of mankind. And in this matter we must undoubtedly follow the guidance of nature and promote things which are commonly useful for all" (Marsilio, DP, I, 1, 4).

7.8 There is a utilitarian concept at the basis of Marsilio's political thinking and the reference to Cicero shows the interest in private law, which would ensure the relations between the citizens of the community. It should not be forgotten that Marsilio was the son of Bommatteo de' Mainardini, the university notary. Human nature is made manifest in the concrete, in the search for the useful and for wellbeing. For this reason, when he speaks of the socially-oriented nature of man, this "no longer has that finalistic character previously assumed in Aristotle's *Politics*" (Vasoli, 26), but simply signifies that by living together in orderly fashion, everyone can come nearer to attaining his own expectations and obtaining his own advantages. Marsilio not only does not set out to celebrate ethical objectives; as a realist he has no illusions at all that real life can be free from conflicts as if it were the life of paradise.

7.9 Contestations, insults, disputes and scandals are always in the air, and explode wherever the coercive force of the law fails, and with it the order which should, by means of the laws, be the guarantee of the organs of the state. So there is no human organisation which can do without rigorous norms guaranteeing justice (cf. Vasoli, 27). Put another way, this brings us back to the central idea of Cicero's reflections, in which outside a juridical context there exists a multitude but not a people: *ubi societas, ibi ius.* Without political authority it is not possible to give coercive effect to any system of order. In short, the state structure becomes a necessity and "is only of value according to Marsilio on the basis of the perfect functioning of the norms and principles which it is capable of inculcating and imposing on all" (Vasoli, 29). What political structure is the best, and succeeds best in this task, is a different question; what counts is that we cannot do without it. Without the binding force of the law, society disintegrates, and no-one is any longer in a position to pursue what is useful. This is so because the law is the fruit of the will and tradition of individuals. Here too the reference to Cicero is unmistakable, and it is Marsilio himself who makes it. The civil government has its roots in the mutual pledge and in the faith of the subjects and the governors. "This faith, as Cicero states in his treatise *De Officiis,* Book 1, 'is the foundation of justice, and anyone who attempts to destroy this bond between subjects and governors is only intending to acquire the capacity to overthrow at his own will the power of all those who govern, and hence reduce them to his own servitude'" (Marsilio, DP, II, 26, 13). To sum up, law is the expression of a social bond, and those who do not undertake to safeguard legality are committing a major injustice. Marsilio says, again with reference to *De Officiis,* that "It is not only those who inflict an injustice on others who are unjust, but also those who, while having the knowledge and the ability to prevent harm happening to others, do not do so" (Marsilio, DP, I, 19, 13). This means – and here we are drawing near to a description of the form of government preferred by Marsilio, that everyone possesses civil responsibility.

7.10 "The law, then, is (...) an ordinance created by political prudence around things which are just and advantageous and their opposites, and which has coercive power, and thus for the observance of which a command is emanated which it is obligatory to obey, or which is emanated by means of such a command" (Marsilio, DP, I, 10, 5). This definition permits Marsilio to define not law in general but that law which expresses the only really valid form of jurisdiction. For Marsilio, this law, always referred to the *Corpus juris civilis* belongs to the civil power which, in Marsilio's judgment, is the only power which possesses the capacity to emanate laws and to make them respected. There is one single coercive power, hence a plurality of legislative powers cannot be admitted, and this also applies to jurisdictional powers. If it were to be admitted, "confusion would result from it and disputes between citizens, struggle and separation, and finally the destruction of the state since some citizens would wish to obey one government and others a different one" (Marsilio, DP, I, 17, 5). Here, in fact, Marsilio seems to be something of a slave to his own political passions and to the facts contingent upon his own times; so much so that some critics have rightly remarked on a vision of the state that is monolithic and hegemonic. It may be said that it is by no means liberal, nor is it respectful of those forms of autonomy for which (by contrast) the advancing mercantile society of those days was searching.

7.11 The fact remains that only the civil law, with its positive norms, can judge every dispute and every violation. Marsilio is no longer interested in the hierarchy of laws which saw the divine law and the natural law as the presupposition for the positive law: for him there is only a distinction between divine and human law. What links them together, as we have said, is the power of coercion which, however, only an authority can exercise. Even the natural law in his eyes loses all its force because its real value depends on the fact that men hold it to be useful and therefore observable (cf. Marsilio, DP, II, 12, 7); otherwise it loses all its validity. This strongly utilitarian concept brings to mind quite a number of visions of the last century.

7.12 But who is the user of the laws? To say the inhabitants of the commune or of the kingdom is hardly enough. For Marsilio, who again refers to the Code of Justinian here, it is necessary to define who is a citizen. Such a person is "whoever has that discernment and that undeformed nature which enables him to know, together with all the other citizens what is just and advantageous for the continuity and growth of the civil community" (Vasoli, 44). This definition also includes the emerging classes of artisans, but precisely because it seems to be characterised by a Greek perspective, is clearly still a long way from recognising rights of citizenship to foreigners, which Roman law did in a number of cases – or to women, as Ockham was to propose later.

7.13 It is from this idea of the citizen that Marsilio conceives the authority to make laws to be descended. The authority "belongs only to those who, in making laws, see to it that the laws are better observed, or indeed absolutely observed. But this is nothing else than the whole body of the citizens, and thus it is to them that the authority to make laws belongs" (Marsilio, DP, I, 12, 6). This democratic statement on the one hand anticipates the concept of popular sovereignty, and on the other hand revives that Roman juridical concept which saw the laws as an expression of a *populus* and of its history, and not the charismatic action of some legislator. Marsilio makes this conviction his own, "since, although the laws can be better made by the wise than by those who are less endowed with wisdom, even so we cannot conclude that they are better made by the wise alone than by the whole multitude of citizens, of whom they themselves are a part" (Marsilio, DP, I, 13, 6). The motive for this conclusion is very simple indeed to Marsilio, since the whole citizenry "can discern and will common justice and common advantage, more than each individual part of that same multitude can" (Marsilio, DP, I, 13, 6). The totality is thus seen as superior to the parts because it guarantees an osmosis and a debate which the part, in the nature of things, is forced to redimension. The subject, however, presents a certain trap, linked to the historical condition of the commune in which Marsilio himself was operating. The totality is in fact provided by the *valentior pars,* from which the *vulgus is* to be distinguished because, given its majority position, if it were not opposed by a more homogeneous class which guarantees stability, it would be a grave element of disruption. The *populus* includes both parts and recognises a political role to each of them, while the specific functions of government and judiciary are exercised by the superior class – by the *honorabilitas* which is such only because it has a different intellectual training (cf. Vasoli, 47). Some aristocratic suggestions remain, then, which quite often impinge like certain totalitarian standpoints, on the innovative ideas of Marsilio.

7.14 However, it is an important fact that the law is really more complete, and we might even say better, when it is an expression of a *universus civium* because the intelligences which meet in it are more than the individual expressions of a few legislators. But in reusing for his own purposes the classic distinction of powers, Marsilio clearly shows that the other functions must be carried out by a few individuals, not only because this is more functional, but also because it is more useful. Otherwise a large number of citizens would be distracted from their proper daily activities and this would mean the end of that prosperity of the state which is sought by everybody, and to guarantee which the functions of government are in fact carried out.

7.15 By whom should these latter functions be exercised? What is the best form of government? These questions certainly did not escape Marsilio's notice, because, as has been seen in Dante and Thomas Aquinas, they were subjects which were hotly debated at this time. For Marsilio, as for his more farsighted contemporaries, the best form of government is elective monarchy. We might describe this today as a strong presidential system, but one which respects the will of the citizens and does not go beyond the limits imposed by the law on the exercise of power. We should remember that the laws are not merely the fruit of the contribution and experience of all, but are aimed at the concrete interests of the citizens, and are thus based on real life. Freedom to operate in the search for actual wellbeing must be guaranteed by the law which – precisely because it emanates from the intelligences of the *universitas civium*, cannot be considered as the expression of an external will. "Liberty consists in not being constrained to submit to the command of others, so that the citizen will be truly free only when he must obey the command of a law in the approval of which he has himself participated" (D'Addio, 197).

7.16 We should note that Marsilio has no illusions about the notion that all citizens have the capacity to formulate laws with the due rigour and the due competence. But he is convinced that all can, even so, exercise a function of control. "In fact, although not every citizen (or even the majority of citizens) is capable of discovering the laws, even so every citizen may judge what has been discovered and what is proposed to him by someone else, and can discern what must be added to it, or taken away from it or changed" (Marsilio, DP, I, 13, 3). There are experts in jurisprudence, therefore, who have the task of drawing up and proposing draft laws to the *universitas civium,* which must then approve, add to, or reject them. As we can see, the function of the laws is determining and power must be exercised within the context of the laws. "Given these premises, Marsilio must affirm, to be consistent, the right of the body of citizens, of the *universitas civium,* or its 'better part' (valentior pars), to depose the governing power which has violated the law, or to deprive it of its mandate" (D'Addio, 199). In Marsilio's opinion, in every state there must be provision for the prerogative, on the part of the legislature or some other body designed for this purpose, to judge any transgressions which may occur on the part of the governing power (cf. Marsilio, DP, I, 18, 3). This conclusion is reached in the line of thought inaugurated by John of Salisbury, and followed by Thomas Aquinas; a line of thought which had already been occupying the best brains of Europe for about two centuries.

7.17 The concept of the *universitas civium is* probably Marsilio's greatest innovation in the theoretical sphere. It follows first of all from this concept that the state is understood as a fully autonomous corporation of all the citizens. This means that the supposed distinction – and at the same time, interdependence – between the natural plane and the supernatural becomes a net dichotomy as far as Marsilio is concerned. The political field becomes strictly the domain of the reason and the criterion by which happenings in the earthly city are to be judged becomes scientific (cf. Ullmann, 283). If the latter truly aspires to peace, it can only find one guarantor capable of bringing it about, and that is the civil power. This is the real meaning which underlies the *Defensor Pacis,* but even this, it would seem, was a subject of very lively discussion in the fourteenth century. According to Dante's reflections, numerous texts had been written advocating the complete autonomy of the civil power from the religious. We need only mention Engelbert of Admont who, in his *De ortu et fine romani imperii* advocated the reconstitution of the Roman Empire for the purpose of reestablishing peace and justice (cf. Ullmann, 279). The political dimension was being more and more presented as a self-sufficient entity, capable of realising human objectives in human terms. This objective emerges clearly in Engelbert's other work, *De regimine principum* the title of which recalls other works of the period.

7.18 We can now understand why the Church, as an institution, is robbed of any power in Marsilio's thinking. Judgments, rewards and punishments are prerogatives of the civil power. The jurisdiction of the Church does not concern the temporal order but only the future life beyond this earth, precisely because this comes directly under the full and direct jurisdiction of Christ himself. It should be very clear that the divine law is binding, but not in the earthly dimension (cf. Marsilio, DP, II, 8, 5), and this is so because we are not in the realm of reason but of faith which cannot in any way be coerced.

7.19 For Marsilio, then, it no longer makes sense to speak of the Church as a unique and hierarchical institute. When several of the faithful are gathered together, they constitute a Church in whose vitality all participate in the same way, including the laity. The Church is thus reduced to a totality of individuals, of groups and communities which, as in the future USA or as in ancient Rome nevertheless have the obligation to observe the laws of the state understood as the sole and true guarantee of social peace. Marsilio's whole analysis was conducted with a very specific purpose – that of avoiding the sad and lasting conflict between the Empire and the Papacy. But in the opinion of quite a few critics, he ended by giving the state responsibilities which go well beyond what is legitimate in a democratic dimension such as the one from which (with all the limitation of the democracy of the communes of his time) he had set out. In the end the civil power becomes too intrusive, and it is hard to see who is able to limit this intrusiveness. The concept of limitations seems somehow to have escaped Marsilio. To posit the civil authority even in matters regarding faith, even above the general council of the faithful, gives prerogatives to the civil power which go beyond its own nature. It should not be forgotten that in Marsilio's opinion, "the general council is made up of a representative of the faithful from each state, elected according to the norms laid down by human legislators, and including both priests and laity especially skilled in matters ecclesiastical" (D'Addio, 202). This clearly shows that Marsilio, in his undeniable effort to give autonomy to the political dimension, may, perhaps more than many other thinkers, be too tied to his own time, and thus incapable of seeing behind the end of mediaeval dualism the danger of an over-strong political power of the state, which was to become all too evident in the absolutism of the succeeding centuries. However, it remains a fact that his contribution to the rationalization of politics seems undeniable. So also does the fact that political activity must move within the context of "legality", that is of well-defined norms which are known to all. Both these aspects were to be handed on down to modern societies which claim to be open and democratic.

7.20 Many attempts have been made to compare and approach the thought of Marsilio to that of William of Ockham, even though the latter sought on numerous occasions to distance himself from his contemporary. There are in fact some similarities between the two, but the elements of diversity are so many that to force the comparison would probably be counter-productive. In Marsilio the elements of novelty, although undeniable, are united to a number of traditional elements, so that it is often difficult to draw a clear distinction. William of Ockham, on the other hand, succeeds, with his undoubtedly provocative individualism, in eliminating many of the most established notions of the mediaeval period (cf. Chevallier, I, 343).

7.21 Ockham, in company with Thomas Aquinas alone, bases his concept of politics on a strictly philosophical reflection, even though this has completely different premisses from those provided by Aquinas. The latter differed from William from a logical standpoint. Ockham not only did not accept universal concepts, but held that they could not correspond to any reality. His nominalism, which took unqualifiedly individualistic form, shows the individualist presuppositions with which he was to be led to defend liberty at all costs.

The first certain information we have concerning **William of Ockham** mentions his presence at Avignon in 1324, for reasons connected with the Inquisition. He is assumed to have been born between 1295 and 1300, and to have obtained a degree from the University of Oxford. From Avignon, where he met the general of Franciscans, Michele da Cesena, he went with the latter and other followers to Bavaria, to seek the protection of Ludwig. From there, and together with Michele, who was subsequently deposed, he upheld imperial policy. Only in the latter years of his life did he adopt a more moderate position, even reaching the point of asking to be readmitted to the Franciscan Order, from which he had been expelled. He died either in 1349 or the following year. He composed notable works of philosophy and theology. In terms of political thought, mention should be made, among others, of: *Opus nonaginta dierum* in which he confutes the rejection of evangelical poverty by John XXII; *An rex angliae* where he holds that fiscal impositions on Church property are legitimate, and *Octo quaestiones de potestate papae,* and *Breviloquium de principatu tyrannico.*

7.22 Another by no means secondary issue in understanding the thought of Ockham is the fact that he belonged to the Franciscan order which had not only always sought to stimulate a genuine reform in the Church, but whose leading representatives in that period were in sharp conflict with the Avignon papacy. The latter had proved deaf to the call to poverty expressed by the Father-General of the Order himself. The controversy was not merely a religious one; it also affected the field of culture (because it became a question of defining the respective spheres of reason and faith), and the field of politics. A clear distinction arose from this between theology and philosophy, removing from the latter any possibility of enquiry into, and thus of demonstration of, the existence of God. Faith came to enjoy a complete autonomy. All this did not mean, however, an "irrational kind of fideism: quite the contrary, the strict distinction between reason and faith recalled that all our judgments are founded on the correct use of reason" (D'Addio, 205).

7.23 From the above, it becomes clear that even on the political plane, the distinction between temporal and spiritual power seems more complete than had ever been suggested in the past. For Ockham, evident reason "demonstrates the contradictory nature, from the rational point of view, of the arguments with which the *plenitudo potestatis* of the Pope were maintained and defended" (D'Addio, 205). For Ockham, this power meant the negation of the basic liberties of conscience which are guaranteed by the divine law itself. It can be argued from this that there exists a kingdom of God which has need of its own laws and thus of a power which will cause them to be respected because, as Jesus states quite plainly, "The Kingdom of God is not of this world".

7.24 A completely different argument applies to the civil power. Latin and Imperial Roman tradition, to which Ockham constantly refers, held that this power depended on human will and the laws which it expresses. If conflicts should arise within the laws, those who have a voice in the settlement must be those who are expert in temporal questions, not the leaders of the Church. To the latter, the theologians, on the other hand, belongs the right to discuss the legitimacy, the nature and the limits of the pontifical *potestas* (cf. Ockham, I, 7 and 2). These limits are clear to all, since if the Pope had indiscriminate power by command of Christ, "We would have to say that the Christian law involved a horrifying servitude, far worse than that of the old Law. In fact all Christians, the emperors and kings like their subjects, would be slaves of the Pope, in the most rigorous sense of the word" (Ockham, II, 3). And this is contrary not only to the Gospel' but also to natural law.

7.25 It must be remembered that as well as speaking of horrifying slavery not only for the political power but also for all Christians, he maintains that the power of the Pope must meet with some restrictions even on the spiritual plane. It is not possible in fact that those rights which were recognised as such "even before the explicit institution of the law of the Gospel (...) rights which in normal circumstances the Pope cannot overturn or diminish without motive and without blame" (Ockham, II, 16) should be submitted to the papal power. This was also stated by Christ himself when he said that what belonged to Caesar should be rendered to Caesar, who represents the legitimate authority in the civil field. All "the words and the actions of Christ, and the evangelical and apostolic teachings, prove clearly that the Roman Empire at the time of the infidel emperors, at least from the time of Christ onwards, was a true and legitimate empire, *de jure* and not merely *de facto*" (Ockham, IV, 10). This support given by the philosopher to the imperial power does not place him in the same camp as Marsilio, because in Ockham there is no unconditioned taking of refuge in the imperial authority. For him, authority may be of differing types and it is not obligatory that it should be exercised always by an emperor. Furthermore, it must always be backed up by consensus. This was so for the emperor in the days of ancient Rome, but it was not always the practice of the imperial authority in the middle ages.

7.26 On the question of the importance of consensus, the words of Ockham leave us in no doubt: "The freedom of the evangelical law consists in fact in this: that nothing may be added to the obligations deriving as a result of the law itself, especially if it be burdensome, without blame on the part of the subjects, and without their consent, unless it is required by urgent necessity or manifest utility" (Ockham, II, 17). The Emperor himself, or any other authority, meets with well-defined limits in the exercise of his mandate. It is hardly necessary to point out, on the basis of what has been said in the preceding chapters, that, with Ockham, that recovery of the idea of a secular civil authority which had been evidenced in Roman thought virtually reached its conclusion. As noted in chapter 2, the Roman Emperor was tied to the laws, and could not dispose of the territory of the state as if it were his own property (no marriages exist which permit the cession or acquisition of territorial extension by heredity, unlike in mediaeval and later Europe). He had to allow to all their own freedom of religious choice, provided that it did not damage peaceful civil coexistence, and thanks to the explicit guarantees of private law, everyone was free to pursue his own utility, by carrying out his own activity (this is an aspect which we shall shortly find re-emerging in the thought of Ockham).

7.27 This appeal to Roman juridical notions should not seem forced, because it is Ockham himself who makes it, not only when he noted that Christ himself and the Apostles acknowledged the full legitimacy of the Roman Empire, but also when he maintained that it is from the Roman juridical teaching that the opportunity to recognise laws superior to the Emperor himself is derived. Precisely because of these laws, the Emperor can be relieved of his duties. In the first case, Ockham recalls that Christ specifically commanded the payment of tribute, that he accepted the judgment of the Roman magistrate, and advised his followers not to become subversives, but where possible to appeal to Caesar, as the example of Paul reminds us (cf. Ockham, IV, 14). With regard to the second case, Ockham reminds us that "it is the task of the Romans alone, or of those to whom it pertains to establish and make the laws regarding the Empire, like the prince-electors of the Emperor, (if we hold that they have inherited the functions of the Senate), to raise and discuss the whole legal cause, issue the sentence, and carry it out" (Ockham, V, 2). In this quotation, the reference to the authority of the Senate should be noted, since it stamped the whole of Roman history with its particular mark; however, we should also note the question, the reply to which does not seem all that eirenic, as to whether the "prince electors" do or do not possess the ancient prerogatives of the Senate. It is clear in any case that the supreme head of the civil power must not govern in arbitrary fashion, because in that case he would be subject to deposition. Ockham is convinced that this is the precise way in which the people show their control over the executive power, and their full sovereignty. His words leave no doubt on this: "the definitive sentence of condemnation, however, and its execution, belongs to the Roman Senate, or those who deputise for the Senate, or for the Roman people" (Ockham, V, 2).

7.28 Thus the people are the safeguard of legality, and this is substantiated by the fact that even in the Roman Empire, authority and sovereignty derive, as Ockham repeats frequently, from the free will of the people who had first constructed the republic. As time went on, and the state attained greatness, they had delegated to others many of their own functions, but had never alienated their own rights. In short, as I stated several times in earlier chapters, the Emperor was far from being a Leviathan, but constituted a guarantee of respect for legality, otherwise he could and should be removed.

7.29 Thus power is conferred by the law alone. God had established this, according to Ockham, when he conferred on man, to satisfy his natural needs, the dominion over the whole of nature. This is why it can be said that: "the possession of material goods and the ability to exercise any power are two aspects of a single *potestas,* the exercise of authority is indistinguishable from property (...) *dominium is* both the right to dispose of or claim something in the court and the right to govern over things and persons" (Ghisalberti, 97). Both things are necessary and useful for a peaceful and orderly life. Furthermore, just because it is guaranteed by law, it can be said that property was introduced by the will and is therefore the product of reason; thus all the norms which regulate the manner of acquiring and transferring property belong uniquely to the human law and do not come within the framework of divine law (cf. D'Addio, 207). This means that property implies, for those who possess it, the right to dispose of it freely in that law guarantees the full entitlement to goods. However, we are speaking of civil law and lay property, which is very different from its ecclesiastical equivalent. The latter does not confer full entitlement on anyone, because it is not concerned with personal goods. The goods belong to the Church, and are thus destined for its purposes and needs (cf. D'Addio, 207).

7.30 From what has been said, there follows not only the logical distinction between temporal and "spiritual" power, but also their differing legitimisations. No authorisation is needed for the temporal power to act within its specific civil context. The positive laws are justified by the simple will of individuals, including non-Christians, because the need to be governed in secure fashion and by known laws, agreed and respected by all, is a need of all human beings. It should not be forgotten that for Ockham, "power is founded and legitimised by the will and consent of those over whom it is exercised" (D'Addio, 208). But power guarantees harmony, and here we return to the question of Roman jurisdiction, between the public and the private sphere without ever prevaricating on the latter, but rather considering it the most authentic context of the personality. In other words, even before being a political animal, and without being completely summed up in this description, the individual is an expression of economic, interpersonal (and thus social) activities which only private law, and not public law and political systems, can guarantee.

7.31 We can now understand why, although he recognises various forms of power, when he speaks about Empire Ockham gives it special preference because of its universality. Here we are again faced with motifs which were already important to Dante, because the universal dimensions of Empire, considered as a genuine supranational government, make it possible to attain peace – above all durable peace – and hence justice, which constitute the basic presuppositions for realising the aims which those associating have set for themselves. It is worth remembering in this context that while Dante and Ockham are in agreement on the need for a government above parties to guarantee peace, they are not in harmony about the aims which such a peace must pursue. Dante favours final purposes which we could describe as intellectual, while Ockham has a more utilitarian vision of such peace from a civil point of view. Assuring peace generates prosperity and safe enjoyment of goods; it stimulates productive activity, as we should say today.

7.32 We are not confronted here, therefore, with an imperialism of a modern type, and even less so of an absolutist type. On the contrary, this is a concept of a power *super partes* which by assuring legality, guarantees full local autonomy. Here too the reference to the Roman system cannot be avoided: the Empire under consideration is one which, we might say, safeguards a basic principle of the republic, i.e. the federal principle. In Ockham's view, "the Roman people have not conferred the power on the emperor so that he can institute a despotic government, but so that he can administer the *res publicae* in the interests of all, with respect for the rights of all and the liberties of all. Ockham lays special stress on the defence of autonomies, privileges and rights, of the liberties of individuals and of orders, of communities, feudal lordships, principalities, and kingdoms – this, he says, is the preeminent function of the emperor in which he must not fail, on pain of deposition by the people" (D'Addio, 209). This long quotation sums up quite well the way in which Ockham sees humanity as the ever-growing articulation of a unity which, however, never goes so far as to suffocate the freedom of the individual and his or her dignity. It is precisely to safeguard individuality that such an elaborate articulation exists in the social fabric. Otherwise, what sense would there be in speaking of distinctions of function and roles in the context of power?

7.33 We can now readily understand why, as some scholars have rightly noted, Ockham really never gave any precise definition to imperial power, the necessity of which he recognises, as we have seen. The fact is that Ockham was not interested in defining a jurisdiction so much as recognising the checks and limits which could guarantee the free self-realisation of the individual in the most concrete possible way (cf. Sabine, I, 235). If this is the case with the civil power, which can in some way limit its "action", the same applies to the spiritual power which can limit its "*essere*" – that which in mediaeval thinking constituted the existential fullness of the individual. For this reason he could not tolerate a papal authority which went beyond the – quite restricted – limits of its mandate. "The Pope, who indeed is called the *servus servorum dei*, has become nothing else than a tyrant" (Sabine, I, 236).

7.34 Ockham is convinced that a right use of reason, an honest and healthy culture, lead to the knowledge of God, and thus to salvation, far more than all the decrees of the Popes. However, he does recognise in the spiritual authority the undoubted merit of being able, where necessary, to contest the temporal power. This is a dualism which gives greater guarantees to freedom. But religious authority too, like civil authority, is subject to a series of limitations which help it to avoid any dangerous prevarications. Because of this, the ecclesiastical government must be the expression of a general council, which represents the totality of Christendom.

7.35 In Ockham's view, the Council should be an expression, and the most representative one possible, of the people of God. In this he goes far beyond the convictions of Marsilio. All that comes within the scope of the Church, corporations, monasteries, parishes, etc., must be represented. Even women, because of the importance of their role within the Church, should be properly represented. It should not be forgotten that "the General Council was possibly suggested more directly to William by the government of the two major orders of mendicant friars" (Sabine, I, 237-8). The latter had already for some time been experimenting with and testing the elective method which was also present in many mediaeval parliaments which allowed representation to the boroughs and towns. We must remember too that Ockham was speaking from personal experience. Apart from the elective method of the mendicant orders themselves, as an Englishman he knew the notable role played in the middle ages by the English parliament (cf. Sayles, Ch. XXVII). Certainly he would not have forgotten what *Magna Carta* had signified in limiting the power of the English monarchy.

7.36 Recently the value of *Magna Carta* has been reassessed in no small degree in terms of a path towards a real constitutional system, but we cannot ignore the fact that it nevertheless made fundamental contributions to the assertion of a concrete notion of legality. How can it be forgotten, for instance, that Article 39 states that "no free man shall be arrested, imprisoned (...) or harmed in any manner other than by virtue of a legal judgment by his peers, and according to the laws of the land"? Certainly, the reference is above all connected with certain classes of citizens, but it is, even so, a first glimmer of what an individualist such as Ockham would seek to render more universal, to guarantee the freedom of all. We now understand why Ockham certainly does not show a tendency to eliminate an institution such as the Church, but seeks rather to reform it – not only to render it more adapted to his times, but also to outline precisely its competence, with the aim of making for greater freedom of conscience in matters of faith, and greater capacity for opposing absurd pretensions of the civil power when they appear.

8. Classical Historiography Miscellanea.

8.1 When confronted with events occurring in antiquity, we must accept the requirement of modern historians who, in the case of great events or characters such as Alexander the Great, "make a clear distinction between the tendency to mythicise and a more realistic one: simply to relate what happened". This method is necessary not only for the sake of objectivity, but also because there were, at times, reasons for making judgments different from today's. These evaluations have often led even renowned thinkers to bequeath stereotypes that end up erroneously characterising an entire era and civilisation. This, for example, is what happened in the case of the great Aristotle, to whom we owe the "the conflict between Greeks and Barbarians" in a famous page dedicated to Alexander (cf. Mazzarino, PSC, II, 6 and 39). We also owe the characterisation of slavery to the Stagirite, for whom it was a natural institution. Despite a few distinctions made, this qualified an entire culture even if various exponents of Hellenism made not a few distinctions. Then came the Latin world which actually codified in laws, verdicts and in manuals a problem that concerned daily life in its every facet. Even before Tiberius Gracchus dealt with the difference between free labour and slave labour, the problem echoed throughout Roman tradition. Not only did people take pride in having kings of servile origin, but even considered the twins that founded Rome the children of a slave. This should come as no surprise. Despite the fact that many times there appeared in Rome a distinct "party" in favour of the Greek world and culture, there was always another segment of the Roman population decidedly opposed to Greece. The latter felt that Rome's Trojan origins were a way of opposing the Greeks, but there was more to it than that. The problem of genealogies had already set forth distinctly different premises for the two worlds: "the great ancestors of Rome were men and not gods". The *gentes* and among these the *patres* were of greater importance than the divinities. Hence the importance of the iconography given to the *imagines maiorum* or, from the civil point of view, the highly human *cursus honorum* (cf. Mazzarino, PSC, II, 54 and 60-63). It is easy to understand why a certain "idealising" tendency was viewed with suspicion in Rome by those who would later be called the conservatives in contemporary historiography. They never wanted to lose sight of their down-to-earth origins, typical of shepherds and farmers, who were at the roots of their civilisation. Nor did they wish to forget them when the Urbs was on the way to becoming a world power.

8.2 The concreteness and humble civil situation of some exponents of origins led them to recall that freedom had long been the prize awarded to anyone who had demonstrated valour. This was one of the major themes in the tradition to the extent that anyone who wanted to write a Roman history, above and beyond the role played by Servius Tullius, "had to keep in mind the fact that – whatever group he belonged to, the slaves, and above all, the freedmen, played an important role". It is important that no one among the historians had ever wanted to call into question the servile origin of the ancient monarchy as if to say that valour was as fundamental as social origin. This fact surely made contemporaries marvel as well. Suffice it to reflect on what Philip V of Macedon said in a letter: "The Romans give freedom to the slaves, allowing them to become citizens, and having them take part in the legislatures". This enabled them to expand and found colonies. Not a few scholars have been inspired to say that however much Roman culture was southern Italian Greek, the social and institution structure was profoundly different from that of the Greek world (cf. Mazzarino, PSC, II, 76-77). From Roman, this matter gradually became Italic as some have emphasised, recalling subjects already present in a poem by Ennius, the *Bellum Poenicum* which, unfortunately, has been lost, and which was written before the *Annals*. This is certainly not a strained interpretation. Cato, himself can be considered the creator of this "*Italian* trend; he was the first to attempt to test the new method: narrating Roman history departing from its 'Italian' premises". An idea was indeed spreading that: "it is impossible to write a history of Rome without a history of Italy, which is the essential premise; whether this history of Rome is called decidedly at the 'origins' of the Italian city and the peoples as in Cato, or whether it is placed at the beginning of the normal *Annals*, as in the work of Gellius". The idea of Italy can already be found in the fourth century B. C. in the treaty between Rome and Carthage. Before the two cities came into conflict, Italy was understood to be the peninsula where Roman expansion could take place (cf. Mazzarino, PSC, II, 87-88).

8.3 The question of slavery and that of the Italian, or rather, Italic vision, involve all of Roman historiography and, in this respect, mark its originality. The Greek models, that of Thucydides *in primis*, could be useful for other subjects, but certainly not for explicitly Roman-Italic ones; "they could only be written in a Roman environment, and the era of the Gracchi. (...) Dissatisfaction with certain common forms of injustice was widespread; and enlightened people partook in them with no exceptions" (Mazzarino, PSC, II, 108). That was probably due to social conflicts that were becoming harsher and harsher as much of ancient historiography, and the *Roman History* of Appianus, in particular, demonstrate. These problems were also exacerbated by the conquests that required considerable time to settle and the crises arising from unforeseeable problems. Polybius, for example, recalls the wild price fluctuations at the time of the wars against Hannibal during which, in the most critical phases, certain merchandise was sold at low prices in some areas of Gaul, while those in Rome were extremely high.

8.4 These crisis themes, which Polybius had already examined in the transition from the Monarchy to the Republic, are also examined by Lucretius. Aside from the different way of expressing himself, the poet underscores very different reasons: "the discovery of property and wealth is involved (...) property and gold mark the end of the era in which honour was conferred on 'strong and handsome' (*validis et pulchris*) men, who, at the same time, succeeded thanks to their wits". Lucretius was deemed to have found the origin of law in the crisis that followed and in the transition from the Monarchy to Republican institutions, explicitly stating: "Now there were those who taught people to elect the magistrates, and they instituted law, so that one would proceed in accordance with the law". For Lucretius, law was founded thanks to the revolution against the kings. In other words, for him, the initial core of law was created with the Republic, whereas for Polybius, the kings had already set up the first rudimentary juridical institutions (cf. Mazzarino, PSC, II, 167-169). Both are right for various reasons since there are forms of continuity between the two different institutional forms, but the differences are also considerable. It is a question of viewpoints. In any case, Lucretius shows the pessimism typical of one who is living in a period of transition and is nostalgic about that *rusticitas* that had given greatness to a Republic that had prospered thanks to the hard work of its forefathers. Certainly, if we compared this poetry to Ovid's exaltation of the *Ars amatoria*, we would see the difference between the eras and the social problems: the confidence and stability of the Age of Augustus is in contrast with the crisis of the Republic.

8.5 In the light of Mazzarino's studies, the reflection on Lucretius enables us to offer another important consideration on what are called the *exempla*, the facts that constitute the *leitmotiv* for political action. To refer to these episodes "is classic, that is Greek and Rome at the same time; but the creation of typical *exempla* is not something loaned by the Greeks to the Romans; if anything, it is the opposite, in some cases". Examples such as those between the Curiatii and the Horatii and still others could be mentioned. The fact remains, however, that the *exempla* in Roman historiography are permeated with profound pessimism because the a-temporality that they describe almost always comes into contrast with present events. In other words, the "austere, primitive and victorious Rome" is always opposed to the "later depravity". There is the awareness that lost ideals built the Republic, whereas the present "disorderliness" is accompanying it to its end. This is why Sallust could point out that, after the destruction of Carthage, wealth came to replace the virtues even if he did not want to resign himself to that observation. The age of Sallust "wanted to return to the archaic *virtus* , yet it had reached a social and political phase" that no longer made it possible to restore ancient institutions (cf. Mazzarino, PSC, II, 325-327 and 374-375).

8.6 When Rome came into contact with the Hellenistic world, its historians began, little by little, to acquire a taste for "that theoretical position, which had been that of historical Greek thought in the sophisticated age of the "antilogies": both points of view can be defended. This taste for the antilogy did not, however, have the tragic tone of Thucydides' 'agons of discourses': it is juridical and rhetorical". Even in prominent historians like Sallust, it is shown that every party doubted its own position and *veritas* (cf. Mazzarino, PSC, II, 179). The juridical component, however, revealed not insignificant differences which the Hellenistic and eastern worlds in general were totally unaware of. On this subject, read Caesar's famous speech to the Senate quoted in Sallust, the *Plot of Catilina*, Ch. LI. "Ever since the age of the Gracchi the history of Roman public law had been the object of commentaries and debates". The analysis of *libertas* itself came into this context and was seen as a sort of "restrained liberty". In other words, this liberty was kept within the limits of the law. Although Caesar himself orients institutions towards a Principate, he shows, not just in the speech referred to above, that he lives "in a world dominated by faith in democratic traditions, and likewise by a degree of fervour for the institutions of the Archaic Era". This is the tradition-innovation pair existing throughout Republican history and even into the beginning of the Principate. That is nothing to marvel at. Caesar turns to this approach again to justify, for example, the war against the Venetians for which he "offers a juridical and religious explanation (...) for the economic interpretation we find in Strabo", even though, the latter, probably takes this reflection from Asinius (cf. Mazzarino, PSC, II, 187-189 and 196).

8.7 The juridical and religious explanation continues throughout Roman historiography to Livy who ascribes considerable importance to the publication of the splendours and the *ius civile* closely connected to the development of Roman culture in general. Above and beyond all that "one point is certain, albeit vague: in Archaic Rome the history of law and that of historical thought go hand-in-hand" (cf. Mazzarino, PSC, II, 278). It is this juridical sensibility that induces Caesar to approach and describe peoples in a way the comes as a surprise to the moderns. The radical differences in governing he perceives between Germans and Celts are no less astonishing than the differences between Germans and Celts in their understandings of religion (it is the juridical and religious interpretation that comes back). His reflection on the priest caste existing in one of the peoples and not in the other, with its consequences, led to the observation that "the human spirit has rarely reached such a high degree of sociological sensitivity" which makes it possible to distinguish between peoples generally confused with one another. I think that these considerations should be the point of departure in acquiring an understanding of why, in future, "the conflict between Rome and the *nationes* was to be calmed, and even overcome" thanks to the creation of a ruling class more and more open to the various provincial bourgeoisies (cf. Mazzarino, PSC, II, 204-206 and 211). In other words, if, in Roman thought, something a-temporal is analysed, it always ends up being linked to precise, tangible references; Suffice it to think of Varro's no less important distinction among three types of theology, "mythical, physical, and civil" where everything is integrated and gains practical value in the noblest sense of the term.

8.8 Reflection on the binomial history and law was also typical of Tacitus, who, even in his unquestionable greatness, was resigned to the end of Republican institutions. Perhaps for this reason and from a position of aloofness from political strife, he condemns those who take the sides of either the reaction or the revolution because, in their bloody struggle, they favoured the birth of the Empire, which eventually became necessary in order to ensure peace. The judgments pronounced on Tiberius and Augustus, practically accusing them of hypocrisy are understandable in the light of this, since, in their declaration of homage to the Senate, the two wanted only to give the impression of keeping the basic institutions of the Republic in function, knowing full well that these were about to disappear forever. For this reason, the story of law itself shows "that the Empire departed from a situation of terrible corruption", but, above all, on the obvious weakness of late Republican institutions. Even the theory of a mixed government, truly an innovation in the Roman world, seemed to Tacitus practically a utopian doctrinarian formula (cf. Mazzarino, PSC, III, 72-75). Social and economic changes seem real to him, in which *novi homines* and their families gain importance over the old Senatorial families. Tacitus thus replaces the Polibian palindrome involving institutions with the economic cycle as a force for renewal. This was a true innovation in ancient historiography (cf. Mazzarino, PSC, III, 82-3). Tacitus sees in the struggle for liberty, an eternal theme in his histories, eminently practical aspects, and these will lead in future to the myth of pure tacitism, for example, when Machiavelli returns to the modern myth of the *Princeps* (cf. Spigarolo, 28 ff.).

8.9 The juridical approach of Roman historiography was indeed that tie that guaranteed peace and harmony. The governments which succeeded in attaining this goal, by moderating the claims of the nobility and the hunger of the plebians for innovation were good ones. This was a characteristic aspect of the Augustan Age aside from what many critics have called self-exaltation written for propaganda purposes, and it can be found several times in the pages of Livy. If, on the contrary and as has been properly observed, historians like Sallust still live in a revolutionary age, Livy lives in an age in which the "social classes" have asserted themselves and give legitimacy to the establishment of the Principate. They make an effort to see them tied to tradition as much as possible (thus, it is no accident that Livy can be called a great Ciceronian). Obviously these differences must take into account the attachment of the historians to Roman institutions even though one of them felt a pressing need for reforms, while the other did so to a lesser degree. This explains, for example, why Sallust ends up closer to Cicero than to the "excessively" revolutionary Catiline (cf. Mazzarino, PSC, III, 15 and 20). Yet Sallust was horrified by the reactionary dictatorship of Silla. He was in favour of the innovative politics of Marius, but this *homo novus* is justified in the light of the ancient *virtus* that any authentic Roman spirit would have accepted. In Marius's speech as quoted by Sallust there is "the defence of the rights of *virtus* against the blood rights of the nobility"; these words could warm the hearts of not a few Romans since they certainly were not alien to the values on which Roman tradition was based (cf. Mazzarino, PSC, III, 28-31).

8.10 The historian Didorus Siculus, writing in Greek, likewise shows constant attention to the conquest of the plebs, a conquest seen in the constant anti-tyranny perspective of Roman history. All the peoples who were integrated with the Romans began to consider politics from this point of view. Their concept of "barbarian" was quite different from that of the Greeks. Diodorus uses the distinction between Greeks and barbarians several times, as did many other Greek writers. He noted the differences and cruelty of the latter among whom he included the Carthaginians as they confronted the Greek populations of Sicily (cf. for example Diodorus, XI, 7, 4 and XIII, 57, 1-6). He adds, however, a reflection on the value of social peace, which the barbarians had been threatening, but which enhanced prosperity and well-being (cf. Diodorus, XII, 1, 4; XII, 26, 4 and also the *Introduzione* by Miccichè as well as the numerous text notes). That concept of utility typical of all Greek and Roman historiographical tradition is present here. Another difference emerging from the pages of this century, between the eastern-Mediterranean perspective and the Latin one, concerns the development of law. This law, in the cities of Magna Graecia as well, is almost always written by extraordinary figures with vast culture such as the legislator Caronda, or Zaleucus of Locri, the disciple of Pythagoras. The same can be said of Diocles and still others (cf. Diodorus, XII, 11, 3-4; XII, 20,1 and XIII, 33, 2). The Latin approach, as Diodorus himself knows and which he admires, from the so-called *Twelve Tables* is quite different. "That legislation written and formulated in a sober and incisive style, continues to be admired even today" (cf. Diodorus, XII, 26, 1). It should be noted that that sober and incisive style underscores the emergence of legislation governing daily life, from that *mores maiorum* which everyone recognised and which constituted the basis of law.

8.11 The conflict between Sallust and Livy, rather than conflict between two political orientations, is the conflict between two generations, the first still plunged in civil wars while the second has the goal of definitively putting an end to them. Yet, in both, that fear of the decline of the ideals of *libertas* can be perceived, and this, in the final analysis, they have in common with Tacitus. In Livy the theme of harmony predominates. At times it is introduced with the pride of one who wants to claim the authenticity of his tradition. There are those who have even perceived traces of nationalism. Suffice it to think of Numa's description. According to some, Numa was trained in Pythagoran disciplines. Livy has him trained in that of the ancient Sabines, peoples of Latium, and who must therefore be considered on a level with Romulus. Both had assimilated various peoples as would subsequently happen for other Italic ones and, as in Livy's era, was happening for the Mediterranean populations. This miracle that the Roman Empire represented, offered, according to Livy, any local "bouregoisie" the possibility of obtaining important positions in the life of the State. Despite what has been said, Livy cannot be considered the spokesman and propagandist for Augustus' policies, which he did not totally accept. If, on the one hand, his policy of faithfulness to tradition is exalted, on the other hand, this is all counterbalanced with the negative judgement that the historian gives of Caesar as well as the exaltation of Brutus and Cassius, who certainly did not fall within the political views of Octavian Augustus (cf. Perelli, I, 12). This explains a certain fact: although Augustus seems to many the recognised heir of Caesar, the defence of tradition and the various cultures that tend to become integrated becomes apparent, and will end up exalting the image of Cicero as well as his death, praised by many as an example of the Roman spirit. Here too, Livy's description can be enlightening. Cicero is "the true denominator of Roman life at the end of the free age". His life exalts the "religion of liberty" and becomes the expression of the fact that "the idea of a noble death is, for a man of Roman culture, equally as tragic as that of liberty lost" (cf. Mazzarino, PSC, III, 67-68). This idea will be carried on through future centuries.

Anyone who might want confirmation of this has only to read the great authors, starting with Cato Uticense of Dante up to the Roman heroes of Shakespeare.

8.12 Livy remains an impassioned defender of Republican liberty. Like any true Roman, he is hostile to any attempt to reconstitute the *regnum* and sees the *princeps* as the antithesis of the tyrant as well as defender of Republican institutions. Scipio Africanus can be recalled. Livy shows a certain impatience with him, when he sees embryonic forms of a Principate taking shape. The highly-exalted Camillus himself is criticised for several excessively haughty deeds for a man at his moment of triumph. Augustus himself is rarely praised, especially when his political and constitutional reforms are examined (cf. Perelli, I, 12-14). Augustus is given recognition for the regained harmony which, as has been said, is presented as one of the salient features of Roman tradition (cf. Livius, IV, 3 and 4) together with *pietas* and *religio*. This harmony prevents the dangerous breaks in civil society (Livy himself uses this expression *societatem civilem*) and brings about the prosperity of institutions (cf. Livius, IV, 4, 4-10 and the question in V, 4, 10; see also V, 7, 10; V, 10, 4 and VII, 21, 5-8 where it is apparent that the solution of the problem of debts set the scene for "harmony among the spirits". Subsequently, interest was reduced from eight to four percent, cf. VII, 27, 3). Harmony is facilitated by religious tolerance since the Romans not only respected the religion of their ancestors, but also brought in foreign and created several new divinities (cf. Livius, V, 52, 10).

8.13 An analysis of the problem of harmony provides an opportunity for further considerations. First of all the Principate instilled cooperation between the two sides: the *optimates* and the *populares* who contributed to achieving that constitution, a mixed expression of the aristocratic Republic that was to have such great fortune among the considerable number of liberal spirits of the contemporary world. This cooperation had existed since the beginning to such an extent that Tarquinius Superbus had the reputation of being tyrannical, because "he had no other right to rule than by force, having not been elected by the people and approved by the Senate" (Livius, I, 49, 3). This would all lead to the creation of an *élite* which would ensure continuity in political action. Secondly, implementation of the *moderatio* in dealings with the other peoples (a subject explored above all in the Fourth Book), which would ensure the solidity of the State. This certainly cannot be called a propagandistic motif if it is true that many other writers, starting with Cicero, complained of a change in attitude towards allies and subject peoples (cf. Perelli, I, 42-46). History serves as a model here, too, and it recalls no less than the Curiatii and Horatii, to point out that, "before the duel began, a pact was made between the Romans and the Albans" (Livius, I, 24, 3). This pact was read and approved by the respective peoples who then abided by what had been set forth. It hardly need be repeated that the pact was called *foedus*, the foundation of that Italian Federation that was to be one of the cornerstones of the Republic. History thus has a moral purpose, in the sense given to this word by the Latin peoples. Hence we can intuit that decadence came to be identified with the coming of riches from the Orient, which corrupted ancient customs. This is why in Livy, the conviction of the civil role of religion comes out, and it would be of great interest to Machiavelli, since it was considered the basis of the virtue of the Roman people. It could thus be said that the "history of Livy unrolls in the light of ideal values", and

Humanism as well as the Renaissance, like Machiavelli, perceived in this the ideal humanity for which it became almost the paradigm of classical antiquity.

8.14 Right from the beginning, association would be the way to integration. Various kings from various peoples assumed command and this proved to be Rome's good fortune. This fortune was certainly not by chance (this aspect, too, was to be of great interest to Machiavelli) as the first Latin writer whose name is recalled, Appius Claudius Caecus points out. He is accredited with the famous judgment *fabrum esse suae quemque fortunae* (each is the creator of his own destiny) (cf. Perelli, I, 34-38). This destiny is fulfilled within the limit of the laws, and liberty manifests itself within these laws. It is always open to new prospects. As Livy believes and writes in the first chapter of the Second Book, "the authority of the laws is above that of men" (Livius, II, 1, 1) lamenting the fact that without these, despotism is sure, hence political offices, even limited in time, must be subject to limitations (cf. Livius, II, 1, 7; cf. the enlightening passage IV, 25, 4 and VI, 35, 4-7 where he speaks of curbing the authority of the various magistrates). The law places everyone on an equal basis: "*aequari summa infimis*" (cf. Livius, II, 9, 3) which sounds quite similar to the verse of Virgil *parcere subiectis et debellare superbos* (for the verb *debellare* see point 1.5; it should be recalled that that subject is dealt with by numerous historians, among whom is Titus Livius). From their first recording, these laws were not only approved through the comitia of the people, but also became the source of all public and private law (cf. Livius, III, 34, 6-7). This distinction has always been at the heart of Roman jurisprudence and daily life based on the cooperation among the public and the private for the performance of various works (cf. Livius, VI, 4, 6).

8.15 This harmonisation between public and private was to bring out the "dimension of a State not paternalistic, not a welfare state, but solid in its internal order" (Fiore, 16) which find the guarantee and support of every action in law. The Roman federative system which, for Livy, represents the strong point ensuring the integrity of the Roman world is based on this law (cf. for ex. Livius, IX, 19, 17) but it was gradually becoming disarticulated as the moral premises behind daily life became less solid. When these were secure, it was "not necessary to set forth a punishment. The sanction of moral condemnation was sufficient to ensure obedience of the law" (Perelli, II, 27). I do not think that these writings are propagandistic. Doesn't everyone know that in certain periods a handshake is all that is needed, whereas in others, not even the criminal code is enough? Only when the ideal Republican no longer exists, can admiration for people like Marcellus be understood. He had always been conscious of the limitations of the *ius* and the *potestas* associated with his office (cf. Ramondetti, 17). Going beyond that body of criticism that has always called into question the reliability of Livius as an historian – indeed some have even considered him a "poet" – two other points outlined in his histories should be recalled. The *first* concerns the moment when Titus Quintius Flamininius confirmed to the delegates from all over Greece that the Romans intended to give them back their ancient freedom. In this crucial passage from Book XXXIII, 32, Livius maintains that those statements are sincere and what comes up in the book that follows seems to confirm the fact. The Roman ruling class had no intention of becoming involved in a new foreign policy, too risky at the time, hence it tried to steer clear. The Republic was obliged to become directly involved, since Greece was now incapable of pursuing an autonomous policy (cf. Pecchiura, 10-11). The *second* concerns the entire first part of Book XXXIV where abrogation of the "Oppia" Law is described. This provided for strict limitations on women's luxuries. It had been passed under extraordinary circumstances, which no longer existed, so Roman women demonstrated publicly and the recriminations of authoritative people like Cato were to no avail (cf. Pecchiura, 15-16). The ample space he devoted to the subject not only bears witness to his sensitivity towards far-reaching social matters, but also shows how law was conceived of in Rome: the severity of some rules were compensated for by the flexibility of others, always in a position to interpret the feelings and moods of the population.

8.16 Josephus Flavius points out several times, even without explicit references, that the transition from the Republic to the Empire was possible only because the intermediaries, that is, the nobles, were eliminated between the people and the Emperor as well as the military forces who supported him. The Republican experience in Rome was based in the Senate, which limited the excesses of populism, and which was limited by the people. When the Senate and the tradition of the *Gentes no longer existed, populism and militarism supported an Empire which was becoming more and more Helenised and orientalised.* Thus it was that the future Caligula thought to "deprive the country of the cream of its nobility" (Josephus, II, 10.1), as was confirmed by Suetonius himself (cf. De Vita C, Calig., 23-35). It is no accident that during the rise of Claudius to the throne, the Senate, led by the Consuls voted to provide armed opposition, thinking that "either an aristocratic government had to be reinstated according to the old constitution, or a man worthy of governing the Empire had to be chosen by vote" (Josephus, II, 11, 1). The quotation brings out the aristocratic character of the Republic, and records one of the several and extreme attempts to perpetuate the Republican system.

8.17 The Empire prevailed because it managed to maintain the stability and peace that no other institution could guarantee, despite internal resistance. The various populations as well as the Judeans themselves, "asked the Romans for that security that they despaired of finding in their own country" (Josephus, IV, 7, 1). The Romans were well aware of all that and, indeed, they recognized the internal autonomy and religious practices of the various peoples as long as these remained within the bounds of the law. When these bounds were exceeded, as in the case of the Judean War, the "laws of war" were to apply (Josephus, VI, 6, 3). War itself had its own rules: *Bellum* had been considered a veritable duel with very precise rules, from the Republican era onwards. This is all proven by the fact that the rights of the Judeans in every other part of the Empire were guaranteed even during the Judean War. Indeed, the authorities prevent banishment of them from the cities as well as confiscation of their property (cf. Josephus, VII, 5, 2 and VII, 10, l). It is all the more extraordinary when one thinks that not only were the Jewish people at war with the Romans, but there were so many populations in the Middle East in open conflict with the Jews – and Josephus Flavius mentions this at various points.

8.18 "The practical Romans generally flee from any metaphysical lucubration (...) It is important to understand that law, being (...) 'true, tangible, real philosophy', cannot but be expressed in the tangible reality of the world of phenomena, of what appears and what occurs: law, like philosophy is an interpretation of reality" (Giomaro, 9-10). To be convinced of this, one need only read what the sources of law are in any commentary whatsoever. For example, Gaius maintains that "all the law of which we make use concerns persons, things, or actions" (cf. Gaius, I, 8). Gaius deems it suitable to open his treatise with the words: "All the peoples who rule themselves by laws and customs (*mores*) used their own law partly, and, partly, a body of law common to all people". The first is set up for the utility of the people itself and is called *ius civile,* the other is called *ius gentium* since all peoples use this. The Roman people also use both (cf. Gaius, I, 1). This dual path led to the flexibility of a law when then laid the base for a civilisation of law, thanks, as well, to aphoristic statements that have almost become postulates. For example, Gaius also calls law "that which the people set forth and establish" and he immediately explains the origin, succinctly, thanks to the *lex Hortensia* (287/8 B. C.), it was established that plebiscites would be binding on the entire people, including the patricians (cf. Gaius, I, 3). In addition to what was set forth on slavery (cf. the first chapter), it was then established that "women of mature age handle their own affairs" (Gaius, I, 190) and possess the same rights as men as far as inheritances are concerned (cf. Gaius, II, 124), a demonstration of the fact that flexibility in the Roman legal mentality took into account what was new and emerging in the society. From the above, the protest of women against the law becomes understandable (cf. 8.15).

8.19 Concerning particular societies, as indeed, society in general, it can be said that these last "as long as their members continue to insist on maintaining the agreement" (cf. Gaius, III, 148-151) otherwise they dissolve, whereas for general ones, one might say that they become disjointed with confirmation of the legal basis of community living:

ubi societas tbi ius. As these particular societies established relationships with the general one, the ingenious distinction referred to by Ulpianus between public and private law (cf. point 1.17) was brought out. Further considerations are based on this. From the first lines of Justinian's *Digest*, in which Ulpianus' ingenious statements are to be found, the dominant features not only of Roman law, but in the way of understanding the politics and lives of all Latin civilisation become clear. When it is said that jurisprudence seeks to separate "what is just from what is unjust, distinguishing the lawful from the unlawful" (*Digesta*, 1, 1, 1), the law *appears as extenuating circumstances,* in other words, as able to mark that *limit* which constitutes *the area* in which to operate, to put into practice one's own liberty. It must operate within the precepts of law which are: "*honeste vivere, alterum non laedere, suum cuique tribuere*" (*Digesta*, 1, 1, 10). It is thus a liberty which guarantees not only itself, but also that of others, of third parties. One might, indeed one can say "of the greatest number of people" because, as is written further on in the Digest (1, 1, 11), "*ius* is what responds to the *utilitas* of all or most of any social community".

8.20 Was the transition from Republican to Imperial institutions inevitable? Was it possible to govern a territory that had become so large under principles that still guaranteed the liberty of Roman tradition? These are the questions that Cassius Dio attempts to answer. From the Revolution of the Gracchi to the Battle of Philippi Republican ideals had sung their swan song and suffered defeat. "At Philippi, they themselves, the Roman people, won and were defeated, they fell and were toppled". As in the case of Tacitus, Dio realised he was face to face with a new era, which had to be studied using a new method (cf.

Mazzarino, PSC, III, 201-3). Dio had a clear picture of what had happened and he set it forth in the famous Book LII of his *Roman History.*

8.21 Cassius Dio's long history has never been considered a masterpiece, even though it has always been seen as quite useful, because, at times, it fills in the gaps left by other historians reputed to be more important. Aside from this, however, *Roman History* has considerable importance, since it brings out one leg in that slow but sure journey that enabled Rome to build a civilisation. This work is no longer one written by a Greek who contemplates and admires the Roman world and institutions, like those of Polybius or Dionysius of Halicarnassus; it is not as yet the work of a Greek who will write in Latin, having been captured by the world-wide importance of Rome. It is somewhere in between all that: born in Bithynia, a province which had always been permeated with Greek culture, he was a Roman citizen, magistrate and historian, as well. This middle road taken is such that he is not always clear. His style becomes "intricate and confused when Cassius Dio wants to explain certain Roman laws and customs" (Norcio, 55), but when it becomes a question of exalting the glories of Rome, he his extremely clear and filled with pride. Furthermore, and this is perhaps the most important question, Cassius Dio is the expression of that particular moment when "the two worlds, Greek and Roman, at first distinct and separate, tended to blend in a single, large social organism" (Norcio, 13) both becoming rich, but also mutually honing down certain originalities.

8.22 Like Josephus Flavius, our historian often exalts, for example, the Roman war machine, considering it a source of stability and peace, but these do not come so much from tradition as from the monarchical political institution. As a good easterner, he considers these the safest and most stable ones (cf. Norcio, 44). Everyone, in fact, has something to gain from such a strong State, and it is easy for anyone to be ruined when the State weakens. On this subject, his statements are perfectly clear: "No man has such a solid private situation that he will not be ruined if the State fails; on the contrary, a fortunate State remedies even the misadventures of its citizens" (Cassius Dio, XXXVIII, 36, 8). Of course this does not mean that any type of State is acceptable, if it ensures order. Cassius Dio praises monarchy, convinced that "if a State based on democracy has flourished, that has occurred for a short time, as long as the people had power or strength, due either to the violence resulting from well-being or the envy arising from ambition" (Cassius Dio, XLIV, 2, 3). With these statements, he shows that he is more aware of the reasons for the decay of the Greek City-States than of the reasons for their splendour. As he thinks further, however, he realises that the result of this decadence was "the destruction of democracy and the creation of tyranny" (Cassius Dio, XLVI, 34, 4) to which he certainly does not feel that he must submit. Hence that praise of liberty and security (cf. Cassius Dio, XLV, 18, 2-3) as expressed by Cicero in a speech which can clearly be called the swan song of the Republic. He feels that for it to be more efficient, it needs cooperation from the best, and that can come only from the Senate. Furthermore, as long as the Senate operates, political debate takes place openly and everyone can participate; otherwise, the monarch who operates on his own, isolated, carries out a policy of power whose measures become known once they have been taken and are already in force (cf. Norcio, 43 and 46). This, it can be said, is why Cassius Dio favours a moderate monarchy.

Suffice it to read a few pages of his Book XXXVI when he points out that the Senators, during the first century B.C., tried however they could to limit the power of anyone who attempted to turn power to personal ends and, with popular support, thought to assign Pompei to carry on the war against the pirates, the Senators "preferred to suffer any harm from the pirates rather than grant so much power to Pompei" (Cassius Dio, XXXVI, 24, 1). Catulus' speech in the Senate, in the chapters of the book mentioned above from 31 to 36, is noteworthy and telling. As far as Pompei is concerned, the speech is summed up in words that leave no room for doubt: "If you need this sort of law, you can, without breaking laws and without neglecting the interests of the State, elect Pompey or anyone else as dictator, provided that his rule have a normal term and that it not be exercised outside of Italy" (Cassius Dio, XXXVI, 33, 2). It is the last murmur of a Senate and a Republic that is still seeking to abide by the rules, which, in any case, are not at all unknown by those who are attempting to change the institutions. Proof of this is the fact that the support of authoritative personalities capable of gaining consensus was sought, as well as armed assistance. Caesar himself not infrequently grasped this point (cf. Cassius Dio, XXXVIII, 4, 5). As the prestige of some personalities waned, as a result of a continued reassessment of the Senate's role, weapons gradually took on a different importance, until, with the passing of time, "legal force was ascribed to their violence" (Cassius Dio, XLI, 34, 5). Thus, with nostalgia for the past and reflecting on the experience of his times, our historian reminds the reader that Octavian Augustus "was of the opinion that the commander should do nothing against his own will, compelled by the violence of his troops, because the soldiers always put forth new claims" (Cassius Dio, XLIX, 13, 4).

8.23 The greatness and decline of Rome occurred not by chance. Institutional rules gradually revised, then, unfortunately, no longer abided by, dictated its history. There is no Fate or Destiny that can erase the merits and demerits of a civilisation. Even though the Romans had built a temple in honour of Fortune, our historian advises us that that temple was "given a name that the Greeks could not understand, considering that mankind must ponder and reflect on present and past matters, and not forget whence it all began, and where it ended up" (Cassius Dio, XLII, 26, 4). Fortune lasts a long time only if accompanied by moderation (themes that Titus Livius was fond of coming back to) and if power is held within proper limits. Fortune deprived of these and other virtues does not provide security, only suspicion and reproach (cf. Cassius Dio, LXIII, 16, 3-4). It is certainly not by chance that echoes of Virgil can be heard in the historian's account: the Romans were "by their very nature inclined to bring down the strongest and aid the weakest" (Cassius Dio, XLV, 11, 3).

8.24 What must have struck Cassius Dio most of all was the behaviour of those Roman politicians who, against tradition, acted as if they were eastern sovereigns. Suffice it to think of the contempt of Mark Anthony's citizens as he gave away territories and islands as if he owned them, to Cleopatra and offered possessions to his children (cf. Cassius Dio, L, 25, 4 and 28, 5), whereas for a long time after the Empire had been established "none of the Emperors considered worthy of any honour dared to do anything of the sort in Rome or any city in Italy" (Cassius Dio, LI, 20, 7-8). It is appropriate to emphasise Rome and Italy, because such things did happen in many cities in the East and in Greece, as the historian himself points out.

8.25 It has been justly observed that Book LII of Cassius Dio's work is an unusual one, since he abandons the usual method of narrating events to dwell on a dialogue that is said to have taken place between Agrippa and Maecenas in the presence of Octavian Augustus. While the former seeks to defend democracy, the latter examines the qualities of the monarchical institution which Augustus is inclined to prefer. For the historian, it is justifiably an epoch-making event, and can even be considered the rebirth of Rome. The monarchy was necessary given the political ineptness of the masses and widespread corruption. However, the then young Emperor does not emphasize that and, indeed, tends to show that it is his intention to carry on with Republican institutions adapting them to the needs of the present (cf. Cresci Marrone, 9, 11 and 20). In other words, that mixed constitution, that created Rome's greatness, will live on adapting itself to the needs that call for ample institutional renovations (cf. Cassius Dio, LIII, 19, 1-2) to govern a State that is not only immense, but now multi-ethnic and of many religions. Continuity will be ensured by a Senate that is more and more open to the diverse components to be found all over the Empire. Dio takes a look at this attempt to form a "liberal and constitutional" monarchy indicating, with great interest, that a Senator like himself, coming from Bithynia, could also be considered completely integrated like many others. There is, however, a bit of nostalgia for a world that seems to be disappearing given the increasing influence, as early as the third century, of the army (cf. Cresci Marrone, 26-27).

8.26 Obviously, Agrippa's defence of democratic ideals must be understood in a Republican sense, referring, that is, to the aristocratic Republic of which Cicero had spoken. Dio seemed quite interested in this and he advocated bringing into politics the best elite from all over the Empire.

This is why the possible arbitrariness of judgments and the distinction of public and private judgments requiring rules must be defended, and the same is true for court conflicts and completely diverse judgments (cf. Cassius Dio, LII, 7, 5). Furthermore, dangerous concentrations are to be avoided since they end up hampering the efficiency of the State. This is why various administrative districts are proposed not just for the remote parts of the Empire, but also for nearby Italy. Functionaries and magistrates must be permanently established in their districts and assisted by a suitable number of individuals to enable many people to gain familiarity in managing the affairs of State and benefit as a result (cf. Cassius Dio, LII, 22, 6 and 25, 4). It is noteworthy that Cassius Dio suggests the sale of all that public terrain that is not strictly necessary and useful to avoid excessive financial burdens on the State. The revenue would then be reinvested through moderate-interest loans and it would be guaranteed that the fields were used by autonomous owners. Another basis of stability is showing that economising on expenditure on the political apparatus is to the advantage of the community. All this led to that security and prosperity that favoured financial dealings with places as far off as India (cf. Cassius Dio, LII, 28, 3-4; 29, 3 and LIV, 9, 8). In addition, in order to avoid arousing discontent and to gain consensus "it is also advisable to speed up the proceedings involving controversies among private citizens and arrive at the verdicts as quickly as possible" (Cassius Dio, LII, 37, 9). No less important is allowing anyone to choose his assistants when called upon to fill particular positions (cf. Cassius Dio, LIII, 14, 7).

8.27 Cassius Dio's most important conclusion is that the Principate of Augustus was accepted by the Romans because it combined "the monarchy with the Republic, preserved their liberty and laid a foundation for order and stability, hence (...) they could live under a system of moderate freedom in a monarchy that was not oppressive, governed by a king without being slaves and being part of a *respublica* free of civil strife" (Cassius Dio, LVI, 43, 4). It was possible to live in freedom with the necessary authority. This reflection is important when offered by a Greco-Roman such as Cassius Dio who, writing in his mother tongue, realises how difficult it is to explain certain concepts to the Greeks: "The nuance of the term *auctoritas*, indeed indicates that understanding and it is thus impossible to translate it into Greek with just one word that can convey the meaning" (Cassius Dio, LV, 3, 5).

8.28 Legally and institutionally speaking, extension of Roman citizenship is the characteristic that distinguishes the Urbs from Sparta and Athens. In Rome, there is, in other words, a universalistic seed not on an ideal level as can be encountered in many other civilisations, but on a concrete one that opens up the way to Christian universalism. One need only consider the unifying theme linking Saint Augustine with Cicero and Varro without which the *City of God* would be quite different. The so-called Latin authors, together with Sallust, constitute "an introduction to the Christian era" (cf. Mazzarino, PSC, II, 483). The latter, however, gives rise to a history that can no longer be called uniquely a history of humanity. There is a history of the Church and Christianity that is to be distinguished from profane history. Thus, it is quite strange that Augustine has so long been related back to Plato when he is backed by a surprising realism, not only historically and politically speaking. As Cicero analysed the crisis of the Republic, the Bishop of Hippo would do the same for the Empire. There are no ideal *polis* to be created or better governments to imagine, there are crises to be understood and legality to be restored. Furthermore, Saint Augustine himself tells us how important Cicero was to his development. Speaking of *Hortensius* he tells us that that book changed his whole way of feeling and praying: it aroused new aspirations and wishes leading him to desire other types of wisdom (cf. Aug., Conf., III, 4, 7; on this subject see point 3.26).

8.29 Several times, Saint Augustine himself takes his distance from an immutable world that the philosophers would like to create at all cost, which, rather than a terrestrial paradise, would create an inferno, not only because Saint Augustine is generally critical of any sort of utopia, but also due to the fact that he is anti-Plato in the premises on which his philosophical thought is based. One should read *De vera religione.* Here the mutability of things is not at all considered an evil and, art itself is not criticised because it imitates perfect models. If anything, it can be criticised if we love it as a thing in itself (cf. Aug., DVR, 22, 42 ff.). Concerning love, I have dealt with (cf. Ch. III) the two aspects *of the love of God* and *the love of oneself.* I should like to recall that Saint Augustine often speaks of three types of love, to be more precise "divine love and human love; licit and illicit human love" (Aug., S, 349, 1). The latter is the selfish one, which ruins individuals as much as peoples and the institutions that govern them. This is what ruined Rome, turning it into a Babylon. Rome would have ended up like Sodom had it not been for the martyrs and the just who lived there. "The destruction that fell upon this city is not that of Sodom" (Aug., S, 397, 2.2). The Biblical city disappeared forever. Rome was transfigured almost thanks to Christianity. Rather than a punishment, the crisis of Rome seems like an evangelical trimming to Saint Augustine. "The city, rather, was punished by God who makes right, not destroyed (...) Thus, Rome, too, bore only a single tribulation, in which pious men were freed or purified, and the impious condemned" (Aug., S, 397, 7.8 and 8.9).

8.30 As far as Saint Augustine's thought is concerned, it should be emphasised that all of Latin civilisation finds in it an element essential for its comprehension and, in particular, Latin civilisation that we could call more authentic and more closely linked to his juridical and jurisprudential view, this term meaning a philosophical understanding of existence. Suffice it to think of the relationship that the Father of the Church has with Cicero who, by his own admission, gave birth with *Hortense* to his arduous journey towards conversion. From Latin civilisation Augustine "learns to understand *sapientia* as the goal of all of human struggles and toil; simply as the goal of life" (Ratzinger, 15). This means that the more mature Augustine does not remain fixed on the Platonic perspective, but, moving on to the Holy Scripture, finds in Saint Paul, then in the juridical tradition, all those elements that led him to develop that concept of the people that would be so important in his more famous works. The fundamental components of this singular journey become *credere-auctoritas-humilitas* without which it is impossible to attain that wisdom that is the condition for salvation. To this can be added that on this path, Augustine builds that need for unity that is closely connected to the need for love, because he who loves necessarily wants to become at one with the object of his love (cf. Ratzinger, 18-19 and 51). It must be recalled that it is on the subject of love that all the disputes against the different heresies are centred.

8.31 Aside from Cicero, Varro and many others, Augustine intends to deal with the components of that world that seems to be falling into ruin. Hence, the importance of *religio* in relation to *civitas* does not escape him. The latter "is the true *obiectum formale* of the Roman and Pagan religion as well as the subjective *religio* of the Romans, *pietas,* is the synonym of national feeling (...) *Civitas* is the community, and as such, is called *corpus* (...) The *lex* for this is *mens* and *animus* (...) It would be fascinating to explore the extent to which the Roman idea helped to form the Christian one" (Ratzinger, 266-267). The later also has its own juridical unit and with its cosmic vision, even though its basis is sacred, scriptural and transcending. There is no doubt, however, that the very idea of a people of God owes a great deal to the conception of *populus,* of Roman and juridical origin, with which it has dealt for a long time, and which differs from Old Testament and Hellenic ones. I briefly mention the fact that all these differences, between eastern and western culture, lead to a substantial difference theologically speaking as well.

8.32 It would be interesting to see how the idea underlying that of *populus* in antiquity was quite different – and it is still Ratzinger who points this out – from the one that generated the world *populi* in the plural. The singular also emphasised a particular way to salvation, but this has been forgotten because Latin civilisation and Saint Augustine himself have always been viewed from behind "philosophical blinkers". This is why people fail to understand that "the evolution of Augustine from Seneca to Cicero", in the sense that he abandons a "purely philosophical concept of a people of God", which he had had in his youth after the conversion, to arrive by analogy at the concept of *populus* juridically understood in a Ciceronian sense (cf. Ratzinger, 269-271). Hence the concept of *res publica,* an obviously *Christian one,* characterised all of the Medieval period and more. It is certainly no accident that "Augustine followed Cicero totally in all the concepts concerning the doctrine of the State" (Ratzinger, 302 note 44), even though he necessarily distinguished the two different systems of law as he distinguished the state of man from that of the Church, he also and necessarily distinguished between the two different systems of law.

8.33 Idealism, and much of the contemporary culture that it brought about, seems intentionally to have neglected a considerable part of the ancient world given the fact that it is unwilling to understand what is uniquely Roman and which, in general, is not highly appreciated. The fact remains that "Roman spirituality in its own precision has its own status with respect to the metaphysical spirit of the Greeks" (Ratzinger, 198). Failing to take all that in consideration means that one will end up failing to consider the importance that "Roman spirituality" had in the theological and political tradition of the medieval as well as the modern world and one ends up forgetting that, from the nineteenth century on, there was a critical tendency, unilateral to say the least, afflicting Latin civilisation (cf. Manzo, 27 ff.) Yet, one of the main merits of that conception was its genuinely realistic spirit, not in the sense that would be given to this word by Machiavellism, but in its ability to take refuge from any claim of "perfectism". This, for example, is what emerges in what Lothaire of Segni wrote (1160-1216) in, *De miseria humane conditionis.* According to him, some reflect awareness of the poverty of medieval man, whereas others believe that they will pave a way to a description of the human dignity revealed by Pico della Mirandola after a necessary realisation and purification (cf. Carena, L-LI). Lothaire pointed out that justice was too easily confused with injustice as well as the illicit with the licit, and what really served the poor to satisfy the desires of the rich was neglected. This was not just a pious reflection since, for the future Pope Innocent III, it could call into question one of the mainstays of Medieval political thought. His words leave no room for doubt. "If it is true that every power comes from God, the haughty do not, however, rule by the will of God, as the prophet says: They ruled not by my will, they were princes but I did not recognise them" (cf. Lothaire of Segni, 54-57 and 97-98). These statements were permeated with that concept of resistance to tyrants that would be forgotten at the very beginning of the modern era, in the sixteenth and seventeenth centuries.

8.34 The reason for decadence is another theme reflected upon not only by the Bishop of Hippo, but his entire era, on many of the problems, obviously elaborated upon, of the crisis of the Republic. Suffice it to think that, over and beyond the invasions of the Barbarians, "the western part of the Roman Empire, fell under the blows of the senatorial aristocracy, whose estates become more and more independent of the central power". The potent lords of these families weakened the central power in various ways, taxation for one thing, and tended to divide up the territory more and more, creating veritable, larger and larger oases of independence. According to Olimpiodorus, a fifth-century historian, these families lived in villas that might have seemed like cities. They arranged marriages that tended to found families in themselves extremely powerful and we can infer that they managed, on their own, wide secure areas, having, as they did, veritable armies. These very powerful individuals, almost always senators, aroused the ire of not a few observers among whom was Ammanius Marcellinus. When many senators converted to Christianity the conflict within the senatorial class became sharper and, in some cases, irremediable. Aside from that, it can be said that having reached a certain point, the senators themselves no longer wanted reconstitution of the Republic because *on the one hand* some of them actually aspired to the Principate (if not for themselves at least for their descendants: on this subject, one can think of the polemics of the *Principate pueri)*, and this aroused not a few conflicts between senators and the army, *on the other hand,* many senators thought more about their business than institutions, and desired only wealth and leisure (cf. Mazzarino, PSC, III, 215-219 and 296-300). At this point, however, Rome was withdrawing within itself and it was far from that open city that had communicated with different cultures and religions for over a millennium, a city so, far from entertaining racist feelings that Cicero was able to say that in the Roman World "whatever the definition of mankind might be, it was valid for all. This suffices to show that there is no dissimilarity in the human race, since, if there were, a single definition could not embrace all people" (Cicero, DL, I, 10). This statement was proven many times in actual fact. Suffice it to think that, the millennium of the Urbs, was celebrated by the Emperor Philip the Arab, the son of a sheik born near the boundary between today's Syria and Iraq.

8.35 Yet, the goal of reconstructing civil life based on the premises of Latin civilisation was pursued. Flavius Magnus Aurelius, known as Cassiodorus (ca. 485-580) made one of the most serious attempts. He tried to save classical culture, by blending it with Christian culture. His *Institutiones,* considered authentic bases for the rebirth of a civilisation, were an invaluable premise for the foundation of the Medieval universities. Of particular interest to us are, above all, his *Variae,* letters to his contemporaries on the most diverse subjects, which show his commitment to renewal of society and good government. In order to succeed in this intent, a sense of legality must be restored, otherwise all political systems fall apart (cf. Cassiodorus, Variae, III, 3). Legality guarantees peace and development. It is noteworthy that Cassiodorus recognises the legitimacy of honest earning, which is to the benefit of everyone. "Why should we not make use of what can become a source of income? Seeking gold through war is an abomination (...) Honest earnings are those obtained without harm to anyone" (Cassiodorus, Variae, IX, 3). As Caruso points out, the considerations on the supplying of raw materials are also of interest, especially when they are necessary for the survival of the population (cf. Cassiodorus, Variae, XII, 23-26). The reflections on the conditions of prisoners and the death penalty, likewise in Book 12 or the *Variae,* are equally interesting. These anticipate not a few of the thoughts of Cesare Beccaria.

9. The Roman and Augustinian Heritage and others.

A) *Liberty and will in Duns Scotus*.

9.1 Some components of Augustinian thought can be found in the reflections of John Duns Scotus (1265/6 – 1308), but they are unquestionably original. One need only think of subjects such as liberty and will, dealt with, to be sure by classical antiquity, but treated in a new way, and capable of opening up to modernity. The sense of limit that the Latin world placed in a juridical framework to give a concrete definition to the sense of liberty, is enhanced in Duns Scotus by a metaphysical reflection. "LIberty is an explanation of its own: *vult quia vult*. (...) If it express the boundary of God, which cannot be traversed, liberty represents the boundary of man, which cannot legally be trespassed". Liberty, furthermore, "is also an expression of the transcendence of man" who would otherwise be subjected to "the necessary logic of nature", like every other reality in the world. In the light of this danger, it is easy to understand why Duns Scotus "attempts to free the individual from the universalising logic of categories" believing that "each individual entity is radically different from any other" (Todisco, 59). In other words, every will is freely determined due to the very fact that an inner logic exists within it, a "rational component", which gives the will the ability to love an object, hence to evaluate and choose it. The will possesses a rational orientation in addition to the natural one, which means that it is impossible to speak of the indeterminism of the will, but which confers on it "an intention" on behalf of good (cf. Meziére, 60-61). Moreover, will is characterised not only by *affectio commodi,* which impels it to desire its own well-being to the highest possible degree but also *affectio iustitiae* which, makes it truly free, by making it capable of loving the well-being of others for their own sakes. From this comes the habit of choosing righteously which reduces the dilemmas of choosing (cf. Meziére, 62 e 64).

9.2 The metaphysical root of the sense of limits comes from a consideration as simple as it is fundamental: violating the limits involves a sense of disorder, not only an inner one, because the will ends up orienting liberty wrongly, as Saint Augustine had maintained concerning the two loves (cf. Duns Scotus, Ord. II, dist. 6, q. 2, nn. 4-5). If there were a certainty of not going beyond limits there would not be any need for law, or even property, in protection of wealth "since no-one would seize what was necessary to others, nor would it be necessary to take possession of it through violence, but each could use for his needs what he had occupied first" (cf. Duns Scotus, Ord. IV, dist. 15, q. 2, n. 4). Since, however, the limit can be continually exceeded, and since "evil and avid man would take possession of more than what was necessary", even through violence, it has become opportune to establish property rights, not only for the good of people, but also of things. An extremely important reflection follows from this. Indeed, Cicero had already expressed it: "the present division of goods cannot appeal either to natural law or divine law (...) it is more reasonable to think that that principle does not come from natural law, but from positive law" (cf. Duns Scotus, Ord. IV, dist. 15, q. 2, n. 6). In other words, *law* is a means of *control,* to avoid disorder, and *to rationalise* life.

9.3 The discussion of law brings us immediately back to that of authority, which can be called just only if it is based on consensus and is capable of freeing us from a state of disorder. All this enables us to understand why the real point of reference of Duns Scotus is Saint Paul, over and above any other philosopher from the past *philosophus noster*. The latter teaches us that the question of faith may be madness, but not alienating, not attentive to human freedom, but moving it towards that divine freedom on which it depends in an ontological sense. In this case it is liberty sustained by a will that loves in the sense that God intends it, recognisable only in those who love and who love as he wishes (cf. Lauriola, 40-43). Being is thus "perceivable only in terms of love and liberty" (Lauriola, 47). All of that is not easily understandable due to that very tension in a state of disorder due to original sin which, however, will must and can strive to overcome. Thus, Christianity does not resign itself to the "Greek and Arab necessitarianism as ontologically incorrect and misleading in a gnoseological sense. God and the world are not a homogeneous unity brought together by necessity, but a heterogeneous one united by liberty and love" (Lauriola, 66). Indeed, *there is a choice between two, radically different forms of anthropology:* one based on the concept of necessity, the other on that of liberty.

9.4 Man thus appears as a *viator* with a capacity for an ethical dimension which, from the point of view of love, manifests itself in the giving of oneself. That is possible because ethicality does not have its roots in man as such, but in man as "finalised". This mean, in short, that there can be no ethics without metaphysics (cf. Lauriola, 88-90). Man is called into existence, according to Duns Scotus by a free and gratuitous act of God's love towards which every person feels irresistibly attracted. This is the source of the dignity of man and the fact that there is in everyone "a degree of positive perfection that distinguishes him from any other creature". For this reason, the tendency to be attracted to the Other marks the relations with others. Society thus becomes the place where the conditions for existence and development, both material and spiritual, are fulfilled. This is why society is also the place of liberty and will, which are identified with one another here, since the latter "is a free faculty, which moves itself" (cf. Lauriola, 93-98).

9.5 In the light of this, it is understandable why authority, which for Duns Scotus is always the result of a proxy, is the expression of will and men have recourse to it because they feel the need to ensure respect for rights and duties, a respect upon which civil life is based in pursuit of the good for all. However, this authority cannot feel itself to be above the law which legislators themselves must abide by, even when the private good is considered. This must be considered in the perspective of the good for all of which it feels itself to be a part. Every person may exercise his right to property, whose roots lie in positive law (cf. Duns Scotus, Ord. IV, dist. 15, q. 2, n. 9), only on things, insofar as they are without will, and not people who, to the contrary can and must express liberty through will (cf. Lauriola, 100-101). This may be limited only when it constitutes a public hazard and that explains why Duns Scotus, called upon to comment on slavery, takes his distance from the Aristotelian perspective accepting in its entirety that of Roman law. From this point of view, the main purpose of politics is to maintain peaceful co-existence. It is indeed lawful for rulers to make laws to keep the peace and their subjects must obey them, as long as they are not repugnant to divine law (cf. Duns Scotus, Ord. IV, dist. 15, q. 2, n. 6).

B) *The role of the aristocracy and the importance of not feeling oneself superior.*

9.6 Brague, it seems to me, brought out with great clarity the guiding motivation for this study of mine, and which I summarised in the two opening sentences found in Thucydides and Sallust. The Greeks maintained that they owed nothing to anyone while "the Romans were willing to admit what they owed to others. Unlike the Greeks, who proudly claimed their own autocthony, the Romans trace their origin back to a non-autocthony (...) Being Roman meant experiencing the ancient as something new (...) the experience of beginning as (re)beginning" (Brague, 48-49). The two groups, then, are two anything-but-similar entities and, only in one of the two, is there the conviction that nothing has been invented, but that people have managed to transmit what they have been capable of absorbing. The proud do not understand this verb. Latin civilisation has not wanted to set itself up as a model distinct from other cultures. It has never had anything to do with the ever recurring Marcionism even in minds above suspicion, like that of Spinoza (cf. Brague, 119 e 231-232).

9.7 The Latin world was great as long as it could resist the temptation to orientalise itself, thereby falling into that nationalization that is the end of any liberty and any right. The third Rome would never succeed in escaping this "temptation", Moscow was the direct heir of Constantinople, despite the fact that it had had the missing parts of the Bible translated not from the Greek of the Septuagint, but the Latin of the Vulgate. Despite that, both the "second" and the "third" Rome sought to put themselves forward as models for the continuity of the Roman spirit, to the extent that even the Sultan of Istanbul claimed the title of "Sultan of Rome" (cf. Brague, 17-18, 31 and 34-35). For these reasons, it is absurd to place our civilisation merely in the wake of Jerusalem or Athens, because there is also Rome (cf. my article in *il Domenicale* of 24 July 2004). The first two cities do not want to be contaminated by other cultures because they do not think there is anything worth imitating. On the contrary, belonging to Latin civilisation "means having behind oneself a classicism to imitate and looking forward to a barbarism to subjugate". Saving the classics was a point of honour for Medieval Latin civilisation as represented by the Church which took upon itself that need to imitate what was really worthy of mankind (cf. Brague, 55, and 108-109). In this respect, Christianity is the true heir of the Latin world because it was able to interpret what Brague calls the criterion of "secondariness". It would be more correct to say Catholicism because it is only in the West that Christianity has always meant being an obstacle to the ambitions of kings, emperors and tyrants of other sorts. The Orthodox clergy was, on the contrary, brutally brought into submission by the Czars. An attempt of this sort was also made in the West after the various reforms (cf. Brague, 204 and 219).

9.8 There are those who have seen in the existence of a tie between Latin tradition and the Medieval Church, a possible justification for making power sacred and its origin divine. They forget, however, that even "in 'Pagan' Rome the origin of the power of life or death *(potestas vita necisque)* was divine. In the Republican era, the Roman people lived under the protection of their Gods, among which *Roma* was deified" (Werner, 210). There are also those who have wished to emphasise that the Roman world, then that which associates itself with it, was a highly hierarchical one, far from the criteria of equalitarianism and tied to the privileges of heredity and property. That must be said, because, in the perspective that I have tried to bring out, the criterion of heredity was not at all bound to that of power, whereas the criterion of property and social hierarchy are perhaps more disguised today, but certainly no less important (cf. Werner, XXII). The *nobilitas* in Rome was something quite different and came from that need for liberty which the *patres* had as they struggled against the monarchical tyranny, whose very name was intolerable to the citizens of the cosmopolis to come. Moreover, how can one forget that the features of this *nobilitas* are multi-faceted and not bound by blood ties but by *honor, dignitas, potestas, militia,* etc. All of these characteristics not only moulded the military hierarchies, but also the administrative ones and went far beyond the Empire (cf. Werner, XVI-XXIII and 7). The fact that the Roman spirit never exalted the superiority of one people over another bears witness to this point. The Romans never entertained "the racist concept that Germans and other barbarians were condemned to remain inferior, unworthy of the *civilitas* romana" (Werner, 33). It must not be forgotten that the duty of citizens "increased hand in hand with the degree of dignity". If the "new arrivals" wanted to replace others in the ranks once reserved to other elites they could do so, taking on all the burdens. This happened in the process of democratisation, called barbarisation at times, for the military structures (cf. Werner, 149 and 175).

9.9 One of the features basic to understanding events, as well as social conflicts of future centuries, leads to a consideration of the continuing social role of the Senatorial order. This was so despite the fact that after the Republican crisis, its autonomy was sharply curtailed, but it never totally lost its prestige. Indeed, in some periods and in various forms, it seemed once again to grow. This all enabled a certain "style of governing" to survive, because the most vigorous Senatorial traditions managed to come together "around the monarchical power and in face of this". That happened on a social level as well, where *the praefectus urbis,* the highest official of the Senatorial class was, in many circumstances, the only one capable of ensuring a minimum of legality (cf. Tabacco, 9-12). This Senatorial aristocracy had now spread all over the territory of the Empire and particularly in Gaul. It would enable the setting up of Roman and barbarian kingdoms which, without functionaries of Roman heritage, would have torn each other apart in their internal struggles. The new unifying vision of Christianity associated itself with this aristocratic tradition and its strong sense of institutions, and constituted the spirit of the new world about to be born. "The Catholic structure now functioned as a potent underlying fabric of a society which, albeit internally torn apart by severe economic inequalities, refused any action harmful to a certain cultural unity" (Tabacco, 26-27). It must be recalled that what differentiated the territories, once under Roman law, was the different way the barbarians related to the senatorial class which, wherever it survived such as in Gaul, would consolidate the structures of the nascent kingdom.

9.10 This is further confirmation of the fact that no power, not even the highest court of the Empire ever became "hereditary by law" despite the de facto attempts to make it so. This was also in the ancient Etruscan-Roman tradition, but was abolished as time went on. Public power was never involved with principles of heredity, even for other offices. "The Romans considered *civilitas* from a more cultural point of view and deemed it accessible to people of the most diverse sort" (cf. Werner, 405, 497 and 9). The example of Philip the Arab (cf. point 8.34) is unequivocal proof of this. What Dante thought, centuries later, might also be recalled. He "placed his hopes in the person of the Roman Emperor Henry VII (a French-speaking 'German'), a mystery which the moderns cannot fathom, and who are only familiar with the nationalities, conveniently calling what seems incongruous to them *Medieval*" (Werner, 38). The fact is that a mixed elite governed Europe for some time, which had inherited the ability of the Roman world to govern a variety of peoples. This happened thanks to Latin that, for seven to eight more centuries, was the only language of the entire administration, in addition to being that of culture for many centuries thereafter. Latin, which had been given to many pre-Roman populations, was now becoming the language of the "post-Roman" people (cf. Werner, 123 and 191).

9.11 Finally, it must not be forgotten that the *nobilitas* was also a real chance to oppose that power which was tending to centralise and absolutise. It is no accident that its importance was greatly diminished with the rise of absolutism, and that where, in Great Britain for example, it held out, modern liberalism developed. Elsewhere, often ambiguous terms were used, and we try to ascribe an often innovative meaning to them, which actually did not exist. In the Roman world, the "*potestas publica* was the incarnation of the State and legality. Nor did the alleged inventors of sovereignty, such as Jean Bodin, possess different formulas for describing public power; as far as the neologism *potestas absoluta,* is concerned, it can be found in a few thirteenth-century documents, equal to 'souveraineté', a formula used in the vulgate by judges in reference to the lords of the era" (Werner, 224).

10. The Greek Heritage in Medieval Islamic Political Thought.

10.1 With works such as *The Philosophy of Plato, The Laws of Plato, The Philosophy of Aristotle* and others, al-Fārābī (870-945) laid down the foundation for Arab political philosophy that would survive into the twentieth century. He was educated not only in Islamic circles, but also Christian ones, whether Nestorian, neo-platonic or the entire Greek tradition in general, and reached the point of sustaining that not only are Plato and Aristotle useful in the study of revealed religions, but that a continuity as well as an unbreakable link exists between the two as far as the philosophical and political conception are concerned (cf. Mahdi, 9-11). This is all shown in a work, the only one of its kind, the *Book of the Concordance between Plato and Aristotle.* For al-Fārābī the two represent two great masters of philosophy, hence their theses cannot be antagonistic to one another. If that were possible, it would mean that philosophy carries within itself the seeds of discrepancy among opinions, the true premise for scepticism. On the contrary Aristotle represents the implementation of Platonic theories and, for both, political life represents the fulfilment of the human ideal (cf. Cruz Hernández, 235-237). But the Islamic thinker seems to go further maintaining that, the two Greek philosophers are in full agreement, too, as far as the gnoseological question is concerned. The role of memory is fundamental not only in Plato, since Aristotle himself ascribes great importance to it along with the sensations. The role of metaphysics must be added to this. Both try to demonstrate the existence of God through metaphysics which, for al-Fārābī, is better proven departing from God himself, since: "when you know the truth, you know its opposite at the same time; but when you know falsehood, you only know this, without knowing the truth" (cf. Cruz Hernández, 239 and 242).

10.2 In addition to the bonds between philosophy and politics, al-Fārābī examines the close ties between these and religion. As clearly comes out in the *Book of Religion* (which was not published until 1968), there is a need to set political science in relation to jurisprudence and theology in order to examine the relationships between the city *(medīna)* and religion *(milla)*. Political science traces rules to arrive at those models explained in the *Virtuous City* and the *Political Regime* which make it quite clear that politics need a theoretical approach if they are to delineate the characteristics of the virtues typical of regal art. Here is where the ties with Plato, who is credited with the merit of having fought against the falseness of opinions in the name of truth, become particularly clear. This aspect cannot be excluded by anyone who wishes to deal with politics from an extremely concrete perspective as the Aristotelian one can be (cf. Mahdi, 15-18).

10.3 It must be recalled that al-Fārābī, not an Arab but a Turk, was imbued in Greek culture, and, like all Islamic philosophers, was first of all Moslem then a rationalist thinker. This conviction tends to bring Islamic political thought, according to some scholars, back into a religious context which, then, borrowed Ancient Greek philosophy (cf. Campanini, 5-6). Personally, I think that it is not so easy to draw a boundary between the two worlds insofar as Islamic political thinking makes use of a certain political thought, because it finds that it corresponds with its own premises, otherwise it would have totally rejected it. "The *theorein* of al-Fārābī is the contemplation of a light which is sublimely intellectual; a radiating light, to be sure, of neo-platonic origin, but which, in the end, coincides with the transcending light of Islam" (Campanini, 6). This consideration can certainly be more readily shared. It explains why Moslem tradition accepted the Neo-platonic and Aristotelian philosophical coordinates. Indeed, al-Fārābī, upheld by an *"acuta vis razionalistica"*, ended up by following Aristotle's theoretical processes to the point of acquiring the title of "second master". This title distinguished him as a philosopher from others such as an-Nasafî, Abû Hâtim ar-Râzî, or Abû Ya'qûb al-Sijistânî, who operated more from a theological point of view (cf. Campanini, 9-11) enhancing the reflection of the isma'ilite schism.

10.4 The role of theology remained central in this entire context. This discipline defended divine law, whose truth, the fruit of a revelation, laid the basis for the authenticity and rigour of the legislator's mission. Theology is, thus, not a field of research and so it is viewed with some suspicion by jurists who, like theologians, have the task and duty of seeing to it that politicians do not claim the power to attribute divine powers to themselves, or, worse yet, that they are not so presumptuous as to found law on bases different from that of the revelation of God as his Prophet expressed it (cf. Mahdi, 33-34). It should be recalled that if any theoretical aspect of divine law needs an interpretation, that is the task of philosophy more than theology. Islamic philosophy itself considers political theology as something having an additional function (cf. Mahdi, 67-68). In addition to that, al-Fārābī, whose research constitutes the basis of all of Islamic thought, reminds us that politics is modelled as much on the cosmos as on the human body seeking to imitate a project which is not corrupted, here too, in a typical Platonic perspective. It must be scientifically known before it is politically implemented in the city (cf. Mahdi, 20-22).

10.5 What has been said about the relationship between theology and philosophy must deceive anyone about the true role that the latter must have in Islamic tradition. In general, it is a widespread conviction that philosophy alone cannot convince anyone. Even for a thinker like al-Ghazālī (1058-1111) thinking otherwise would be the equivalent to pursuing a specious and dangerous form of reasoning to such an extent that he compares anyone who wishes to be convinced of the credibility of the Prophet to a man who, warned that he has a lion behind him, answers that he will not turn around until he is convinced of the truth of the statement and, so doing, ends up being eaten. It is to be deduced that rather than philosophically investigating the truthfulness of the Prophet, one needs only to be convinced that "God sent a Prophet as the leader of men and granted him the right to perform miracles to establish his authority" (Leaman, 207). It thus remains certain that discussion favours doubts and reflections of various sorts. For many men of science these doubts contributed to developing philosophical research which, however, ended up endangering the orthodoxy of faith. al-Ghazālī ingeniously proposes a middle position, maintaining that philosophy by itself can be considered *"bien inférieure à la foi par expérience spirituelle"*, but faith can, in any case, be considered *"raisonnable, en ce sens qu'elle correspond à un sain usage de la raison"* (Caspar, 20 and 12). Here too, one is struck by the impartial position of al-Ghazālī who does not reject the reflection of philosophy and theology, but maintains that that reflection performs the same function of control as armed troops on a pilgrimage. This is a function, therefore, that sustains faith which, however, can never be placed before it, or worse yet, attempt to justify it (cf. Leaman, 24-25). It is thus not the denial of reason, but its use in the context of the Koran, that is a support to faith.

10.6 al-Ghazālī also criticises an anthropological approach based on a certain philosophy that he deems dangerous. There could be the danger that philosophers place man too much in the centre of their analyses at the expense of the divinity. Man must be known in relation to his Creator or, rather, "must first recognise himself as an image of God and, from that point, come to know God". This is the "theory of the *internal correspondence* existing between man and God, and based on a truth of revelation according to which man is the image of God" (Moussalem, 935). This correspondence is not only internal but also secret between the creature and his Creator "made up of two elements: the first, which can be disclosed, is the possibility of being close to God conforming to His customs in accordance with the teachings of revealed law; the second cannot be spoken of, but is experienced when one is well along the ascetic path, and it consists of "the fact that man is the image of his Creator" (Moussalem, 936). God remains totally inaccessible and indescribable, but one can have a sort of indirect awareness of him by advancing the practice of perfection by seeking to conform to his teaching. The role of the God of the philosophers is thus totally secondary if they do not sort out and purify their reason through faith. The conclusion is that *the independence of reason cannot in any way involve the Islamic religion* and it is the logical consequence of a basic approach: the difficulty of "reconciling two types of beings – God and the mortal creatures – which have nothing in common" (Leaman, 95-96).

10.7 For al-Ghazālī it is extremely important to conserve the orthodoxy of faith. From this conviction arises his perplexity about philosophical reflection, the fruit of conflicts and compromises among a number of philosophical schools and sects. These differing opinions are the cause of disturbance and doubt, especially for the simplest spirits, rather than being a source of enrichment. This became an inalienable premise of al-Ghazālī's faith, which was based on three fundamental beliefs. The first are quite obvious: they are God and, naturally, prophecy and judgment. The third is salvation which "cannot be attained through logic and dialectic, but from faith". The importance of faith is, however, not an end in itself. It is important because "it makes virtue possible and virtue elevates the heart of man to the contemplation of God" (Cruz Hernández, 344). It is a faith that serves for good actions and it expresses rather well the idea of that moderation which avoids any dangerous extremism. It can be said that al-Ghazālī was so concerned about the integrity of faith because when it "seems to fall apart, that is due to the impiety of the philosophers, the blind credulity of sects, and the immoral as well as bureaucratic conduct of the doctors of Islam and the exaggerations of the Sūfī masters" (Cruz Hernández, 345). They are all basically presumptuous and incapable of understanding the importance of moderation, even in evaluating their own personal abilities as well as those of the school to which they belong.

10.8 This tells us that religion is as it is, because of the free will of God. Only reason illuminated by faith can be useful because it recognises its own limits and thus becomes "a just means" for acquiring awareness. al-Ghazālī is extremely clear on the subject and he also points out the methodological presumption of the philosophers. Those people "reason, departing from things and not from God (...) The enlightened thought of faith comes from God and not his testimony; pure reason cannot obtain valid results because it was not created by God to act alone, but rather to operate enlightened by faith" (Cruz Hernández, 351). *It would, however, be a serious mistake to believe that this faith constitutes a subjective premise that allows anyone to believe in his own way.* This is another exaggeration that al-Ghazālī cannot accept. Subjectivism is basically an extreme position that comes out of another philosophical approach. Faith must be supported by the Koran and sure tradition, otherwise the most sincere of faiths can be lost in the approach to truth. This can happen because truth "is not manifest, but well hidden: it is easy to lose one's way. Hence, a master is needed to guide us and enable us to avoid dangers (...) reason kept away from error can then receive the divine light of revealed truth which enters the heart of man" (Cruz Hernández, 352). That implies that al-Ghazālī not only opposed the philosophers, but also concerned himself with opposing all the sects that were threatening Islamic orthodoxy.

10.9 Returning to al-Fārābī's political thought, we can easily find what has been said up to now if the premises, the logical method of his political works are considered, in particular, the *Virtuous City,* all of them aimed at "establishing a satisfactory framework for speculation in which revealed Islamic truths would not contradict theoretical ones" (Campanini, 14). Furthermore, in classifying the sciences, al-Fārābī was already tending to establish a hierarchy for Islamic theology, then dividing divine science into three parts which, in turn, are separated from revealed theology itself. Revealed theology cannot do without political science and jurisprudence. These two disciplines "strongly characterise Islamic epistemology where religion, law and the state are closely interconnected terms, whereas, on the other hand, it is difficult precisely to define the boundaries of theology" (Campanini, 14-15). This also leads to a close tie between metaphysics and politics, both aimed at seeking truth and thus, happiness. Here, too, we find ourselves face to face with a premise, albeit revised and brought up to date: Greek culture. Suffice it to consider the *Attainment of happiness* a framework essential to al-Fārābī's political design.

10.10 Hence, there is the need to reconcile the philosophical and political vision with Islamic doctrine. As a result, after the need for politics in the *Citta virtuosa* has been indicated, the types of virtuous leadership are examined, then a distinction is made from those that stray from the perfect model. Then, in a typically religious and Islamic perspective, reference is made to the great beyond to underscore the unavoidable eschatological theme. This is what guarantees the superiority of a society based on religion, the chance for peace and cooperation among men (cf. Campanini, 23-24). However, for a Moslem like al-Fārābī, the only perfect society can be that which is based on the revelation of the Koran which, especially from a Shiite point of view characteristic of the later al-Fārābī, so that the *Virtuous City,* rather than being the "ideal" and state nowhere to be found, is the only "real" and feasible one (cf. Campanini, 25). This explains that constant reference, entirely Platonic, to the one who orders the universe to which the ruler of the Virtuous city must refer. From this conviction arises the other one, no less platonic, of politics understood in terms of an architectural science as set forth in the *Book of Political Science*. To this must be added, in Aristotelian terms as well, the idea of a universal order, of a cosmos, from which the truth can be reached, by studying its cosmological and metaphysical bases. To conclude, the concept of the unattainable divine transcendence *(tanzīh)* refers to that negative theology which, from Plotinus on, had played such a considerable role in Middle-eastern speculation (cf. Campanini, 28-30). This theology stresses the idea of an unrecognisable and unattainable God. All of this to return once again to Plato, the one who refers to the Agent, in which all is perfected to the greatest possible degree, the prophet-philosopher for whom philosophical truths, like religious ones, have universal value.

10.11 As a Prophet-philosopher, this extraordinary individual feels himself authorised to be the king, because he is the only one capable of taking upon himself the political governing of the city. It is truly curious that for Plato as well as Aristotle, monarchy was, in the final analysis, the best form of government. It would be absurd not to select such a "perfect" individual as the political leader. "The Imām-Prophet-philosopher-king, ruler of the virtuous society could, then, be quite similar to the Shiite Imām, especially in the Isma'ilite version. The Imām and the terrestrial city indeed seem like Shiite theophanies (...) Walzer himself cannot but recognise that al-Fārābī considered the Prophet Mohammed a metaphysical philosopher and, at the same time, a legislator who had taken advantage of the gift of his vision" (Campanini, 40 and 42). It is the Islamic thinker himself who agrees that such a politician is exceptional: "The ruler of the virtuous city cannot be just any person (...) Thus, it is not possible that the art of ruling the virtuous city is simply a skill, or aptitude (...) Thanks to what arises from the power of imagination, he becomes a Prophet, one who foresees the future and announces particular events of the present" (al-Fārābī, 215 and 219).

10.12 In al-Fārābī, the ethical and political question has considerable gnoseological implications as well. Suffice it to think that "will is free, but it has a cause; man may choose, but only from what is possible, even though he may also wish for the impossible (...) Human liberty thus consists in the human ability to desire what is possible insofar as it is understood to be possible; The problem then becomes that of the limits of human knowledge" (Cruz Hernández, 253). It will always be fragmented because we cannot know the cause of all actions. Only rarely, thanks to the "legendary wisdom of the Rasidiin Caliphs" was it possible to bring about that ideal, for a certain period of time. This consideration gives rise to the criticism of real society which, in some models, is characterised as imperfect societies, if not dissolute ones. Tyrannical societies are to be considered among the latter, pleasure and wealth-seeking ones (also criticised by some Greek philosophers). All are to be condemned, whereas those based on honours and the criterion of electability of the leaders as well as the liberty of all citizens can be tolerated. It should be noted that the latter two types do not belong to the area of perfect societies. Moreover, it is to satisfy immediate needs that people have decided to set up some types of societies that al-Fārābī calls imperfect (cf. al-Fārābī, Ch. XXIX). Those forms, among which family, tribe, clan and others can be recalled, are called imperfect because the social relations on which they are based are established on the principle of the struggle for existence and not the search for the good of all. A model to overcome these contradictions becomes necessary, an ideal society capable of bringing about perfection and a destiny appropriate to human nature (cf. Cruz Hernández, 255-258).

10.13 The politics of this perfect city is aimed at creating a body of law that can keep the order necessary for the distribution of all the greatest potentialities existing in societies. For al-Fārābī, here too in the perspective of a form of politics seen as an architectural science, this means that every individual must be considered and must behave as the member of a single body, and be integrated in this to give rise to the mutual provision of services. Obviously, in such a society, each person must take the place that is suitable for him in order to attain not only happiness for himself, but that of the entire political system. In this typically Platonic approach, it is assumed that a designated authority is established that bases its role on knowledge and power. al-Fārābī realises that a simple authority cannot carry out such a difficult task: "It is difficult the find all these qualities together in a single man" (al-Fārābī, 223). Hence, to avoid the ruin of the city, he suggests a Senate made up of sages who can assist the ruler, teaching him wisdom. The Platonic model can be called complete when its political ideal is based on a pedagogical criterion. Only the role of the laws must be added and these come down directly from the divine legislator, which the governing philosopher limits himself to enforcing and, if necessary, to restoring (cf. Cruz Hernández, 258-261).

10.14 These conclusions can lead to dramatic consequences if we simply ask ourselves some obvious questions: what if one did not want to follow a master recognised as such by Islam? what if that master entered into conflict with the pre-constituted authorities? These problems concern our era as well, and this fact is worth pointing out. Furthermore, they are not strained interpretations. "al-Ghazālī himself conceives the political leader as the master of the community; his teachings follow a progressive scale, going from educational demonstration to the function of correction". If he were to show himself to be unworthy, problems would arise that would not be easy to solve. Could a lower authority "call him to task"? Under such circumstances, when "public reproof of a superior who has shown himself to be unworthy and who flaunts his power, thereby compromising the public good takes place, it is necessary to resort to civil war, which, in this case, becomes a duty for any good Moslem" (Cruz Hernández, 362). It cannot be otherwise since no superior authority exists who is capable of solving the matter. Concerning the correction function, it is perhaps wise to recall that this includes "seven successive levels: proper training in the just principles, a warning that those principles must be followed, the condemnation of the corrupt, material suppression of the causes of corruption, intimidation of the sinners with the threat of temporal punishments, private and public rebuke" (Cruz Hernández, 362).

10.15 As for classical western thought, the problem of keeping order becomes one of the basic prerogatives of power. "The sovereign must, therefore, keep this order, using force if necessary, however much it is used in a spirit of charity, in order to dominate the conflicting passions and enable the free performance of the acts that direct man towards perfection" (Cruz Hernández, 363). It is obviously on that use of force that the two traditions diverge, as they do in their understanding of the temporal as opposed to the spiritual. At first sight it would seem that the difference did not exist. "Not only must the sovereign have sufficient and legitimate qualifications, but he must also exercise power according to the laws set forth, demonstrating the force, justice, intelligence and mercy with which he is endowed during the performance of his functions. (...) al-Ghazālī favours the creation of a council of the erudite who can advise the sovereign" (Cruz Hernández, 363), sages who would obviously be experts in the Koran and the tradition. Here lies the difference, and it is not inconsiderable. In Islam, religion and politics are identified with one another, as law and religion. Politics is not taken to be an independent science and the law does not involve natural premises from which an independent positive law can be produced. Politics and law, detached from the religious sphere, become dangerous for the integrity of the Islamic community as if, in their independence, they would come to lose that spirit of moderation typical of the tradition.

10.16 That spirit of moderation involves everyone, the sovereign who must avoid excesses, the sages who must reject the claims of a reason that wants to supplant faith, but it also involves the entire community. It is true that the latter can even rebel if the sovereign or the sages themselves endanger the orthodoxy of faith, but all that is not always feasible. "The ideal of perfection can, at times, require that the duty of rebellion against the tyrant be sacrificed, just as it obliges people to sacrifice their desires and individual rights on many occasions" (Cruz Hernández, 364). In other words "tyrannicide" can be mollified in practice even if it is feared in theory. Perhaps for this reason all the various analyses of "resistance" to power that gave rise to Medieval thought from John of Salisbury to Saint Thomas Aquinas, just to recall the most noted, do not exist. To be sure, historical contingencies oblige al-Ghazālī "to moderate his political and educational ideal" (Cruz Hernández, 364), but, in his era, the distinction between active and passive resistance with all their infinite possibilities does not seem to exist. On the contrary, the forms to resistance to power can be toned down, when it is thought that power is useful to the cause of Islam, and thus has the right to insist upon some actions to maintain orthodoxy. It is easy to find such justifications, based on religious beliefs. The "very spirit of charity must stimulate religious zeal, obligatory in Islam, in warning, correcting and denouncing believers who do not fulfil their religious obligations" (Cruz Hernández, 365).

10.17 At this point, the question of the liberty of human acts and the merit deriving from them arises. A series of questions not only presents itself, but also risks not being resolved, despite the fact that al-Ghazālī favours psychological forms of argumentation (cf. Caspar, 148 and 156). Does merit lie in action, in intention, or in both? Is good performed only because it is imposed, provided that it is indeed good, meritorious for one who performs it or only for one who demands and obliges it? Are these not questions that favour philosophical enquiry over religious subjects? Here too the spirit of moderation seems to come to our aid: Obedience to the dictates of the Koran and tradition seem to merit any sacrifice whatsoever, even that of critical reasoning. Perhaps this explains why al-Ghazālī was deeply attached to dogma since this may have set forth limits to enquiry thereby guaranteeing orthodoxy. "A passage in the Ihyā' explicitly sets these limits: asked to explain what the 'channels' of certitude might be, he explained the following to his interlocutors: 'all that the Prophets have handed down" (Veccia Vaglieri, 18). The use of interpretation, or the *fa 'wīl* was possibly only when following this path, that is the orthodox one of tradition. Indeed, al-Ghazālī "was reproached for having made excessive use of the *fa 'wil*, but he defending himself stating that it kept him within the bounds of dogma" (Veccia Vaglieri, 19).

10.18 It has been said that knowledge that does not relate to faith is dangerous because it causes people to lose faith in God and deceives them into thinking that they can become self-sufficient. For al-Ghazālī, however, there is another danger, that of making man so presumptuous that he closes himself up in his own intelligence to the point of considering works on behalf of others and religious obligations themselves superfluous. al-Ghazālī's warning against the "deceived" is totally clear. "They believe that their salvation and liberation lie in science and that they can thus do without the works. That is the opinion of the philosophers. Good heavens! These blind people do not know that once science has been acquired, and if they do not put it into practice, the accusation against them will be more serious at the moment of reckoning" (al-Ghazālī, F, 51). In other words, to be rewarded, it is necessary to act and to do so properly. This is the assumption underlying the entire work of al-Ghazālī guiding him along the path of renewal of the religious sciences. "The son warns – science without practice is madness. Practice without science is a nullity" (al-Ghazālī, F, 59). This statement is in line with the spirit of moderation that inspires all of Islam, even if it is one of the basic criteria of any religious spirit. It must, however, be emphasised that the mystical experiences of some Sūfī masters are viewed with respect, but here too, the spirit of moderation suggests avoiding explanation of the unexplainable in order not to run the risk of heresy.

10.19 In historical analysis, this view, ends up avoiding an understanding of the intentions and ideas of the adversary. This is the case for the writings on the Crusades which, in fact, are scattered through general annals or condensed in other narrations. They end up exalting a personage or a dynasty as champions of the faith without mapping out the political organisation of the Franks or giving a profile of their culture. There is moderate interest for their customs and ideas (cf. Gabrieli, 14 and 17). For contemporaries, they seemed under the influence of hashish given the serenity with which Franks accepted being massacred. We well know that this serenity came from other convictions, with which Marco Polo was already familiar (cf. Polo, 40), and which drove those fanatics always to act in public and before big crowds, generally in a mosque during prayer or in broad daylight (cf. Maalouf, 121). The same can be said of the description of some Arab leaders which enables us to have a better knowledge of the role they played, not only as defenders of Islam, but also in internal politics as well as in the tools they used. This is the case of the great Nūr al-Dīn (Nuraddin) who set up a veritable propaganda machine, through psychological mobilisation. He involved men of letters and men of faith to gain the allegiance of other Arab leaders and thus obliged them to take his side. Behind a unique religious conviction, the need to keep only one State in existence was encouraged. A veritable personality cult was based not only on his austere personality, but also on this combination (cf. Maalouf, 163-164). History perhaps went a different way, too, as we find out from Ibn Giobair in his travel account. He reported the well-being of all those Moslems who lived together with the Franks, from whom they had acquired a sense of ownership of their houses and their goods. The same was true for the property of funds. This was different from what happened with those of the same religion who lived elsewhere and did not have leaders who behaved "with fairness like the Franks". In other words, the newcomers brought in a society that "gave out rights" whereas, in other Islamic territories, "there existed no limit to the arbitrary power of the Prince". If all that had continued, the Moslems "would perhaps have risked turning their backs on others of their religion". This did not happen because the Franks were inclined to learn Arabic but the Islamics were reluctant to learn western languages, thus, integration remained only on a superficial level (cf. Maalouf, 285-286).

10.20 What had happened on the birth of Islam happened once again. The birth of a new religion meant the realisation of a new body politic which, in turn, was rooted in the conceptions and activities of the pre-Islamic Arabic world. There was an especially strong sense of tribal life in which the group was worth more than the individual (cf. Montgomery Watt, 4-6). The Prophet became the interpreter of this atavistic and still very relevant situation to the point that accepting his message and becoming a Moslem ended up being the same thing. This would also explain the rapid expansion of Islam because, carrying on with the action of the Prophet meant carrying on with the policy of the *Jihād*. Rather than simply being a holy war, this was the development *of the Arabian plunder.* Furthermore, the command itself "obey God and his Messenger", placed the Islamics in the direct service not only of the Prophet, but also those who were his legitimate spokesmen (cf. Montgomery Watt, 17-18 and 23). The Islamic State thus came to be the incarnation of a veritable aristocracy. Suffice it to think that when Mohammed began to be accused of having political aspirations, the expression "custodian" or rather "guardian" is introduced into the Koran to respond to the accusations. It should not be forgotten that if European languages continue to use the word Prophet, in Arabic, one speaks of *rasūl Allāh* that is Messenger (or Envoy) of God. These expressions have a greater practical, hence political sense (cf. Montgomery Watt, 27-28). The noble qualities of Mohammed were thus almost "genetically" handed down through the Caliphate, an aspect that was greatly stressed by the Islamic dynasties. What distinguishes the future Caliphs from the Prophet is that fact that the former lack the ability to prophesy, since the revelation has been definitively concluded (cf. Montgomery Watt, 35 and 42).

10.21 In view of what has been said, a conviction emerges and it will find confirmation in absolutism. In other words, some systems from whatever era and latitude they may be, end up all being alike. The work of Kautilya is a case in point. Weber referred to him as the Indian Machiavelli. The work certainly has not a few Asian characteristics, but, in any case, shows that certain of these are typical of all those systems that seek to achieve perfection on earth. This work, too (Arthašāstra, a writing discovered at the beginning of the twentieth century and dating back to between the fourth and fifth centuries B.C.) deals with the functioning of the State and matters pertaining to public life. The work begins with the upbringing of the Prince, goes on to the wielding of power, then examines the capabilities of officials and all the possibilities they have for degenerating, spies, snipers, secret agents, and so on. Everything is aimed at maintaining power and defending it from the so-called enemies of the State.

Appendices

11. Concerning *Imperium*
Passages taken from D. Nardoni,
Catachanna, Rome, 1979, pp 50-64.

11.1 The *Imperator,* par excellence, is the Senate and People of Rome, depositaries of the *Imperium; rex, praetor, consul, dictator* by delegation; and for the duration of their office all exercise the *imperium*, but not exclusively in the military sphere. There are a large number of sources of *imperium*, of *imperator, and imperare* which have led to the attribution of a valid significance of *imperium* in military language, but one which is not valid in other *sermones* (...). *Imperium, imperare, imperator, imperiosus:* these are terms coeval with the language, with the culture and the civilisation, in short with the Latin people. To consider them as born in the military encampments is to cancel out part of the history of the Roman people. *Imperium* must be studied independently of the "accidentals" which affected it over the years, adapting it to the varying conditions, if we are seeking a definition which is valid both philologically and semantically (...). In *imperare milites* it is possible to discover the idea that will make the analysis easier. In the adjective *pares*, in the adverb *aequaliter,* lies the nature of the *imperium:* "equalisation". By this *rex, praetor, consul, dictator,* distributed the levies on an equal basis: *nova iuvenum examina* among the four legions so that they should be "equal"; this happened, it took place through the coaction which the *imperium* conferred on the magistrate in office; the *imperium* allowed the levy; the *imperium* explains the *animadversiones* against the "*murcii*", the unwilling.

11.2 Nobody except Wagenvoort paid any attention to the *sermo rusticus*. The Roman, first an *agricola*, then a *miles* passed from the hoe to the sword, from the *rus* to the *castra*. And from the camps he returned to the countryside, to the hoe, to service rendered: *emeritis stipendiis*. The *sermo rusticus* adapted to military necessity; the *sermo castrensis* rooted in the soil, the *rus,* source of all sermones. Convinced that *imperare,* to rule, was born in the countryside, and passed from there into the camps (*castra*), we shall seek the meaning of "*imperium*" in *the sermo rusticus.* The sources are very scarce indeed (...). *Exerce tellurem* (...) *imperat arvis* corresponds to the *dura exerce imperia* (...) *ramos compesce* even if the *prius* of the former is the *posterius* of the latter. The earth is worked so that it can then be harrowed, so that the ground shall be "equal". Pruning is done so as to have "equal" shoots, halting the vine which in disorderly growth would lose its vigour (...) thus, substantially, *imperare* means "to equalise" or "to match"; united to a noun, *accidentaliter* it subsumes variations to indicate the specific activities within the framework of the substantial significance. The reading of the Virgilian texts does not exclude the meaning of authority, power, sovereignty, decisional capacity from the word *imperare* (...). But *imperare arvis, imperare vitibus*, the "flattening out" of the fields, the "pruning" of the vines are obtained by the plough in the one case, as it passes over and inexorably breaks up the sods, and by the pruning-hook in the other, as it ruthlessly cuts away the tendrils, which weep by spilling their sap. *Imperare*, then, *substantialiter* on two fronts: the "equalisation" subsumes the "coercion" and is realised by doing so. *Imperare*, equalise, if necessary by force, valid if semantics confirms the philological enquiry.

> *Imperare / im+per+are / im+par+are.*
> (The philological investigation follows at this point, Author's note).

11.3 *Imperium* – "equalisation", "matching", is made into a concrete fact by the "command", *imperium*: power of equalisation, equalisation carried out among peoples, with peoples, and for peoples, on whom and over whom the *imperium* acted with both pacific and warlike means (...). *Imperare* – to "pacify"; *parcere*: "to raise" to equal status; *compescere: debellare* : to "abase" to equal status. The conquered "abased" themselves before the victorious *imperator*; they were "raised up" again by the path which led to equalisation. Rome "raised up" the conquered; it humiliated the proud; it "flattened out" the road to the *imperium* by both peaceful and warlike routes; the use of the *coërcendi vis* was decided on when the peaceful means failed (...). The imperialistic idea is worth applying to modern states and to their policies, their ideologies: it proves inadequate when applied to Rome (...). Romulus who by sealing a pact with the Sabines showed that the population of Rome could expand, welcoming the enemy. Thus many peoples from the Latium: Tuscolani and Lanuvini and other peoples en masse – Sabines and Volsces and Hernices obtained the *ius Romanae civitatis*. The *imperandi ars*: the art of raising the conquered to citizenship, is traced by Cicero all the way back to Romulus, pointing to it as a motive force *ab origine* of Roman policy.

11.4 "*The Romans were usually liberal in their practice of emancipating slaves and of the privileges of citizenship to freed slaves, whereas the Greeks consistently refused to incorporate freedmen into the citizen body*", as Frank points out. Citizenship to individuals, to cities, to populations: the secret of the *imperium*. Unregulated citizenship: the *ius civitatis*: a prize which one had to merit. To individuals, to cities, to peoples, a period of "*probandato*" before becoming citizens. This is expressed in Virgil's words:

> *"By bringing equality to the peoples, Rome, may you rule*
> *Let there be three roads for you: command respect for peace,*
> *Raise up the vanquished and bring the proud down to the ground".*

By its imperial rule, Rome assured to all the freedom of thought, freedom of belief, freedom of religion. Rome, the holy pagan city (...) Septimius Severus venerated in the Lararium: Abraham, Christ, Orpheus – to all these he poured out libations, offered incense, and brought kisses: worship.

12. The case of Aristotle.

12.1. The political thought of Aristotle has been at the centre of attention in the west ever since its rediscovery in the Middle Ages. Many have considered it to be opposed to that of Plato, and to contain more than a few elements of liberalism, while others have placed him firmly in line with his teacher, considering his political thinking to be a deeper exploration of certain themes typical of an already consolidated area of thought. The truth, however, is somewhat different, and it is Aristotle's own disposition which makes this clear. His Ethics, the prelude without which his political thought cannot be understood, are founded on virtues seen as the "just mean", the middle position between two extremes. Aristotle could thus be defined in today's terms as a "moderate": in other words, a thinker who puts forward quite a few innovative points of departure in confrontation with Plato's political thought, but is in no way a revolutionary. He partly introduces novelty into a tradition, but at the same time he remains strongly indebted to that tradition. He criticises Plato and a good deal of the Greek tradition, but as is only natural, he remains bound to its fundamental characteristics.

Born of an aristocratic family in Stagyra in 384 B. C., **Aristotle** moved to Athens in 367 in order to attend the school of Plato, in which he remained for nineteen years in all, until 348 when he married. in 343, at the invitation of Philip of Macedon, he became tutor to the future Alexander the Great. After returning to Athens, he founded the Lyceum, his own school, in 335; the name is a reminder of the proximity of the sacred wood of Apollo Lyceus. In this period he devoted his time to compiling some of his most fundamental works. Apart from the world-famous philosophical works, those most relevant to the present analysis are the *Nicomachaean Ethics* and the *Politics*. He died a few months after the death of Alexander in 322, in Chalchide, where he had retired to put himself out of reach of the accusations of the anti-Macedonian party.

12.2 The aim of politics – or rather it would be more accurate to say of all human actions – is happiness. This is why, if we wish to find a definition for Aristotelian politics, it can be said that it is the science which seeks to apply wisdom to the solution of the problems which man encounters in the environment of the city, the *polis*. "In this view, Aristotle established a substantial link between metaphysics, history and politics, in the sense that the former indicates the meta-empirical principles on which reason is founded, while the latter points out the end to which all human actions tend" (D'Addio, 74). This conception has had its own validity from the time of Machiavelli onwards, following the rediscovery of Aristotle in the Middle Ages. The metaphysical basis on the one hand, and the ethical on the other, both witness to this double relationship of "attraction and repulsion" which Platonic political thought exercised on Aristotle. This explains why the *Politics*, Aristotle's crucial work, "was to pass through three successive stages: study of the ideal constitution on the Platonic model, study of the political constitutions founded on the analysis of real politico-social situations, and study of the ideal state on the Aristotelian model" (D'Addio, 75). The attraction of the concrete, therefore, does not do away with the reflection on the ideal model which remains the purpose of all Greek thinking until the Stagyrites, and this explains the great capacity for and power of abstraction in Greek culture.

12.3 Plato's Ideal is certainly not Aristotle's, and the latter strongly criticised Platonic idealism, based on collectivism. The latter is presented as an unrealisable proposal in Aristotle's view, for he holds the family and private property to be two natural realities and thus impossible to eliminate. But it is in fact nature which is the premise of Aristotelian idealism. Nature contains within itself an end, which gives character to the "process of becoming" of everything, including human action. We may take as an example the relations of command and obedience which are determined by a genuine natural hierarchy of intelligences, from which spring the three different types of authority that a man may exercise over his children, over his wife and over slaves. Aristotle's sentiments on this are very clear: there exists an interest, a mutual friendship between slave and master in the circumstances that they have deserved to be such by nature (cf. Arist., I, 1255b, 12). It is nature, then, which at the very act of birth, does not make everyone equally free, so that not all can equally be citizens: workers, for instance, being devoid of virtue (i.e. not knowing how to command and obey) cannot participate in the life of the *polis*.

12.4 A sceptical attitude towards workers is not an end in itself, but has to be seen within the framework of a typical Aristotelian mind-set, which on the one hand understands the importance of action, but on the other has many perplexities. As a "moderate" he knows that practical activities produce wealth, but he also knows that an excessive concentration on wealth produces tension in the *polis*. Solon is cited with some bitterness, in his contention that there exists no limit to wealth, nor is any perceived by men (cf. Arist., I, 1256b, 34). Wealth, in short, is a disintegrative force in the natural structure of the *polis*. From this comes the Aristotelian suspicion towards commercial activities, seen as activities not aimed at the good of the community but only at the enrichment of individuals. *This conception is radically different from the Roman one which saw trade as a benefit for all, so that those conditions capable of guaranteeing it (safety of the roads and seas, certainty of law, and so on) were to be sought after.*

12.5 The city has its part in the order of nature. The six social classes (farmers, artisans, warriors, those of independent means, priests and magistrates) exist in all cities, and are intended to carry out the various tasks which are useful to the citizens. The good of the *polis* is attained at the moment when "there is co-participation in rights and benefits" among equals (D'Addio, 80), unless nature predisposes some exceptional figure to whose will all must submit: such is the case with Alexander the Great, for instance. The words of Aristotle leave us in no doubt: if there is someone superior in virtue and practical capacity in the most important actions, it is a good thing to follow and obey him. However, it is necessary that he should possess not only virtue but also the capacity which renders him effective in action (cf. Arist., VII, 1325b, 10-13).

12.6 One of the most profound and fortunate points in Aristotle's reflections is the sense of limit, to which all those who act within the *polis* must conform. But even here we are faced with a consideration that was suited to its time, though taken up by later tradition. The sense of limitation in politics derives from the fact that the *polis* was considered a genuine living organism, which in its own nature made its limits perfectly clear; they could be described as organic. From this the specific relations between city and surrounding territory are derived: choice of a suitable place which guarantees economic independence, facility of trade and possibility of defence. A city measured not only in external but in internal terms: the Platonic suggestion of controlling both the health of births (by suitable matrimonial laws) and the disproportionate increase of population, both reappear. Furthermore, with regard to the quantity of the population, we said that it should be embraceable in one single scan, and likewise with regard to the territory; to be able easily to embrace it in a single scan means being able to defend it easily (cf. Arist., VII, 1327a, 1-4). Aristotle adds immediately after that this means constructing the *polis* according to "the ideal".

12.7 The reflection on population is of some importance; from it emerges the constitution which governs the *polis*. The constitution is the expression of the tendencies and values which inspire the *polis*. It should not be forgotten that Aristotle had carried out the first comparative study of constitutions, which unfortunately has been lost. It pointed out the various factors, including geographical and "sociological" ones, which contribute to their formulation. Constitutions cannot, therefore, be imposed on different peoples, because each of them must be an expression of its own people, which in turn is an expression of their own interests and their own aspirations.

12.8 The various constitutions are gathered by Aristotle into three models, which form the three "perfect" constitutions: monarchy, aristocracy and *politeia*, or democracy of the free. Three other types arise from these as a result of degeneration: tyranny, oligarchy and demagogy, or democracy of the mob. These models certainly do not exhaust the whole range of constitutions: it would be doing a great wrong to Aristotle to think they do. The analysis is in fact supported by various sub-species, but a constant datum, almost of a psychological nature, shows that Aristotle too in the end preferred a balanced constitution based on aristocratic-elitist values. The multitude, incapable of living according to "virtue", does not know the sense of limits, and in the end is capable of committing every kind of absurdity, due to passionate and even animal-like motives. In these moments, the multitude ends up by stamping the law beneath its feet. For Aristotle, law is in fact order (cf. Arist., III, 1287a, 19), and when it loses its strength and its will, it witnesses the breakdown of the stability of political order, and the passions of the multitude finally prevent the triumph of virtue. Ethics no longer regulate political life.

12.9 From what has been said so far, it seems clear that Aristotle, despite his notable and original institutions, has a distinctly aristocratic bias, charged with no small element of Platonism. Proof of this can be found if we turn our attention to other facts. To belong to the *polis* every man must assert himself in his fullness. The *polis* is thus prior to the individual; it generates him. The individual is no more than a part of the whole. It should not be forgotten that the citizen, for Aristotle, is the person who lives in the *polis* and for the *polis*. Those who act mainly outside the walls, like those who devote themselves to trade, live a life "without nobility and contrary to virtue"; the same goes for the peasants. This is why certain critics have been able to maintain that Aristotelian equality is in substance inequality, within which freedom is often reduced by submission. Aristotle himself suggests these considerations when he writes: "it is impossible for all the citizens to be equal (...) the state is the result of differing elements, like the living being, for example of soul and body, – the soul consisting of reason and appetite – and the family of man and woman and the property of master and slave" (Arist., III, 1277a, 1 and

6-9). *It is true that many of these diversities are accepted by the whole ancient world, but it is also true that here they are justified because they are unequivocally established by nature.* This was to be incomprehensible to Roman thought which, as we have seen, did not consider slavery a natural thing, and would allow many individuals the possibility of redemption. In Greece, "we must remember that, according to the tradition, Antisthenes was 'a bastard' (his mother came from barbarian Thrace), and that he taught in the Athenian gymnasium reserved for 'bastards'. Or (...) at least in Plato's (and Aristotle's) time, the problem of egalitarianism was clearly seen to be connected with two fully analogous distinctions: that between *Greek and barbarian* on the one side and that between *master (or free man) and slaves* on the other" (Popper, 277-278, n.47 and n.48).

12.10 Thus it is little wonder that, following in the paths of Plato, there are quite a few idealistic notions in the *Politics*. We have only to remember that the ideal city must enjoy certain material conditions not only as far as the composition of its inhabitants is concerned, but also with regard to its geographical position. "If it is to be constructed according to the ideal, it is desirable to site it conveniently in relation to both sea and land" (Arist.,VII, 1327a 4-5). But Aristotle is even more Platonic when it comes to the governors. These must be the best, even in the physical sense (cf. Arist., VII, from 1334a to 1337a). When the best govern, there is nothing that needs to be done apart from letting them guide according to their virtue. The whole teaching process must be oriented towards this virtue, and in Aristotle's view, it can only be undertaken by the state.

12.11 The fact that no pedagogical role is ascribed to private individuals should not surprise us. The idea of the private finds no place in a reflection in which the whole directs the part, since the latter must logically be oriented towards the whole. Education, Aristotle says, since it must be the guarantee of stability, is the best instrument for making a constitution last. Therefore it is not an instrument of political criticism, but an instrument for the governing class. Reflection on this argument is enough to make us realise that Aristotle, when he is speaking about tyranny, although he criticises it, distinguishes two different types: the first makes use of violence and is clearly oppressive, while the second, for which Aristotle shows a certain preference, makes of the tyrant one who sets himself up to be the "true" ruler of the *polis*, seeking to appear a genuine king.

12.12 This is what is said as regards the Greek citizens of the *polis*, while for the "barbarians" a similar pretence would be completely pointless. It should not be forgotten that Plutarch states that Aristotle advised Alexander to govern the Greeks as a "just" military chieftain, while he should govern the barbarians as a despot (cf. Chevallier, I, 181, note). We may add to this the now famous notion about slavery. As we have mentioned several times this is seen by Aristotle as being an intention of nature, which has established a kind of hierarchy of intelligences in ineluctable fashion. We are a long way here from the Roman conception, so well expressed by Cicero, that nature has provided everyone with reason, and that in the same way everyone must pass through a confused awareness to one which gradually permits the exercise of virtue. It was Seneca who later maintained explicitly that natural equality extended to the whole human race, slaves included.

12.13 This explains why in Greece, an institutional notion such as the *res publica*, which apparently means "of the people", could never have arisen. This is confirmed by the fact that as Chevallier has rightly pointed out, in Rome the "forms of government may be different, there may be a different organisation of power, but what always remains intact is that the *populus* is the possessor of sovereignty (all three *régimes* are differing forms of *res publica* and a *res publica* is a *res populi*" (Chevallier, I, 211).

12.14 The reasons for this difference, however, are also to be found on the theoretical plain as well as on the practical one of political life, and they provide a final confirmation that there is no contradiction between the two levels. This goes generally for the entire body of Greek thought and for the political theory of Aristotle, which belongs within a precise gnoseological context, as it did for Plato. Popper pointed out very clearly that the fear of the mutable, of daily instability, which certainly had its justification dictated by historical contingency, drove Plato to go beyond the analysis of the sensible, to seek to arrive at the essences. Speaking of political Platonism, we may thus speak of methodological essentialism, which was then to have numerous followers. "Many of the later methodological essentialists, for instance Aristotle, did not altogether follow him (Plato) in this, but they all agreed with him in determining the task of pure knowledge as the discovery of the hidden nature or Form or essence of things" (Popper, 31). By its nature, this essence would appear to all those who in one way or another link their ideas to Greek thought, to be static. Such a notion is in sharp contrast to what serious political analysis should be, for by its intrinsic nature, it repudiates every kind of methodological immobilism, since it is linked to the process of becoming. "If we are to believe Aristotle's report, then the theory of Forms or Ideas was originally introduced in order to meet a methodological demand, the demand for pure or rational knowledge which is impossible in the case of sensible things in flux" (Popper, 37-38). If change is embraced within this way of thinking, it can only be change conditioned by determined premises and with a very precise direction.

12.15 In the light of what has gone before, and despite the various passages in which Aristotle maintains that justice is something which is referred to persons, the role of the individual, even in the moral context, is always played down. It could hardly be otherwise when we remember that for Aristotle "to take care of virtue is the business of a state which truly deserves this name (...) [but] what we need and what we want is to moralize politics, not to politicize morals" (Popper, 112-113). But Aristotle could not have understood this, for in his view "the essential end of the state is to make its citizens virtuous" (Popper, 114).

12.16 Aristotelian sciences, therefore, are always referred back to theoretical sciences, despite their separation from the latter. In speaking of ethics and politics, the thinkers of the era of the crisis in the *polis*, Aristotle among them, seek to re-present models and hypotheses derived from the scientific conception of the times. It can thus be asserted easily "that Plato *was one of the first to develop a specifically geometrical method* aiming at rescuing what could be rescued from the breakdown of Pythagoreanism (...) a re-reading of Plato, Aristotle, Euclid, and Proclus, in the light of these hypothesis, would produce as much corroborating evidence as one could expect" (Popper, 319-320). Moreover, a thread linking the political thought of Pythagoras, Plato and Aristotle does exist, and can be seen in the thoroughly aristocratic conception – and I would also add practice – of all three of them.

12.17 The aristocratic position of Aristotle shows through clearly on more than one occasion. When he is speaking about oligarchic systems, he holds that if one wishes to subjugate the people more easily, one must avoid open hostility. "He thinks it wiser that 'true Oligarchs should *affect* to be advocates of the people's cause'; and he is anxious to give them good advice: 'They should take, or they should at least *pretend* to take, the opposite line, by including in their oath the pledge: I shall do no harm to the people'" (Popper, 296, n.13). We seem here to be reading the paradoxical recommendation by Machiavelli to his Prince when he suggested that to command is to make believe. Anyone who thinks that this conclusion is a little forced has only to read what Aristotle wrote in his *Politics*: "The aim is clear, in any case: it is necessary that he appears to his subjects not as a tyrannical chief, but as an administrator and royal ruler, not a usurper, but a tutor who follows moderation in his way of life and not excess (...) that he lives sheltered from hatreds and fears but also that his government should last longer, and that he should be either well-disposed to virtue in his character or at least half good and not perverse, but only half perverse" (Arist., 1315b, 1-10). This is certainly not an "ideal" position. Aristotle hastens to add that both tyranny and oligarchy are short-term constitutions. But his aristocratic notions frequently emerge, even if they are less marked than those of Plato. It should not be forgotten what is for Aristotle the best form of government, or the ideal form. That government, in Popper's view, is the one which manifests "a 'moderate' programme, viz., that of the 'paternal state'" (Popper, 299, n. 26), which I believe, without exaggerating too greatly, can be seen as the forerunner of the Welfare State.

12.18 Aristocratic nature is typical of the Greek mentality, and thus closely influences their political reflection, which is shown to be barely open at all to other cultures, judged always and in all ways to be "bastard", and thus incapable of making suggestions and contributions. In connection with this, we need only recall what Plato said with regard to foreigners. The frequent mixing of the citizens of one state with those of another by nature confuses together customs of every kind; strangers to one another, they cannot avoid being the occasions of mutual novelties and innovations in their respective states. This would bring about the gravest damage of all to the states which are well-organised and founded on good laws (cf. Plato, 949e-950a). Everyone can assess how distant this is from the Roman conception of the city which was open to the world, expressed in the first chapter, and summed up so well by the conviction of Ennius recorded at the beginning of this work (cf. point 1.2).

13. Letters from K.R. Popper and I. Berlin.

13.I The first chapter of this book received the following comment from Professor Popper:

(p.1)
                                                                12-1-93
    My Dear Pezzimenti,

    I received your letter and your marvellous first chapter this afternoon; I read it at once, and I was deeply impressed by it. I cannot quite express my sense of admiration, and my conviction of the importance of this chapter. And, what is less important, my deep agreement.

    It is only in recent years that I have realised the importance of the Roman tradition, and of Cicero. My attack on Plato was, I believe, necessary. But I knew too little of Cicero.

    Thank you again for your splendid paper. Your English is excellent, forceful throughout.

    I found a few printer's mistakes. See the other page.
    Yours sincerely,

                              Karl Popper.

(p.2)
                                                                12-1-93
    A few printer's mistakes
p. 122, line 3 from bottom
    imited → *limited*
p. 124, last line: "solutions" ?

p. 124, line 7 from top: "suspended laws against the debtors":
   I found this ambiguous and incomprehensible (cf. I.14).
p. 125, 1.17, line 3: quotation marks closing without a beginning.
p. 133, line 1: last two words are printed without a space between them. p. 136, lines 14 to 13 from bottom <u>very</u> good (cf. I.42-I.43).
   line 2 fr. b. Lawsand → laws and
p. 138, last 6 lines of 1.47: <u>very</u> good.
p. 139, line 1 onemind → one mind
   I.50, line 3 live → lived
   (I have recently put this: "There are two possibilities. A rule of violence and fear – or The Rule of Law.")
   1.51, line 1 thealleged → the alleged
p. 140, 1.52, line 3 third volume → third book.
   1.52, line 13 closing quotation marks, but no beginning ones.

The two points in brackets regarding p.124 and p.136 have been added by me. The notes written by Prof. Popper bear witness to the very close attention with which he read the manuscript.

13.2 For the sake of the record I should add that the comments on my excellent English should be attributed to my friend Brian Williams, Professor of European History at John Cabot University in Rome, with whom I have gone over the text sentence by sentence to ensure its comprehensibility.

13.3 At the beginning of Chapter III I stated that the relation between religion and politics is certainly one of the most controversial in western history. In pointing out the extreme viewpoints, I mentioned on the one hand those who attribute to religion, which is here referred to the Judaeo-Christian tradition, the credit for having given western civilisation the seeds of that liberty and equality which were to be at the basis of the liberalism of the future, and on the other hand, those who see in religion the justification for the *status quo* and a great many forms of absolutism.

13.4 On this issue I put two questions to Professor Popper a long time ago, basing them on two passages from his work on the Open Society: 1) "The view that norms are man-made is also, strangely enough, contested by some who see in this attitude an attack on religion. It must be admitted, of course, that this view is an attack on certain forms of religion, namely, on the religion of blind authority, on magic and tabooism. But I do not think that it is in any way opposed to a religion built upon the idea of personal responsibility and freedom of conscience. I have in mind, of course, especially Christianity, at least as it is usually interpreted in democratic countries: that Christianity which, as against all tabooism, preaches, 'Ye have heard that it was said by them of old time (...) But I say unto you (...)' opposing in every case the voice of conscience to mere formal obedience and the fulfilment of law" (Popper, 65). Despite a number of assertions to the contrary, does this conclusion not demonstrate that a certain metaphysic which we might call 'open' – i.e. not crystallised, never satisfied with itself – such as may be at the basis of scientific development, may also lie at the basis of a democratic society? By this we mean a metaphysic unlike the static Platonic conception, but of a dynamic kind which demands constant renewal, as you yourself said when you quoted: "You have heard what was said (...) but I say to you (...)".

13.5 "The starting point can be described as a *naive monism*. It may be said to be characteristic of the 'closed society' The last step, which I describe as *critical dualism* (or critical conventionalism), is characteristic of the 'open society'. The fact that there are still many who try to avoid making this step may be taken as an indication that we are still in the midst of the transition from the closed to the open society" (Popper, 59). If we may refer, after this affirmation, to the previous question, could we not say that a metaphysic understood in this way (i.e. open, dynamic, etc.) is capable of making a substantial contribution to critical dynamism, and thus to the open society?

13.6 From Popper's reply, prior to that quoted in point 13.1, I have only reproduced the first part here, since the second is related to a totally different problem concerning the philosophy of science.

> *Dear Mr Pezzimenti.*
> *(1) What you say is very good, as always. But one should not make too much fuss over terms like "metaphysics". I certainly do not wish to say that one should not talk about metaphysics. But what has been usually called so was not of a critical (and as you call it, "dynamic") character. But I have no objection to what you say about my Open Society, p. 59 and p. 65.*
> *(...)*
> *Congratulations and best wishes,*
> *Yours,*
> *Karl Popper.*

13.7 On the central theme of this work, I sent Professor Isaiah Berlin a number of questions of a general character. His replies were of the greatest value to me, above all for Chapter VII and for the authors who will be examined subsequently in my next volume. These are the questions (the work by Berlin which is referred to is *Four Essays on Liberty).* 1) Almost at the end of the first paragraph of your introduction, you ask: "But is casual behaviour not perhaps the exact opposite of liberty, of rationality and responsibility?" I would ask: "does liberty, in order to emerge and defend itself and grow, need an appropriate culture, which is not atomistic, casualistic or dispersive, or not? How can those who preach improvisation, instinctuality or even worse, violence, defend liberty? It has been said that liberty can be lost through liberty, but only if, devoid of any guarantee, it is confused with arbitrariness. I am almost tempted to say that liberty is defended by a culture which has its own metaphysic, with irrevocable and indefeasible principles".

13.8 2) Again in the introduction you maintain that individual liberty is the safeguard of those boundaries which no authority may violate, and that it is a conquest of our modern world. I see no objection to this, but I do wonder whether such a liberty was not contained, *in nuce,* in those private rights of the Roman world such as, for instance, private property which could not be damaged either by third parties or by public authorities. As Carlyle made very clear in his classic study on the middle ages, it is specifically the rediscovery of the Roman jurists which opens the way to modernity. Montesquieu, too, before writing *L'Esprit des Lois,* examined the reasons for the greatness and the decline of Rome.

13.9 In your third essay you maintain several times that persons must be inviolable, and that these personal rights should be considered absolute. This is what the liberal tradition teaches. The concept is clear, but I remain a little uncertain about the term 'absolute'. It brings to mind, for me, something of Kant's *a priori* requirements of morality. I do not believe that it should be understood in this sense. Unfortunately, morality does not have given universal principles, but slow conquests; perhaps the history of law shows this too. The concept of the person is itself a conquest of western history. A Chinese friend of mine, after the events of Tienanmen Square, told me that far fewer deaths would have meant the fall of a western government. But in China, the same concept of the individual was yet to become acceptable. *Pace* the Kantians, the formulae of the categorical imperative are *not* universal, they are only empty words where no liberal tradition (of a slow historical development) exists and is given vitality by the certainty of law.

13.10 These are Berlin's replies to the above questions (NB In the text which follows, numbers of notes are included. These are references to certain clarifications, included below, which Berlin himself wished to make, and which were contained in the kind letter in which he gave me permission to publish the following):

> *Dear Professor Pezzimenti,*
> *Thank you for* Metalogicon, *which I haven't had time to read – I have so much piled up on my desk that I cannot promise to read it, for at any rate a few weeks, but I will then.*
> *Thank you also for your letter of 24 November. I shall try and answer the questions you ask as best I can, although I am afraid that – as a result of the lack of time I have at the moment – the result may be somewhat amateurish and confused.*
>
> *1. Casual behaviour the exact opposite of liberty, etc. Well, of course, it depends on the kind of liberty we are talking about. For me, liberty is basically the absence of restraint. Of course, if anyone is allowed complete liberty in this sense, disaster will follow. The wolves, if given liberty, will slaughter*

the sheep – the pike, the carp. So restraints have to be imposed. Now, liberty in the ordinary, personal and political sense, of course only means liberty in certain respects, not in all respects – and of a limited, not unlimited, kind. That I fully accept. Given this, there must obviously be (rules ⃞1⃞) criteria for limiting it. Since I believe in a multiplicity of ultimate values, and since I believe that some of them clash, it is clear that if a certain degree of liberty on the part of X deprives Y and Z and A and B and C of their security, it must be restrained; and there are other values with which liberty can collide: justice, happiness, the dissemination of the truth, security, man's need for food and drink and shelter – all these things are ultimate values, which we cannot do without. But in such cases agonised choices may be necessary. Unless there is a body of criteria which at any rate guide us in the direction in which we have to proceed, liberty in the sense you and I mean it, i.e. social, political liberty – and private liberty too – within a demarcated sphere cannot be obtained. Hence what you call 'casual behaviour', that is to say, behaviour that ignores external circumstances, rules, the structure of a society, other people's needs and rights, etc., will certainly be an obstacle to liberty of both kinds: both of the negative sort, i.e. absence of obstacles to doing whatever I choose, and the positive sort, i.e. my ability to determine myself and not to be determined by others. So I agree with what I take you to mean.

2. *Roman law and property* – is this the notion of individual liberty contained, as you say, in nuce? I do not think so. Of course human beings in ancient Greece and Rome, and many other countries, possessed some degree of individual liberty – they could move about freely in normal societies, whether democratic or not; they were able to obtain food such as they wished, within limits, or shelter or clothes or whatever

it may be. Property does not seem to me to be a particular conception or phenomenon that guarantees, or is even the seed of a guarantee for, individual liberty – any more than the satisfaction of other needs. *If I stop a murderer, I limit his liberty; if I am preserved from him, this guarantees my liberty within certain limits.* Property is only one of the institutions which creates a fence against oppression or interference. What I mean is that the idea of private life or personal liberty was of course not unknown before it was discussed. My point was that neither in Greece nor in Rome was this, [2] so far as I know, explicitly recognised as a human right – it was not something of which men were conscious as a problem, or an end, or a value, against which arguments could be used. That only came when individual rights to privacy were recognised – I don't know when that might have been, I think the earliest is probably Ockham and nominalism and the notion of individuality not covered by generality of any sort. But I do not know; I am not a historian of Rome or of the Middle Ages. It seems to me a typical modern notion. Of course my idea comes from Benjamin Constant, who in his famous essay On the Liberty of Ancients and Moderns, which I am sure you know, says that liberty for ancient Athenians consisted in the fact that anybody could denounce anybody in the Assembly – [3] that anybody could probably look through someone's private window without being punished; whereas modern liberty has something to do with some kind of area within which a man could be safe from interference by the state or other men. That essay made a deep impression on me, that is what in this instance I am talking about.

3. About 'absolute' rights, you are entirely justified in your reservations. Of course, unless you believe in sacred Writs, or Kantian <u>a priori</u>, or other sources of absolute truth, authority, etc., nothing can be regarded as absolutely absolute, if I may

put it like that. There are certain rights which we regard normally, i.e. in post-Renaissance society, as inviolable – the right to life or to movement or to various other things which Grotius summed up under the notion of natural law – ④ *even if one doesn't go along with his or anybody else's actual list of these laws. This is perfectly true. But situations can, of course, arise in which one is justified in setting these rights aside: if I see a man about to commit a murder, of course I do not regard his body as inviolable, I use coercion to prevent him; if a society is so abominably organised that what we like to call basic human rights (which are not 'absolute' in the sense that you mean) are trampled on, then of course one is justified in taking measures against that, indeed in making a revolution if necessary, in order to confer or restore such rights. So nothing in that sense is absolute. All I really meant, though I expressed it badly, is that there are certain values which a great many men, at a great many times, in a great many places, have regarded as ultimate – not means to other values, but ends to be sought for their own sakes. And the denial of such ends was regarded as in some way an offence against the human person – 'natural rights', 'human rights', etc. refer, as does 'natural justice' to often unspoken rules by which men, almost everywhere, but not everywhere, at almost all times but not at all times, have lived, are living, are likely to live. That is all I wanted to stress. Of course you are perfectly right in saying that the Chinese concept of the person is probably different from ours, and that moral rules vary – it was only that I optimistically assumed that they don't vary that much: that variety is not as great as is sometimes maintained, though in theory, no doubt, it can be infinite; that there are certain concepts in the light of which we live, such that these who lack them are regarded as abnormal or mad or the like. In the famous anecdote, when a man said 'I used to know the difference between right and wrong, I know there is one, but I have simply forgotten what it is'* ⑤ *it is as if one were to say: 'I knew the difference between left hand and right hand, but what on earth is it?'. But otherwise you are perfectly right: the notion of the human person, the notions of rights, duties, what is right and wrong, good and bad, what kind of government is just or unjust, all that constitutes justice or happiness or whatever you wish – can be different in different societies. But not, as I say, that different – there is a common core: the notion of right and wrong, of good and bad, has always governed men – what has differed is what content is put into this – the categories are comparatively unvarying, the contents can vary a great deal, and are subject to persuasion, argument, destruction. etc.*

I do not know if this answers your questions, I can only hope that it does.

Yours sincerely,

Sir Isaiah Berlin

13.11 In order to explain the references made in the preceding lines, I am reproducing here only a part of a recent letter by Professor Berlin, since a substantial part of it concerns reflections on the thought of Vico, which I will analyse in the next volume. Obviously, in addition to the numbers, references to pages, lines and paragraphs in the first letter will also be found; for this reason also, (and to make comparison easier), it is reproduced with the others at the end of this appendix.

22 May 1995

Dear Professor Pezzimenti,

Thank you for your letter of 11 May, and for the copy of the long letter which I wrote you in 1992.

In this connection, I would like to make certain corrections if you want to publish the letter – it was written in some haste and therefore contains a certain amount of amateurism and inexactness.

1. *p.1, para 3, line 10:* '*...obviously be rules for limiting.*' I think the word '*rules*' won't do. There cannot be precise rules about how to draw a frontier between individual liberty and standards of living or security or equality of treatment and the like – these things must be done in accordance with some kind of rational decision about what would be best within the limits of what might be called a decent society – '*rules*' cannot possibly be drawn – the same applies to the use of '*rules*' further down, line 19.

2. *P.2, line 15:* between '*...Rome was this...*' and '*explicitly*', would you put in '*,so far as I know,*' – after all, as I say, I am not an ancient historian and this is merely my impression. I do not believe that <u>Jura</u> means '*rights*'.

3. *Line 26:* the word '*but*', following '*Assembly*', should be '*that*'.

4. *Para. 3:* half-way down, where I say '*though I don't go along...*', it would be more modest to say '*even if one does not go along...*'.

5. *P. 3., line 24:* for '*as well to*', you should substitute '*it is as if one were to say...*'

Line 28: for '*that*', perhaps '*all that*' should be substituted.

Otherwise I don't think I want to withdraw anything, but I should like to add this:

Apart from political liberty, negative or positive, there is a more basic liberty which people sometimes confuse with it, namely the fundamental liberty of choice: something that human beings must possess if they are to be human at all. Even if I lack negative liberty, if I am in prison or tied to a tree or threatened with death by someone, I must retain the minimal possibility of choice, of whatever it may be –

to open or close my mouth, to resist or die quietly, to cry or be silent, etc. That is neither positive nor negative, but an essential human trait without which one would become dehumanised, could not be counted as a member of the human race in the full sense.

Perhaps that hardly need be said, but it does have to be in this context because the view that minimum choice is indispensable to being human is not irrelevant to the later uses of liberty, whether negative (i. e. how many doors are open to me?) or positive (who is master?).

(...)

Yours sincerely,

Sir Isaiah Berlin

13.12 In my reply to Prof. Berlin, in relation to the second point in his letter, I pointed out the fact that it would be a grave error to continue to use the Graeco-Roman binomial as if it were indissoluble. I also wrote, as I then tried to demonstrate in my study, that the first mediaeval autonomies were reborn as a result of the rediscovery of Roman law. This always favoured the development of mercantile society, and, as time went on, the work of Vico, Montesquieu and those who opened the way to modern thought.

Sir Karl Popper, CH, FRS, FBA

136 Welcomes Road,
Kenley, Surrey
CR8 5HH

12 — 1 — 93

Dr Rocco Pezzimenti
Borgo Vittorio 74
00193 Roma, Italy

My dear Pezzimenti,

I received your letter and your marvellous first chapter this afternoon; I read it at once, and I was deeply impressed by it. I cannot quite express my sense of admiration, and my conviction of the importance of this chapter. And, what is ~~perhaps~~ less important, my deep agreement.

It is only in recent years that I have realized the importance of the Roman tradition, and of Cicero. My attack on Plato was, I believe, necessary. But I knew too little of Cicero.

Thank you again for your splendid paper. Your English is excellent: forceful throughout. I found a few printer's mistakes.*

See the other page

Yours sincerely
Karl Popper

Sir Karl Popper, CH, FRS, FBA

136 Welcomes Road,
Kenley, Surrey
CR8 5HH

12 — 1 — 93

A few printer's mistakes

p.122 line 3 from bottom
         imited → limited

124   last line: "soleteions"?

124   line 7 from top: "suspended laws against the debtors". I found this ambiguous and incomprehensible

125, I.17 line 3: quotation marks closing without a beginning.

133   line 1, last two words are printed without a space between them

136   lines 14 to 13 from bottom, *very good*
   "   2 fr. b. lawsand → laws and

138, las 6 lines of I.47: *very good*

139   line 1   onemind → one mind
      I.50 line 3   live → lived
      (I have/put this *recently*: "There are two possibilities: A rule of violence and fear — or the Rule of Laws.")

      I.51 line 1   thealleged → the alleged

140, I.52, line 3   third volume → third book
     I.52, line 13 closing quotation marks, but no beginning ones.

Rocco Pezzimenti
Borgo Vittorio 74
00193 Rome, Italy.

136 Welcomes Road
Kenley, Surrey
CR8 – 5HH.

The Post Office
has changed this ⤴

Dear Mr Pezzimenti,

(1) What you say is very good, as always. But one should not make too much fuss over terms like "metaphysics". I certainly do not wish to say that one should not talk about metaphysics. But what has been usually called so was not of a critical (and, as you call it, "dynamic") character. But I have no objection to what you say about my *Open Society* p 59 and p. 65.

(2) I did not like so much "Verification and Falsification". First, I of course do not hold Galileo's method outdated! (But he does not know how to describe it correctly; nor do you.) But you try to relegate as unimportant or unnecessary the **asymmetry** between falsification and verification. Of course, if you say we do **not** mean by "verification" anything that can ever be final; we merely mean the same as (what) I call "corroboration", then the whole is (apparently) a question of terminology, and my results, which are results of importance (not only in my opinion) become uninteresting. (I know that this is not your opinion.) Incidentally, the Chaos people have merely rediscovered what Hadamard found in 1898 and I rediscovered in 1948 (approximately). Of course I agree with you on Feyerabend

For section 34: But we seek for absolute truth, even though we cannot test for absolute certainty that it is very important.

Congratulations and best wishes
yours Karl Popper

HEADINGTON HOUSE
OLD HIGH STREET, HEADINGTON
OXFORD, OX3 9HU
TEL. OXFORD (0865) 61008

30 November 1992

Dear Mr. Pezzimenti,

    Thank you for *Metalogicon*, which I haven't had time to read - I have so much piled up on my desk that I cannot promise to read it, for at any rate a few weeks - but I will then.

    Thank you also for your letter of 24 November. I shall try and answer the questions you ask as best I can, although I am afraid that - as a result of the lack of time I have at the moment - the result may be somewhat amateurish and confused.

1.   Casual behaviour the exact opposite of liberty, etc. Well, of course, it depends on the kind of liberty we are talking about. For me, liberty is basically the absence of restraint. Of course, if anyone is allowed complete liberty in this sense, disaster will follow. The wolves, if given liberty, will slaughter the sheep - the pike, the carp. So restraints have to be imposed. Now, liberty in the ordinary, personal and political sense, of course only means liberty in certain respects, not in all respects - and of a limited, not unlimited, kind. That I fully accept. Given this, there must obviously be rules for limiting it. Since I believe in a multiplicity of ultimate values, and since I believe that some of them clash, it is clear that if a certain degree of liberty on the part of X deprives Y and Z and A and B and C of their security, it must be restrained; and there are other values with which liberty can collide: justice, happiness, the dissemination of the truth, security, man's need for food and drink and shelter - all these things are ultimate values, which we cannot do without. But in such cases agonised choices may be necessary. Unless there is a body of rules which at any rate guide us in the direction in which we have to proceed, liberty in the sense you and I mean it, i.e. social, political liberty - and private liberty too - within a demarcated sphere cannot be obtained. Hence what you call 'casual behaviour', that is to say, behaviour that ignores external circumstances, rules, the structure of society, other people's needs and rights, etc., will certainly be an obstacle to liberty of both kinds: both of the negative sort, i.e. absence of obstacles to doing whatever I choose, and the positive sort, i.e. my ability to determine myself and not be determined by others. So I agree with what I take you to mean.

2.   Roman law and property - is this the notion of individual liberty contained in, as you say, <u>in nuce</u>? I do not think so.

- 2 -

Of course human beings in ancient Greece and Rome, and many other countries, possessed some degree of individual liberty - they could move about freely in normal societies, whether democratic or not; they were able to obtain food such as they wished, within limits, or shelter or clothes or whatever it may be. Property does not seem to me to be a particular conception or phenomenon that guarantees, or is even the seed of a guarantee for, individual liberty - any more than the satisfaction of other needs. If I stop a murderer, I limit his liberty; if I am preserved from him, this guarantees my liberty within certain limits. Property is only one of the institutions which creates a fence against oppression or interference. What I mean is that the idea that of private life or personal liberty was of course not unknown before it was discussed. My point was that neither in Greece nor in Rome was this explicitly recognised as a human right - it was not something of which men were conscious as a problem, or an end, or a value, against which arguments could be used. That only came when individual rights to privacy were recognised - I don't know when that might have been, I think the earliest is probably Occam and nominalism and the notion of individuality not covered by generality of some sort. But I do not know, I am not a historian of Roman or of the Middle Ages. It seems to me a typical modern notion. Of course my idea comes from Benjamin Constant, who in his famous essay On the Liberty of Ancients and Moderns, which I am sure you know, says that liberty for ancient Athenians consisted in the fact that anybody could denounce anybody in the Assembly - but anybody could probably look through someone's private window without being punished; whereas modern liberty has something to do with some kind of area within which a man could be safe from interference by the state or other men. That essay made a deep impression on me, that is what in this instance I am talking about.

3. About 'absolute' rights, you are entirely justified in your reservations. Of course, unless you believe in sacred Writs, or Kantian a priori, or other sources of absolute truth, authority, etc., nothing can be regarded as absolutely absolute, if I may put it like that. There are certain rights which we regard normally, i.e. in post-Renaissance society, as inviolable - the right to life or to movement or to various other things which Grotius summed up under the notion of natural law - though I don't go along with his or anybody else's actual list of these laws. That is perfectly true. But situations can, of course, arise in which these rights can be one is justified in setting these rights aside: if I see a man about to commit a murder, of course I do not regard his body as inviolable, I use coercion to prevent him; if a society is so abominably organised that what we like to call basic human rights (which are not 'absolute' in the sense that you mean) are trampled on, then of course one is

justified in taking measures against that, indeed, in making a revolution if necessary, in order to confer or restore such rights. So nothing in that sense is absolute. All I really meant, though I expressed it badly, is that there are certain values which a great many men, at a great many times, in a great many places, have regarded as ultimate - not means to other values, but ends to be sought for their own sakes. And the denial of such ends was regarded as in some way an offence against the human person - 'natural rights', 'human rights', etc. refer, as does 'natural justice', to often unspoken rules by which men, almost everywhere but not everywhere, at almost all times but not at all times, have lived, are living, are likely to live. That is all that I wanted to strees. Of course you are perfectly right in saying that the Chinese concept of the person is probably different from ours, and that moral rules vary - it was only that I optimistically assumed that they don't vary that much: that variety is not as great as is sometimes maintained, though in theory, no doubt, it can be infinite; that there are certain conceptions in the light of which we live, such that those who lack them are regarded as abnormal or mad or the like. In the famous anecdote, when a man said 'I used to know the difference between right and wrong, I know there is one, but I have simply forgotten what it is', as well to say 'I knew the difference between left hand and right hand, but what on earth is it?'. But otherwise you are perfectly right: the notion of the human person, the notions of rights, duties, what is right and wrong, good and bad, what kind of government is just or unjust, what constitutes justice or happiness or whatever you wish - can be different in different societies. But not, as I say, that different - there is a common core: the notion of right and wrong, of good and bad, has always men/ governed/- what has differed is what content is put into this - the categories are comparatively unvarying, the contents can vary a great deal and are subject to persuasion, argument, destruction, etc.

 I do not know if this answers your questions, I can only hope that it does.

Yours sincerely,

Sir Isaiah Berlin

Works cited

ACTON J.E.E.D., *Lectures on Modern History*, London, 1906.

ACTON J.E.E.D., *The History of Freedom and other Essays*, London, 1907.

AMMIANO MARCELLINO (AMMIANUS MARCELLINUS), *Le Storie*, UTET, Torino, 1973.

ARANGIO-RUIZ V., *Istituzioni di Diritto Romano*, Napoli, 1987.

ARISTOTELIS (ARISTOTLE), *Politica,* recognovit brevique adnotatione critica instruxit W.D. Ross, Oxonii, 1957.

AUGUSTINI (SANCTI) (AUGUSTINE ST), *Confessionum Libri Tredecim*, in *Opera Omnia*, vol. I, Città Nuova, Roma, 1975.

AUGUSTINI (SANCTI) (AUGUSTINE ST), *De Civitate Dei*, in *Opera Omnia*, vol. V/1, Lib. I-X, Città Nuova, Roma, 1988.

AUGUSTINI (SANCTI) (AUGUSTINE ST), *De Civitate Dei*, in *Opera Omnia*, vol. V/2, Lib. XI-XVIII, Città Nuova, Roma, 1988.

AUGUSTINI (SANCTI) (AUGUSTINE ST), *De Civitate Dei*, in *Opera Omnia*, vol. V/3, Lib. XIX-XXII, Città Nuova, Roma, 1989.

Augustini (Sancti) (Augustine St), *De vera religione*, in *Opera Omnia*, vol. VI/1, Città Nuova, Roma, 1995.

Augustini (Sancti) (Augustine St), *Epistolae/2*, in *Opera Omnia*, vol. XXII, Città Nuova, Roma, 1971.

Augustini (Sancti) (Augustine St), *Sermones/4*, in *Opera Omnia*, vol. XXXII/1, Città Nuova, Roma, 1984.

Augustini (Sancti) (Augustine St), *Sermones/6*, in *Opera Omnia*, vol. XXXIV, Città Nuova, Roma, 1989.

Augustus C.O., *Res Gestae Divi Augusti*, Editori Riuniti, Roma, 1982.

Aa. Vv., *Storia Augustea*, Rusconi, Milano, 1972.

Balmes J., *Antología Política de Balmes*, por J.M.G. Escudero, B. A. C., Madrid, 1981.
The numbers refer to the paragraphs.

Barbero G., *Introduzione* a *Il pensiero politico cristiano*, vol. II, Sant'Agostino, UTET, Torino, 1965.

Bardy G., *La conversione al cristianesimo nei primi secoli*, Jaca Book, Milano, 1988.

Berlin I., *Four Essays on Liberty*, Oxford University Press, 1969.

Boissier G., *La fine del mondo pagano*, Sugarco, Milano 1989.

Brague R., *Europe. La voie romaine*, Éd. Gallimard, Paris, 1999.

BRANIGAN K., *L'influenza ellenistica sul mondo romano*, in *Il mondo di Roma imperiale, La formazione*, vol.I, Editori Laterza, Roma-Bari, 1989.

BRAUND D.C., *L'eredità della Repubblica*, in *Il mondo di Roma imperiale, La formazione*, vol. I, Editori Laterza, Roma-Bari, 1989.

BRAUDEL F., *Il Mediterraneo. Lo spazio, la storia, gli uomini, le tradizioni*, Bompiani, Milano, 1992.

BURTON G., *Il governo e le province*, in *Il mondo di Roma imperiale*, a cura di J. Wacher, *Vita urbana e rurale*, vol. II, Editori Laterza, Roma-Bari, 1989.

CAMPANINI M., *Introduzione* a al-Fārābī, *La città virtuosa (Le idee degli abitanti della città virtuosa)*, Rizzoli, Milano, 2001.

CARENA C., *Introduzione* a Lotario di Segni, *La miseria della condizione umana. De contemptu mundi*, Mondadori, Milano, 2003.

CARLYLE R.W. E A.J., *Il pensiero politico medievale*, vol. II, Editori Laterza, Bari, 1959.

CARRARA P., *I pagani di fronte al cristianesimo, Testimonianze dei secoli I e II*, Firenze, 1984.

CASPAR R., *Theologie Musulmane*, tome II, *Le credo*, P.I.S.A.I., Rome, 1999.

CASSIO DIONE (CASSIUS DIO), *Storia romana*, vol. I, Libri XXXVI-XXXVIII, Rizzoli, Milano, 1995.

Cassio Dione (Cassius Dio), *Storia romana*, vol. II, Libri XXXIX-XLIII, Rizzoli, Milano, 1995.

Cassio Dione (Cassius Dio), *Storia romana*, vol. III, Libri XLIV-XLVII, Rizzoli, Milano, 1996.

Cassio Dione (Cassius Dio), *Storia romana*, vol. IV, Libri XLVIII-LI, Rizzoli, Milano, 1996.

Cassio Dione (Cassius Dio), *Storia romana*, vol. V, Libri LII-LVI, Rizzoli, Milano, 1998.

Cassiodoro F. M. A. (Cassiodorus), *Variae. Per il buon governo della società*, a cura di Antonio Caruso, Edizioni Vivere in, Roma, 2001.

Cassiodori Senatoris (Cassiodorus), *Institutiones*, R. A. B. Mynors, Oxford, 1961.

Cesare C.G. (Caesar C. J.), *La guerra civile*, Rusconi, Milano, 1976.

Chenu M.D., *La teologia nel medioevo*, Jaca Book, Milano, 1972.

Chevallier J.J., *Storia del pensiero politico*, vol. I, *Antichità e medioevo*, Il Mulino, Bologna, 1989.

Cicero M.T., *De Legibus*, in aedibus Livianis, Patavii, MCMLXVIII.

Cicero M.T., *De Re Publica*, in aedibus Livianis, Patavii, MCMLXVIII.

CICERO M.T., *De Oratore, Opera Rethorica II*, in aedibus Livianis, Patavii, MCMLXVIII.

CICERONE M.T. (CICERO M.T.), *De Officis* (Dei Doveri), Zanichelli, Bologna, 1987.

CICERONE M.T. (CICERO M.T.), *Lettere ai familiari*, Zanichelli, vol. III, Bologna, 1983.

CICERONE M.T. (CICERO M.T.), *Lettere ad Attico*, Zanichelli, vol. II, Bologna, 1983.

COARELLI F., *Roma*, in *Il Mediterraneo*, a cura di F. Braudel, Bompiani, Milano, 1987.

CRESCI MARRONE G., *Introduzione* a CASSIO DIONE, *Storia romana*, vol. I, Libri LII-LVI, Rizzoli, Milano, 1998.

CRUZ HERNÁNDEZ M., *Historia del pensamiento en el mundo islámico. I. Desde los orígenes hasta el siglo XII en Oriente*, Alianza Editorial, Madrid, 1996, tr. it., vol. I, Paideia Editrice, Brescia, 1999.

DANTE ALIGHIERI, *Monarchia*, Garzanti, Milano, 1985.

D'ADDIO M., *Storia delle dottrine politiche*, vol. I, ECIG, Genova, 1992.

DIODORO S. (DIODORUS S.), *Biblioteca storica. Frammenti dei Libri IX-X. Libri XI-XIII*, Rusconi Editore, Milano, 1992.

DIONISIO DI ALICARNASSO (DIONYSIUS OF HALICARNASSUS), *Storia di Roma arcaica (Le antichità romane)*, Rusconi, Milano, 1984.

DRINKWATER J.F., *L'urbanizzazione in Italia e nelle province occidentali dell' Impero*, in *Il mondo di Roma imperiale*, a cura di J. Wacher, *Vita urbana e rurale*, vol. II, Editori Laterza, Roma-Bari, 1989.

DUNS SCOTO I. (DUNS SCOTUS J.), *Ordinatio*, Liber secundus, *Opera Omnia*, editio minor, III/2, *Opera Theologica*, a cura di G. Lauriola, Editrice, AGA, Alberobello, 2001.

DUNS SCOTO I. (DUNS SCOTUS J.), *Ordinatio*, Liber quartus, *Opera Omnia*, editio minor, III/2, *Opera Theologica*, a cura di G. Lauriola, Editrice, AGA, Alberobello, 2001.

ENNIUS AND CECILIUS, *Remains of old Latin,* newly edited and translated by E. H. Warmington, M. A., London, W. Heinemann, Ldt, Cambridge, Mass., Harvard University Press, MCMLXI.
(In the note on page 8, it is indicated that the quotation from Ennius, of doubtful attribution, is in fact recorded by Gellius, XVII,17,1).

EUSEBIO DI CESAREA (EUSEBIUS OF CAESAREA), *Storia ecclesiastica*, Rusconi, Milano, 1979.

AL-FĀRĀBĪ, *La città virtuosa (Le idee degli abitanti della città virtuosa)*, Rizzoli, Milano, 2001.

FASNACHT G.E., *Acton's Political Philosophy. An Analysis*, London, 1952.

FIORE L., *Introduzione* a TITO LIVIO, *Ab Urbe condita, Storie*, Libri XXVI-XXX, UTET, Torino, 1997.

FLORO (FLORUS L. A.), *Epitome di Storia Romana*, Rusconi, Milano, 1981.

GABRIELI F., (textes recueillis et présentés par), *Chroniques arabes des Croisades*, Sindbad, Arles, 2001.

GAIO (GAIUS), *Institutiones, I Il Testo*, Edizioni QuattroVenti, Urbino, 1994.

GAUDEMET J., *Il miracolo romano*, in *Il Mediterraneo*, a cura di F. Braudel, Bompiani, Milano, 1987.

AL-GHAZĀLĪ, *Ayyuhā al-walad*, tr. it., *O figlio!*, in AL-GHAZĀLĪ, *Scritti scelti*, UTET, Torino, 1986.

AL-GHAZĀLĪ, *al-Munqidh min ad-dalād*, tr. it., *La salvezza dalla perdizione*, in AL-GHAZĀLĪ, *Scritti scelti*, UTET, Torino, 1986.

GHISALBERTI A., *Introduzione a Ockham*, Editori Laterza, Bari, 1976.

GIACOMO DA VITERBO, *De Regimine Christiano*, Nardini Editore, Firenze, 1993.

GILSON E., *La filosofia nel medioevo. Dalle origini patristiche alla fine del XIV secolo*, La Nuova Italia, Firenze, 1978.

GIOMARO A. M., *Spunti per una lettura critica di Gaio Institutiones, I Il Testo*, Edizioni QuattroVenti, Urbino, 1994.

GIOVANNI DI SALISBURY (JOHN OF SALISBURY), *Policraticus*, Jaca Book, Milano, 1985.

GIUSEPPE FLAVIO (JOSEPHUS FLAVIUS), *La guerra giudaica*, a cura di Giovanni Viticci, Mondadori Editore, Milano, 1974.

Gramsci A., *Quaderni del Carcere*, vol. I, Einaudi, Torino, 1975.

Gramsci A., *Quaderni del Carcere*, vol. II, Einaudi, Torino, 1975.

Green E., *Diritto e sistema legale nel Principato*, in *Il mondo di Roma imperiale*, a cura di J. Wacher, *Vita urbana e rurale,* vol. II, Editori Laterza, Roma-Bari, 1989.

Guarino A., *Il diritto romano: caratteri e fonti*, in *Guida allo studio della civiltà romana antica*, diretta da V. Ussani e F. Arnaldi, Istituto Editoriale del Mezzogiorno, vol. I, pp. 381-406, Napoli, 1952.

Guillelmi de Occam (Ockham William of), *Breviloquium de Potestate Papae*, par L. Baudry, Paris, 1937.

Hassall M., *Romani e non Romani*, in *Il mondo di Roma imperiale,* a cura di J. Wacher, *Economia, società e religione*, vol. III, Editori Laterza, Roma-Bari, 1989.

Homo L., *Les Institutions Politiques Romaines. De la Cité a l'Etat*, Paris, 1976.

James E., *Histoire sommaire de la pensée économique*, tr. it., *Storia del pensiero economico*, Garzanti, Milano, 1970.

Kautilya, *Arthaśāstra*, (L'arte del governo), Bariletti Editori, 1990.

Lauriola G., *Introduzione* a G. Duns Scoto, *Antologia*, Editrice Alberobello, Alberobello (Ba), 1995.

LEAMAN O., *La filosofia islamica medievale*, Il Mulino, Bologna, 1985.

LIVIO T. (LIVIUS T.), *Ab Urbe condita, Storie*, Libri I-V, UTET, Torino, 1974.

LIVIO T. (LIVIUS T.), *Ab Urbe condita, Storie*, Libri VI-X, UTET, Torino, 1995.

LIVIO T. (LIVIUS T.), *Ab Urbe condita, Storie*, Libri XXI-XXV, UTET, Torino, 1995.

LIVIO T. (LIVIUS T.), *Ab Urbe condita, Storie*, Libri XXVI-XXX, UTET, Torino, 1997.

LIVIO T. (LIVIUS T.), *Ab Urbe condita, Storie*, Libri XXXI-XXXV, UTET, Torino, 1995.

LOTARIO DI SEGNI (LOTHAIRE OF S.), *La miseria della condizione umana. De contemptu mundi*, Mondadori, Milano, 2003.

LUCAIN, *La guerre civile, La Pharsale*, tome I, L.B.L., Paris, 1962.

MAALOUF A., *Les croisades vues per les Arabes*, tr. it., Società Editrice Internazionale, Torino, 1995.

MAHDI M., *La fondation de la philosophie politique en Islam. La cité vertueuse d'Alfarabi*, tr. fr., Flammarion, Paris, 2000.

MANZO T., *Scripta philologa*, N. M. R., Roma, 2003.

MARCHESI C., *Storia della Letteratura Latina*, vol. I, Principato, Milano-Messina, 1953.

MARSILIO DA PADOVA (MARSILIO OF PADUA), *Il Difensore della Pace*, UTET, Torino, 1975.

MAZZARINO S., *L'Impero romano*, vol. III, Editori Laterza, Roma-Bari, 1976.

MAZZARINO S., *Il pensiero storico classico*, vol. II, Editori Laterza, Roma-Bari, 1994.

MAZZARINO S., *Il pensiero storico classico*, vol. III, Editori Laterza, Roma-Bari, 1994.

MAXFIELD V.A., *L'Europa continentale*, in *Il mondo di Roma imperiale, La formazione*, vol. I, Editori Laterza, Roma-Bari, 1989.

MEZIÉRE P. M., *Il fondamento metafisico della libertà spirituale in Duns Scoto*, in Quaderni di Studi Scotisti, n°. 2, 2005, pp. 55-72.

MICCICHÈ C., *Introduzione* a DIODORO SICULO, *Biblioteca storica. Frammenti dei Libri IX-X. Libri XI-XIII*, Rusconi Editore, Milano, 1992.

MOMMSEN T., *Römische Geschichte*, Ester Band, Berlin, 1856.

MOMMSEN T., KRUEGER P., SCHOELL R., *Corpus Iuris Civilis*, Volumem Primum, *Institutiones - Digesta*, Berolini, MCMXX.

MONTGOMERY WATT W., *Islamic Political Thought. The Basic Concepts*, Edinburgh, 1968.

MOUSSALEM R., *Aspetto ascetico spirituale dei Nomi di Dio nell'opera di al-Ghazālī*, in *Nuova Umanità*, n. 6, 2001.

NARDONI D., *Catachanna*, Roma, 1979.

NARDONI D., *Sotto Ponzio Pilato*, E.I.L.E.S., Roma, 1987.

NARDONI D., *I Gladiatori Romani*, E.I.L.E.S., Roma, 1989.

NORCIO G., *Introduzione* a CASSIO DIONE, *Storia romana*, vol. I, Libri XXXVI-XXXVIII, Rizzoli, Milano, 1995.

PASSERIN D'ENTREVES A., *Introduzione* a TOMMASO D'AQUINO, *Scritti politici*, Bologna, 1946.

PECCHIURA P., *Introduzione* a TITO LIVIO, *Ab Urbe condita, Storie*, Libri XXXI-XXXV, UTET, Torino, 1995.

PERELLI L., *Introduzione* a TITO LIVIO, *Ab Urbe condita, Storie*, Libri I-V, UTET, Torino, 1974.

PERELLI L., *Introduzione* a TITO LIVIO, *Ab Urbe condita, Storie*, Libri VI-X, UTET, Torino, 1995.

PINCHERLE A., *Vita di Sant'Agostino*, Editori Laterza, Roma-Bari, 1980.

PLATONIS (PLATO), *Res Publica*, rec. J. Burnet, tomus IV, Oxonii, 1957.

PLINI C. CAECILI SECUNDI (PLINY THE YOUNGER C. C. S.), *Panegyricus Traiano Imperatori Dictus*, Firenze, 1949.

POLIBIO (POLYBIUS), *Le Storie*, Rusconi, Milano,1987.

POLO M., *Milione*, Mondadori, Milano, 1982.

POPPER K. R., *The Open Society and its Enemies*, vol. I, *The Spell of Plato*, Routledge & Kegan Paul, London, 1977.

POULTER A., *Gli insediamenti presso i campi militari: "canabae" e "vici"*, in *Il mondo di Roma imperiale,* a cura di J. Wacher, *Vita urbana e rurale,* vol. II, Editori Laterza, Roma-Bari, 1989.

RAMONDETTI P., *Introduzione* a TITO LIVIO, *Ab Urbe condita, Storie*, Libri XXI-XXV, UTET, Torino, 1995.

RATZINGER J., *Volk und Haus Gottes in Augustins Lehre von der Kirche*, tr. it., *Popolo e casa di Dio in Sant'Agostino*, Jaca Book, Milano, 2005.

RIZZACASA A., *Introduzione* al *De Regimine Christiano* di Giacomo da Viterbo, Nardini Editore, Firenze, 1993.

SABINE G.H., *A History of Political Theory*, tr. it., *Storia delle dottrine politiche*, vol. I, Etas/Kompass, Milano, 1978.

SALLUSTIUS CRISPUS C. (SALLUST C. C.), *Catilinae Coniuratio*, in aedibus F. Pesenti Del Thei, Venetiis, MCMLXV.

SAPEGNO N., *Commento* a *La Divina Commedia*, vol. II, *Purgatorio*, La Nuova Italia, Firenze, 1967.

SAPEGNO N., *Commento a La Divina Commedia*, vol. III, *Paradiso*, La Nuova Italia, Firenze, 1968.

SAYLES G.O., *The Medieval Foundations of England*, London, 1948.

SCOTT ANDERSON A., *L'esercito imperiale*, in *Il mondo di Roma imperiale*, La *formazione*, vol. I, Editori Laterza, Roma-Bari, 1989.

SENECA L. A., *Lettere a Lucilio*, Rizzoli, voll. I e II, Rizzoli, Milano, 1974.

SENECA L. A., *I Dialoghi, Della Provvidenza, Della costanza del saggio, Dell'ira*, vol. I, Mondadori, Milano, 1992.

SENECA L. A., *I Dialoghi, Consolazione a Marcia, Della vita felice, Della vita appartata, Della tranquillità dell'animo, Della brevità della vita, Consolazione a Polibio, Consolazione ad Elvia*, vol. II, Mondadori, Milano, 1993.

STEVENSON G.H., *L'amministrazione imperiale*, in *Storia del mondo antico*, vol. VIII, *L'Impero romano da Augusto agli Antonini*, Cambridge University Press, ed it., Milano, 1975.

SORIA C., *Introducciones* a *La Suma Teologica, Tratado de la Ley en General*, B.A.C., Madrid, 1956.

SPIGAROLO B., *Filippo Cavriana. Mantovano del XVI secolo letterato tacitista storico e politico*, Editoriale Sometti, Mantova, 1999.

SUETONIUS T. G., *De Vita Caesarum*, tr. it. *Le vite di dodici Cesari*, Rusconi, Milano 1975.

TABACCO G., *La storia politica e sociale. Dal tramonto dell'Impero alle prime formazioni di Stati regionali*, in Aa. Vv., *Storia d'Italia. Dalla caduta dell'Impero romano al secolo XVIII. La società medievale e le corti del Rinascimento*, Einaudi, Torino, Il Sole 24 Ore, Milano, 2005.

TACITO (TACITUS C.), *Annali, dalla morte del divo Augusto*, Rusconi, Milano, 1978.

TACITO (TACITUS C.), *Storie*, Rusconi, Milano, 1982.

THOMAE S. AQUINATIS (THOMAS AQUINAS), *De Regimine Judaeorum*, in *Opera Omnia*, Frommann Holzboog, vol. 3, Stuttgart, 1980.

THOMAE S. AQUINATIS (THOMAS AQUINAS), *De Regimine Principum*, in *Opera Omnia*, Frommann Holzboog, vol. 3, Stuttgart, 1980.

THOMAE S. AQUINATIS (THOMAS AQUINAS), *Summa contra Gentiles*, in *Opera Omnia*, Frommann Holzboog, vol. 2, Stuttgard, 1980.

THOMAE S. AQUINATIS (THOMAS AQUINAS), *Summa Theologiae,* in *Opera Omnia*, Frommann Holzboog, vol. 2, Stuttgard, 1980.

TODISCO O., *Introduzione* a *Giovanni Duns Scoto filosofo della libertà*, Edizioni Messaggero Padova, Padova, 1996.

TOUCHARD J., *Histoire des idées politiques*, tome I, PUF, Paris, 2008.

ULLMANN W., *Law and Politics in the Middle Ages*, C.U.P., Cambridge, 1975.

VANSTEENKISTE C., *Cicerone nell'opera di San Tommaso*, in *Angelicum*, 1959, pp. 343-382.

VASOLI C., *Introduzione* a *Il Difensore della Pace* di Marsilio, Torino, 1965.

VECCIA VAGLIERI L., *Introduzione* a al-Ghazālī, *Scritti scelti*, UTET, Torino, 1986.

VELLEIO PATERCOLO (VELLEIUS PATERCULUS), *Storia di Roma*, Rusconi, Milano, 1978.

VIANSINO G., *Introduzione* a L. A. Seneca, *I Dialoghi*, vol. I, Mondadori, Milano, 1992.

WACHER J., *Introduzione* a *Il mondo di Roma imperiale, La formazione*, vol.I, Editori Laterza, Roma-Bari, 1989.

WACHER J., *Postfazione* a *Il mondo di Roma imperiale, Economia, società e religione*, vol. III, Editori Laterza, Roma-Bari, 1989.

WERNER K. F., *Naissance de la Noblesse. L'essor des élites politiques en Europe*, tr. it., *Nascita della nobiltà. Lo sviluppo delle élite politiche in Europa*, Einaudi, Torino, 2000.

ZOSIMO (ZOSIMUS), *Storia Nuova*, Rusconi, Milano, 1977.

Index of Names

ABRAHAM, 254
ABÙ HÂTIM AR-RÂZÎ, 233
ABÙ YA'QÙB AL-SIJISTÂNÎ, 233
ACTON J.E.E.D., 133, 147
ADCOCK F.E., 50
AEGIDIUS ROMANUS, 150
AGRICOLA G.J., 74
AGRIPPA M.V., 210
ALBERTUS MAGNUS, 136
ALEXANDER THE GREAT, 48, 63, 91, 187, 255-256, 258, 262
AMBROSE (ST), 104
AMMIANUS MARCELLINUS, 22, 37, 56, 73, 80, 87-93, 217
ANTONY M., 50
ANTISTHENES, 261
APPIANUS, 190
APPIUS C. C., 200
ARANGIO-RUIZ V., 24-26
ARISTOTLE, 37, 39, 99, 136, 148-149, 165, 167, 187, 231, 233, 239, 255-265
ASINIUS, 192
AUGUSTINE (ST), 37, 97, 103-110, 112-117, 121, 149, 212-216, 222
AUGUSTUS C.O. or OCTAVIAN, 50-52, 62-64, 67, 74, 81, 87, 93, 194, 197-198, 208, 210-211,

AVERROÈS, 161, 163
ATTICUS T. P., 48

BACON F., 35
BALMES J., 148-149
BARBERO G., 111
BARDY G., 98
BECCARIA C., 219
BECKETT T., 120-121
BELISARIUS, 157
BERLIN I., 267, 270, 272, 276, 278
BODIN J., 229
BOETHIUS, 96
BOISSIER G., 96, 99-101, 113, 116
BONIFACE VIII, 153
BRAGUE R., 225-226
BRANIGAN K., 61
BRAUND D. C., 62
BRUTUS M., 197
BURTON G., 85-86

CABOT J., 268
CAESAR C.J., 11, 30, 36, 47-50, 56, 90-91, 162, 179-180, 192-193, 197, 208
CALIGULA, EMPEROR, 71, 202
CAMILLUS F., 198
CAMPANINI M., 232-233, 237-239

CANGRANDE DELLA SCALA, 153
CARACALLA, EMPEROR, 63, 82
CARENA C., 216
CARLYLE R.W. E A.J., 121, 123, 271
CARONDA, 196
CARRARA P., 85
CARUSO A., 219
CASPAR R., 234, 244
CASSIUS C.L., 47, 197
CASSIUS DIO, 205-212
CASSIODORUS (FLAVIUS MAGNUS AURELIUS), 218-219
CATILINE L.S., 30, 195
CATO M.P., 45, 107, 125, 189, 202
CATO U., 159, 198
CATULUS Q. L., 208
CHENU M.D., 123
CHEVALLIER J.J., 150, 176, 262-263
CICERO M.T., 13, 18, 26-37, 39-45, 47-48, 51, 56, 59, 64, 73, 76, 80, 86, 89, 91, 95, 99, 106-107, 110, 116, 123, 126, 138, 140-141, 160, 167-168, 195, 197, 199, 207, 210, 212-216, 218, 222, 253, 262, 267
CLAUDIUS, EMPEROR, 71, 202
CLEMENT X, 136
CLEOPATRA, 50, 209
COARELLI F., 54
CONSTANT B., 274
CONSTANTINE, EMPEROR, 82, 90, 100-103
CONSTANS AUGUSTUS, 92

CRESCI MARRONE G., 210
CRUZ HERNÁNDEZ M., 231-232, 236-237, 240-244

D'ADDIO M., 23, 36, 103-105, 110-111, 114, 120, 134-135, 137, 150, 154, 165-166, 172-173, 175, 177, 182, 184, 256, 258
DANTE ALIGHIERI, 153-162, 165, 172, 174, 183, 198, 229
DESCARTES R., 35
DIOCLES, 196
DIOCLETIAN, EMPEROR, 82
DIODORUS S., 195-196,
DIONYSIUS OF HALICARNASSUS, 57-59, 206
DRINKWATER J.F., 83
DUBOIS P., 150
DUNS SCOTUS J., 221-224

ENGELBERT OF ADMONT, 174
ENNIUS Q., 14, 189, 266
EPRIUS MARCELLUS, 79
EUCLID, 264
EUSEBIUS OF CAESAREA, 97, 101-104, 108, 110

AL-FĀRĀBĪ, 231-233, 237-241
FASNACHT G.E., 147-148
FIORE L., 201
FLORUS L. A., 63-64
FRANK T., 253

GABRIELI F., 245
GAIUS, 204

GALBA, EMPEROR, 77
GAUDEMET J., 54-55
GELLIUS A., 189
GERMANICUS, 56
AL-GHAZĀLĪ, 234-237, 241-245
GHISALBERTI A., 181
GIACOMO DA VITERBO, 139, 150-151
GILSON E., 161, 163-164
GIOMARO A.M., 204
GRAMSCI A., 153
GREEN E., 86-87
GREGORY VII, 120
GROTIUS U., 275

HADRIAN IV, 127
HANNIBAL, 190
HASSAL M., 84
HENRY II PLANTAGENET, 120
HENRY IV, 120
HENRY VII, 229
HEROD, 110
HOBBES T., 28, 33, 77, 93, 124, 142
HOMO L., 18, 22
HUME D., 12, 23

IBN GIOBAIR, 246
INNOCENT III, 217

JAMES E., 139
JEAN DE PARIS, 150
JOHN OF SALISBURY, 119-122, 124-133, 173, 243
JOHN XXII, 177
JOSEPHUS FLAVIUS, 202-203, 206

JULIANUS AUGUSTUS, 91-92
JUSTINIAN, EMPEROR, 130, 156-157, 170, 205
JUVENAL, 80

KANT I., 66, 271
KAUTILYA, 248
KIERKEGAARD S., 112

LAURIOLA G., 223-224
LEAMAN O., 234-236
LIBANIUS, 89
LIVIUS T. or LIVY, 192, 195-201, 209
LOCKE J., 12
LOTHAIRE OF S., 216-217
LUCAN L.A., 65-67
LUCRETIUS T.L., 190-191
LUDWIG OF BAVARIA, 164
LUKE (ST), 99

MAALOUF A., 246
MACHIAVELLI N., 79, 92, 122, 125, 130, 166, 194, 199-200, 248, 256, 265
MAECENAS G., 210
MAHDI M., 231-234
MAINARDINI B. DE', 167
MANEGOLD OF LAUTEMBACH, 120
MANZO T., 216
MARCELLUS M.C., 201
MARCHESI C., 40, 67
MARCUSE H., 35
MARIUS C., 195
MARSILIO OF PADUA, 148, 163-176, 179, 185
MARX K., 29

MAZZARINO S., 96, 187-195, 197, 206, 212, 218
MAXFIELD V.A., 60
MEZIÉRE P. M., 222
MICCICHÈ C., 196
MICHELE DA CESENA, 176
MOHAMMED, 239, 247
MOMMSEN T., 14, 16-20, 22, 26
MONICA (ST), 104
MONTESQUIEU CH. L., 12, 15, 22, 38, 41, 54, 105, 125, 130, 132, 143, 271, 278
MONTGOMERY WATT W., 247
MOUSSALEM R., 235

NARDONI D., 15, 26, 251
AN-NASAFÎ, 233
NERO, EMPEROR, 52, 67-68, 71, 77
NORCIO G., 206-207
NUMA P., 197
NŪR AL-DĪN or NURADDIN, 246

OCKHAM WILLIAM OF, 163, 170, 176-186, 274
OLIMPIODORUS, 217
ORPHEUS, 254
OVID N., 191
OZANAM A.F., 101

PANPHILIUS, 101
PASSERIN D'ENTREVES A., 146
PAUL (ST), 180, 214, 223
PECCHIURA P., 202
PERELLI L., 197-201
PERICLES, 11
PETRARCH F., 156

PEZZIMENTI R., 267, 270, 272, 276
PHILIP OF MACEDON, 255
PHILIP V OF MACEDON, 188
PHILIP THE ARAB, 218, 228
PICO DELLA MIRANDOLA, 216
PINCHERLE A., 115, 117
PLATO, 34, 37, 39-40, 42, 44, 99, 212-213, 231-232, 239, 255, 257, 261, 263-267
PLINY THE YOUNGER C.C.S., 65-66, 85
PLOTINUS, 239
PLUTARCH, 102, 262
POLO M., 246
POLYBIUS, 35-39, 77, 87, 102, 190, 206
POMPEY G. MAGNUS, 48-49, 208
POPPER K.R., 13, 97, 261, 263-265, 267-270
POULTER A., 83
PROCLUS, 264
PUBLIUS SERVILIUS, 22
PYRRHUS, 17
PYTHAGORAS, 196, 264

RAMONDETTI P., 201
RATZINGER J., 214-216
RIZZACASA A., 151
ROMULUS, 197, 253
RUTILIUS NAMANTIANUS, 101

SABINE G.H., 65, 124, 184-185
SALLUST C.C., 36, 107, 191-192, 195-196, 212, 225
SAPEGNO N., 156, 160

SARTORI G., 11-12
SAYLES G.O., 185
SCHUMPETER J.A., 35
SCIPIO P.C. AFRICANUS, 18, 32, 35, 198
SCOTT ANDERSON A., 81
SENECA L.A., 39, 61, 65, 67-73, 140, 215, 262
SERVIUS TULLIUS, 17, 34, 188
SERVIUS (JURIST), 98
SEXTUS QUINTUS, 69
SEPTIMIUS SEVERUS, 82, 254
SHAKESPEARE W., 198
SILLA L.C., 56, 195
SORIA C., 137, 149
SPIGAROLO B., 194
SPINOZA B., 225
STEVENSON G.H., 53
STILICONE, 95-96
STRABO G.C., 192
SUETONIUS T.G., 49, 51, 74, 81, 202

TABACCO G., 228
TACITUS C., 37, 52, 64-65, 73-80, 87, 89-90, 92-93, 107, 193-194, 197, 205
TARQUINIUS SUPERBUS, 199
THEODOSIUS, 95
THOMAS AQUINAS, 12, 135-149, 172-173, 176, 243
THUCYDIDES, 189, 192, 225
TIBERIUS, EMPEROR, 75, 194
TIBERIUS GRACCHUS, 26, 187

TITUS QUINTIUS FLAMININIUS, 201
TODISCO O., 221
TOUCHARD J., 62-63
TRIBONIANUS, 157
TULLIUS HOSTILIUS, 33

ULLMANN W., 173-174
ULPIANUS D., 65, 205

VALENTINIAN, EMPEROR, 82
VANSTEENKISTE C., 141
VARRO M.T., 50, 193, 212, 214
VASOLI C., 166-168, 170-171
VECCIA VAGLIERI L., 244
VELLEIUS PATERCULUS, 56-57
VIANSINO G., 71-72
VICO G.B., 12, 79, 276, 278
VIRGIL M.P., 50, 159, 200, 209, 253
VISCONTI M., 164
VITORIA F. DE, 149

WAGENVOORT H., 252
WALZER R., 239
WACHER J., 60, 84
WEBER M., 248
WERNER K.F., 226-229
WILLIAMS W.T., 268

XERXES, 63

ZALEUCUS OF LOCRI, 196
ZOSIMUS, 87, 93-95

www.ingramcontent.com/pod-product-compliance
Lightning Source LLC
Chambersburg PA
CBHW032019230426
43671CB00005B/134